I0203449

Mister Shifter

EDWARD DAVIE

This book is a work of fiction. Names, characters and incidents are products of the author's imagination or are used fictitiously. Any resemblance to actual removal companies, events or persons (living or dead) is entirely coincidental, but if the cap fits...

Copyright © Edward Davie 2013

ISBN 978-1-63041-576-1

All rights reserved
The right of Edward Davie to be identified as the author of this work has been asserted by him in accordance with the Copyright, Designs & Patents Act 1988

www.marzipan-media.com

Designed and produced by Marzipan Media
Typeset in 10/14 Amasis MT

To my long-suffering wife Ann,
without whose patience and computer savvy
this work would not have been completed.
You're a star.

Customer Care Prayer

by Al Borowski

Lord, I beg you, give me strength
With certain customers who talk at length.
Give me patience and the common sense
To listen while the customer vents.
Let me feel what they go through
So I can see their point of view.
Guide my words so what I say
Reaches them in a courteous way.

Open my ears that I might be led
To hear the message left unsaid.
Show me ways to build rapport,
That lets them know we offer more.
Make me always show respect,
And far exceed what they expect.

Remind me that service is but part of my role;
Customer care becomes the primary goal.
Help me to always live by this prayer
To prove to them I really care.
And at day's end, let me look back with pride
That I kept every customer satisfied.

Lord, help me remember that
When dealing with customers leaves me a wreck,
They are the ones who fund my pay cheque.

© www.AlBorowski.com

Prologue

IT'S WITH DEEP FOREBODING that I steer the van between the automated, ornamental wrought-iron gates to our last job of the day. Not one I'm looking forward to, that's for sure. Especially in my condition.

A piano removal. And not a normal ground-floor piano removal. This one's from the second floor. And there's no lift. I know this for a fact. We did a full-scale removal in this same block a couple of weeks back.

Unbelievable. All that money spent to make the building what it is and the developers couldn't think to install a lift. If not for the removers, at least for the residents. Tosspots!

So it's the stairs for Charlie, my crew mate, and me. A lot of stairs. And a lot of graft to get the bugger down safely.

But it's not only the piano I've got to worry about. It's also the apartment block itself. This property's been designed for the well-heeled, with each apartment setting the owners back a cool four to five hundred thousand quid. The building is top of the range and in immaculate condition. So we'll have to be extra careful not to be knocking bits of paint or plaster off the doors, walls or stairway. Any of that malarkey could cost an arm and a leg to put right.

I haven't even seen the piano. Negotiated the job over the telephone because I couldn't be bothered to visit. Not an omission I'd normally make before committing myself to such a job. And oh boy, do I now regret that. Now I've no idea what's facing me.

The automatic gates close behind us and I groan inwardly at the prospect facing us. 'Here we are, Charlie,' I say. Pointlessly I guess, as Charlie-boy is neither blind nor dumb.

He says nowt but continues to sit quietly beside me, staring vacantly into space. What's going on in his mind is hard to fathom. But that's Charlie for you: enough strange matter in there to keep the best brain surgeons in the country bemused for a lifetime.

I carefully manoeuvre my removal van up to the glass-fronted double-door entrance and turn off the ignition. Charlie sits patiently waiting for instructions. Good job I wasn't expecting a thought-provoking discourse. The chance would be a fine thing.

Taking the opportunity for a well-earned breather, I reflect over the course of the previous eight hours, during which we have successfully completed two other removals. Whilst neither was large or particularly difficult, each has kept us well and truly occupied over the course of the day. I don't know about Charlie, but I feel well and truly knackered.

The weather conditions haven't helped our cause, the temperature hanging around the 80-degrees mark. The inside of the box van has been better suited for use as a sauna than for transporting furniture. Large damp blotches are clearly visible on the backs and fronts of our T-shirts and Charlie's feet are beginning to smell like the internal organs of a dead hedgehog. Mind you, it would help if he changed his socks more than once a week. Though that's not something that would be prudent to address at the moment. I don't want him to get the hump or distract him from the job we're about to undertake. Hopefully, his missus will sort him out with a fresh supply of jocks and socks before he shows up for work in the morning.

But that's for tomorrow. It doesn't change the here and now.

It's now my firm belief I've taken on one job too many as far as Mrs Jarrod – and her piano – is concerned. Not only am I whacked, but my varicose veins feel like they're about to pop. And my haemorrhoids aren't in great shape either. It feels like two hot-air balloons have been stuffed up my backside.

'We could well have done without this bloody piano,' I mutter soulfully to Charlie, finally voicing my doubts and looking for solace.

Looking for solace? From Charlie? I should have known better. I must have had a bit too much of the black stuff last night; that, or too much sunshine today. One way or another, it's definitely affecting my grey matter.

I sneak a sideways glance at him as he continues to stare vacantly into space, seemingly oblivious not only to my concerns, but also to the strong odour emanating from within his size elevens.

'Aye, you're right enough there, Frank,' he suddenly responds, surprising me with his eloquence. Having spoken, he then continues to gaze blankly out of the front window.

I give the back of my neck a brief massage, then roll my shoulders to try to ease the stiffness which seems to have consumed the greater proportion of my body.

'Okay, Charlie, let's go.' So saying, I ease myself from the relative comfort of the van – not without some difficulty, given the parlous condition of my rear end. With Charlie dutifully following in my wake carrying the piano wheels, I push the large glass doors open into an exquisite marble-floored foyer.

At the rear of the foyer, corridors lead off to left and right, spokes to the apartments situated to each side of the building. Dominating the centre is a spiral staircase, wending its way to the first and second floors. Open to one side, an ornamental chest-high railing is the only obstruction to a total view of the foyer from top to bottom. This is where the piano will have to come down.

I remove a hanky from my trouser pocket, wipe my brow then slowly wind my way up the smooth surface of the marble stairwell. Apartment number six, we're looking for. Turn left at the top of the second stairwell and the door's along the corridor on the left. Mrs Jarrod made it sound like a doddle in the park.

'We're going to have to be careful with this one, Charlie,' I pant, finally hauling myself on to the second-floor landing. I rest momentarily against the stair-rail to regain my composure. My heart is pounding and my breath comes in deep short bursts. Now I know what it's like to climb Mount Everest.

Charlie squats down beside me, cheeks aglow and sweating, but breathing evenly. He gives me a long searching look of concern. Probably wondering if I'll last the course.

'Here we go, Charlie,' I say resignedly, directing my ageing joints along the corridor towards number six.

I ring the bell, my mouth as dry as an Afghan well. Charlie says nothing – what's new, pussycat? – but stands expectantly waiting for further developments.

A few minutes elapse as I inwardly pray for an aborted entry. Then the door opens. An elderly, sophisticated lady faces me across the threshold. She frowns over the top of her gold-framed spectacles. Her nose wrinkles and her eyebrows quiver at the sight of the apparitions that stand before her.

'Yes?' she questions curtly.

'Mrs Jarrod?' I reply, attempting to appear chirpy and enthusiastic.

'That's correct,' she replies, her accent as clipped as a number-one haircut. There are distinct signs of puzzlement, mixed with concern, as she warily runs her eyes over us. Almost immediately, a look of enlightenment crosses her features as she realises she's not about to be mugged or pillaged.

'Are you here to remove the piano?' she asks, probably recognising the piano wheels in Charlie's possession for what they are.

What the hell does she think we're here for? A nice hot cup of Earl Grey and a hot muffin? To watch the telly? To make mad passionate love in the drawing room?

'That's right, m'dear,' I reply courteously, wisely keeping my inner thoughts to myself. 'If you can just show me where it is, my mate Charlie and I will get on with it.'

Without further ado, Mrs Jarrod turns her back on us and walks down the hallway, Charlie and I trailing in her wake.

The piano is sited in the lounge. As I cast my eyes on the article in question, my heart sinks.

My worst fears have just been realised. The piano's not one of the modern compact ones I'd hoped for. In contrast to the luxury of its surroundings, this one is old-fashioned, albeit still in pretty good nick. As with most pianos manufactured years ago, it's big and unwieldy, with a cast-iron frame. It'll weigh a bleeding ton. Given the size and weight, we could definitely be doing with three of us.

'Can the two of you manage this on your own?' Mrs Jarrod now questions anxiously, as if reading my mind on the matter. 'I know the piano is an old one,' she continues, 'but we've had many years of good service from it and are now passing it on to our grandchildren. It was a present from my husband on our first wedding anniversary and I've got a very sentimental attachment to it. I wouldn't be happy if anything happened to it.'

I give her a look, which, in my own mind, should be sufficient to sink a battleship.

Does she really think I'm going to be jumping with joy if something happens to it, when I'm the one who'll have to pick up the pieces? Literally and metaphorically.

Or if Charlie accidentally drops this big lump of shit on my foot? Or if one or two discs slip whilst we're moving the bugger down the bleeding stairs, leaving me hospitalised for the next six weeks?

Watching proceedings from the comfort of an armchair is an elderly grey-haired gentleman whom I presume to be Mr Jarrod, the wife's piano benefactor. Standing by him are three children. I guess these would be the grandchildren, all now taking an acute interest in the arrival of Charlie and myself. They say nothing, but regard us like we've just landed from Mars, their eyes and mouths wide open. Mr Jarrod looks at us disdainfully over the rim of his spectacles, but also says nothing. Whether this disdain is because of our sweat-stained shirts or the aroma pervading the room from Charlie's feet would be hard to say.

I become aware that Mrs Jarrod is awaiting some response.

'Can the two of us manage your piano?' I parrot, my eyebrows raised. A nervous laugh, more like a hiccup, escapes my lips. 'No problem, m'dear,' I lie, my outer display of confidence masking my inner concerns. 'Charlie and I have moved pianos bigger and better than this one. Isn't that right, Charlie?' I now say, turning to Charlie and surreptitiously giving him an exaggerated wink with my right eye.

Fortunately for me, Charlie is either clued up to the sensitivity of the situation at hand or doesn't give a toss, one way or the other. 'That's right, Frank,' he replies, his eyes darting from me, to the piano, to Mrs Jarrod, on to Mr Jarrod, back to the piano and then back to me.

I detect some signs of unease in Charlie's reaction. But seemingly, our clients are not aware of anything amiss.

'Right, Charlie, what have we got here, then?' I proclaim purposefully, moving closer to the piano. Having had some experience treading the boards in amateur theatrical circles, I've discovered that a bit of posturing can add a sense of occasion when it comes to the removal of a particularly difficult piece of furniture. It even goes someway to justify my removal charges. With this in mind – and aware that I've commandeered the rapt attention of the assembled audience – I stand erect, hands on hips, before slowly moving round the piano, giving it what is intended to be seen as a professional assessment of the task in hand.

Having circled the piano twice and taken my thespian role as far as it can go – milked the dramatic content from the scene to its utmost, so to speak – I suddenly switch to action-man mode, at the same time desperately trying to ignore the burning sensation within my rear passage. 'Right, Charlie, let's go for it. Madam, if you and the kids could step aside, please.'

Then begins the less demanding procedure. Positioning our piano wheels and having removed the kick-board, we duly lift the piano onto the wheels – not without a considerable amount of physical effort and causing an immediate impact to my abused body. Phase one completed satisfactorily, we trundle the piano though the lounge, down the hall, out the front door and onto the stair landing. Two true professional removers, even if I do say so myself.

We reach the top of the stairs, closely followed by Mr and Mrs Jarrod and the three children, all observing proceedings closely. I try to ignore them but inwardly wish they'd bugger off indoors and leave Charlie and me to get on with it, without us feeling under any more pressure than already exists.

'Right, Charlie. Hold it there,' I instruct. 'That's as far as we can go on the wheels. It's my brain and your brawn from now on.' This attempt at a piece of light humour runs off Charlie like water off a duck's back. He's heard it all before. Drops of sweat have now reappeared on his forehead and drip steadily onto the floor.

'What end are you taking, Frank – top or bottom?' he asks, his full attention on the job in hand.

I don't answer immediately. This needs some careful thought.

'Could be a bit of a problem with the back passage, Charlie,' I finally respond. I wink at him knowingly, aware that he's fully conversant with my medical shortcomings. It's unlikely though that the Jarrods will have picked up my coded message. 'I guess I'll take the bottom end, if that's okay with you? I shouldn't have to stretch over so much.'

Casting my eyes over the piano, I can't help but wish we had additional manpower. One at the top end, two at the bottom end, that's what's really needed here. Better still, two up and two down. Nothing can be done about it now, though. 'Okay, Charlie, let's go for it. Make sure you keep a tight hold on the top end and don't let the bugg– piano go, come what may.' I laugh reassuringly in the Jarrods' direction as they continue to observe the scene closely. Why I'm laughing, I don't know. Given the circumstances, a good old bawl would be more appropriate. As for Charlie, his return look reproaches me for suggesting he could possibly do such a thing. But Charlie being Charlie, he keeps his lips closed.

So saying, we duly lift the piano off the wheels and set it down carefully on the marble landing, facing downstairs. Standing on the edge of the top step, my back to the stairwell, I then steady the piano whilst Charlie, at the other end, lifts it from the bottom until it's tilting at the same angle as the stairs. It's admirable the ease with which he does it. The Jarrods certainly seem impressed.

Stage one completed, I position my shoulder against its bottom side, at the same time securing the best possible grip. I bend my back and brace my legs. 'Right, Charlie, off we go. One step at a time! Nice and easy. Ready? Okay, let's go, big boy.'

We commence our downward journey. Rivers of sweat run down my brow and the sinews in my arms and legs are wound up tighter than Jordan's bra strap.

Then the nightmare begins.

My right foot is midway between the seventh and eighth stair when my left foot slips off the edge of the seventh stair. How it happened is easy to explain. At the very moment my right foot is dangling in mid-air, Charlie emits an extremely loud and prolonged fart, causing me to lose concentration.

There was no way to stop the ensuing sequence of events.

Going down backwards – and not having any backup to prop me from the rear – I'm unable to regain a firm footing on the stairway. My right foot follows my left foot over the edge of the marble step, at which point I lose my grip on the piano. My chin and body smash down onto the hard marble stairs and I begin to slide down the smooth stairwell on my stomach, my arms trailing behind me.

Momentarily losing sight of both the piano and Charlie, I find myself mentally detached from the physical aspects of the crisis engulfing me. I'm vaguely aware of the blurred faces of the Jarrods and their grandchildren, peering anxiously through the railing, and watching the spectacle unfold below them with wonderment mixed with incredulity.

'So you've moved pianos bigger and better than this one, Mr Tipple?' I can almost hear Mrs. Jarrod thinking, in response to my earlier boast.

Nice one, Frank. Next time, keep your big gob shut.

I'm also aware of the shock and disbelief on Charlie's face as he sees me disappearing down the stairs. Recognising the predicament we're in, he bravely attempts to support the piano on his own, the veins in his arms standing out like rivers on a map and a nerve above his right eyebrow pulsating violently. I'm thinking he's likely to burst a blood vessel if he continues to hold onto the piano.

Hold onto the piano? I should be so lucky.

A sudden shifting downwards makes me conscious of the fact that Charlie has lost this particular battle, and thus any further control over subsequent proceedings.

The piano suddenly springs from the blocks. Miraculously remaining upright, it begins to bounces downward, picking up speed as it goes.

With chunks of broken marble and wall plaster clattering down the stairwell in my wake, I hit the first-floor landing. My legs crumple underneath me like two pieces of rotting wood. A sharp cracking noise, like the crunch of a nut shell, emanates from my lower leg and a section of ragged bone magically appears through a tear in my trouser leg.

I emit a spine-chilling scream as an unbelievable pain shoots through my entire body. Incapable of any further movement, I writhe on my stomach like a decapitated snake, mesmerised by the relentless progress of the piano as it thunders inexorably downwards.

The piano finally runs off the last stair and momentarily hangs there, suspended over my inert body. I've only a fleeting second to wonder whether the damage to both the piano and myself will be irreparable, when this further example of Newton's law of gravity is concluded. The full weight of the piano finally smashes down on top of me.

I sense, rather than feel, the crunching of bone and bodily organs before …

★ ★ ★

I JERK UPRIGHT in bed, half-awake and disorientated. My body is drenched in sweat, my heart is pounding and my brain feels like it's enclosed in a sticky morass of gooey treacle, totally incapacitating my ability to think straight.

The realisation finally hits me: I've had a nightmare.

A realistic, lurid and detailed nightmare, probably induced by the combination of booze and curry consumed last night.

God help me, when will I ever learn?

Shaking my head at my own folly, I struggle out of my soggy pyjamas and throw them carelessly onto the bedroom floor. Finally, with one last comforting look round the room, I snuggle back under the duvet.

Images of Charlie, pianos and stairs continue to flash through my mind until I fall back into a shallow, fitful sleep.

Had I known that my nightmare was a portent of what the day had in store, it's unlikely that slumber would have found me such a willing bedfellow.

Chapter one

THE INCESSANT RINGING of my alarm clock abruptly awakens me from a shallow, troubled sleep. Groggy, and with a dull ache occupying my head, I slowly manoeuvre my neck through thirty-five degrees. The illuminated panel of my digital clock slowly materialises through bleary, misty eyes.

Six-thirty, Monday: the start of another working week in January 2004. And it's not a promising beginning. I feel like a piece of dog crap, the inevitable result of last night's merrymaking. And how I regret those excesses. God help me and my lack of maturity.

I grope blindly in the darkness and turn off the alarm. But it doesn't stop the ringing in my ears. To make matters worse, the room is revolving, my stomach is queasy and I'm in danger of regurgitating last night's dinner.

Three or four minutes elapse before I drag myself out of bed then unsteadily navigate my way round the bottom of the bed towards the bathroom. With my bedroom light switched off and barely able to see where I'm going, I stub my big toe on the bed-leg.

'Aaaarrgh! Shit and bollocks!' As this convoluted moan of anguish escapes my lips, an instant gut feeling takes a strong hold on me: *this is going to be one of those days*. Not that my gut is in pukka condition. A bit sluggish, you might say. Just like my brain. And now I've got a big toe to match.

That doesn't bode well. With four full-scale house removals scheduled for today and all my resources stretched to the limit, it's not a day to have diminished mental or physical capabilities.

But it's my own fault – stubbing my toe, that is. The trouble is, I *never* switch on the bedside light before hauling myself out of bed; a naive attempt on my part to avoid facing the inevitable reality of another working day. Daft as a brush, I know, but it's my habit, I can do what I like with it, and yes, it does sustain me during those first few minutes of awakening to the real world.

My body shudders involuntarily. The temperature is below freezing. I feel like I've jumped from a jumbo jet at thirty thousand feet, naked and clad in a bag of ice-cubes. I hobble into the bathroom, clad only in my birthday suit, cursing under my breath.

As I struggle to get my arms into my bathroom robe, my remaining teeth begin to clatter of their own accord. Turning on the light, I gaze forlornly into the bathroom mirror through rheumy eyes. Not a pretty sight. My face resembles a turnip, one unworthy of a presence in a soup kitchen for down-and-outs.

'Hell's bells, Frank. What would Jane think if she saw you now?' I ask myself. Grounds for instant separation, I think.

Jane has been my best friend and partner for seven years now. Although neither of us is in any hurry to jump that last hurdle and plight our troth, we're both aware that this is our best chance to secure a relationship till death do us part. But it would truly test her commitment if she saw me like this. Lucky for me she stayed at her own place after the dinner party.

As I retrieve my toothbrush and paste from the bathroom cabinet and begin to vigorously brush my teeth, the thought of Jane has brought a much-needed uplift to my spirits.

At the tender age of forty-eight, she's a down-to-earth lady; one who values substance over style, bless her little cotton socks. With her slim build, fair complexion, long silky brunette hair and delicate features, she's a typical Yorkshire rose, her accent the perfect foil to my broad Irish brogue. She wouldn't say boo to a mouse – unless the mouse nibbled on her last bit of cheese, in which case she'd slay the little bugger just as fast as she could catch it. And with her bare hands. That said, she'll generally put up with my highs and lows in equal fashion, in the main accepting a lack of tolerance which happens to be one of my less appealing characteristics. But if I stray across that certain line she's drawn between what's reasonable and what is plain oafish – like nibble her last bit of cheese without so much as asking – then she'll have my guts for garters.

On that thought, I conclude my dental cleaning then remove my denture from the bathroom cabinet. Carefully inserting it, I peer into the mirror and part my lips. 'That's better, Frank. You're nearly human. But not quite.'

Odd as it might seem to anyone listening, I've developed this masterful ability to hold a conversation with myself. Having demonstrated this quirk yet again, I swill down a couple of aspirin. While it's not a good idea to mix aspirin with alcohol, something needs to be done to cure my present ills. Hopefully this will go some way towards putting me to rights.

Swinging into a well-practised routine, I apply a liberal dose of shaving cream and carefully begin to guide my razor around the contours of my face. Then, for some unaccountable and irrational reason, I begin to take stock of the person I am and how I came to be projected into the world, totally unprepared for the path I was destined to follow.

★ ★ ★

WHEN MY MA and da decided to christen me Francis Frederick Fidel Foster, I can't imagine what was going through their minds. To burden an innocent and defenceless baby with a monicker like that. Well, it beggars belief. But inflict it they did. And God help me, I've had to bear those four F-ing crosses throughout my entire life. If I'd known what was going on when the vicar had me cocooned in his arms, I'd have been happy to be held under the water of the baptismal font there and then, until every last breath had left my tiny body.

It was only later in life that my eldest brother told me that Francis was the result of Ma's ongoing infatuation with Sinatra; Frederick due to Da's obsession with Nina of 'Nina and Frederik' fame (only the strongest of protestations from Ma stopping him from naming me Nina); Fidel because of his left-leaning admiration for a young Cuban revolutionary; and Foster from God knows where, but most likely confirmation of Da's liking for a particular brand of Australian lager.

★ ★ ★

AND NOW, HERE I am – fifty-eight years on and none the wiser – the owner of a small removals business based in the Royal Borough of Windsor and Maidenhead. One tiny cog helping to drive the local economy, propelled by me, three full-time removal staff, my secretary Alice, and a pool of casual workers taken on as and when needed.

Twenty years now the business has been in my sometimes not-so-capable hands as managing director. It says so on my business card, so it must be true.

Not that I'm one of your fat cats. Fat-Cat Francis Tipple, indeed! That's good for a laugh, that is. No fat cat me. More scraggy mouse than fat cat, I'd say.

And as for that job title? A more accurate job description might be odd-job man.

'Yes, that's you, Frank. You wear more bloody hats than you'll ever find in a milliner's warehouse.'

Whatever the name of the hat, I've got it: managing director hat, HGV driver hat, marketing hat, salesman hat, transport manager hat, customer service hat, damage assessor hat, chief buyer hat, warehouseman hat, personnel manager hat, stock control hat – oh, and most important, office cleaner and tea maker hats.

'Yes, no doubt about it, Francis,' I tell my cream-covered reflection in the mirror. 'You're a pretty versatile lad, even if you do say so yourself. If it were not for a lack of the old brain cells and a clearer direction of what you want in life, there's no knowing what heights could be scaled.'

With that confirmation of my willingness to put myself and my achievements down – and recognising the damage I'm inflicting with my razor – I finish shaving then cast an appraising look into the mirror.

'You're beginning to look human, Frank,' I advise myself, drops of water and blood trickling down my chin.

Thanks to the aspirins, I'm also feeling better. My headache has receded and the throbbing from my big toe has settled into a steady beat I could sing along to, if I had the notion. All in all, things are looking up.

I stem the blood with pieces of toilet tissue then turn my thoughts back to business.

With four removals booked for today, all vans will be out on the road; unusual for a Monday, especially in winter time.

And that's given me a problem: I've been hard pushed to round up the required complement of casuals to supplement my full-time lads.

'Please God, let all the buggers turn up,' I mutter quietly, stepping into the shower.

I've just begun to enjoy the revitalising effect of hot water caressing my body, when the faint but persistent ringing tones of my telephone carry up the stairwell.

With a sinking feeling in the pit of my stomach, I listen intently while assessing the need to answer the call. But there's no real choice. A telephone call at six thirty-five on a working day can only mean one thing: trouble. So this is not the time to prevaricate, posture or piddle about in the shower. Inconvenient or not, I need to know who is trying to reach me at this early hour. And why.

Chapter two

SWEARING PROFUSELY and mindful of the need to protect my toe from further damage, I stumble out of the shower. Soapy water flows onto the bathroom floor, creating grey, wet splotches on the sky-blue carpet.

The telephone downstairs continues to ring insistently.

'Hold onto your bloody horses, I'm coming as fast as I can.' Why I'm trying to communicate with a mute telephone installation, I've no idea.

I snatch a towel and wrap it loosely around my waist then frantically crash down the stairs two at a time; not a sensible form of activity, given the state of my physical well-being and also the fact that I'm functioning more or less in total darkness. I negotiate the stairs safely then my injured toe makes contact with the Windsor chair parked in the corner of my hall entrance.

'Aaarrgh… you stupid piece of shit,' I wail. It would be hard to say if this character assessment was directed at the chair or myself. Unsurprisingly, no response is forthcoming from the chair.

The phone continues to ring. In a poor imitation of Skippy the kangaroo, I hop painfully towards my bureau, at the same time trying to preserve my modesty. Why I'm bothered I surely couldn't tell, as no one else is around to take advantage of the exposition of my private parts. And if there were, would I really give a sod? Not exactly a prime example of the crown jewels I'm displaying at my age.

The shrill ringing tones are blasting the silence of early morning and reawakening the devils in my head. But whoever the caller is, he's determined to make contact, no matter how long it takes.

I snatch up the telephone. 'Hello, who's that?' I bark tersely, my telephone answering skills temporarily deserting me.

'Hi, Frank. It's Beryl. Pete won't be in for work this morning.'

This stark, straight-to-the-point, no-nonsense declaration leaves me feeling like I've been gutted with a samurai sword. My worst fears have been realised: an employee unavailable for today's operations. And one of my full-timers at that.

My towel slips to the floor in a soggy heap while a residue of soapy water continues to trickle down between my thighs. 'Oh, and why's that, Beryl?' I ask tremulously, attempting to retain a note of civility to my voice. Pete has been in my employment for eight years now. More significantly, he's an important cog in the highly greased machine I hope to be putting on the road in an hour or so. Beryl, his dear wife, has all the social and conversational skills of a gorilla – and the physique to match. At five feet ten inches high and three feet six inches wide, she's not one to be trifled with. The story doing the rounds is she's had a trial as a Japanese sumo wrestler – not said within her, or Pete's, hearing. She's a formidable lady and protects Pete at all costs from what she perceives to be an ungrateful and self-interested employer.

'He's been throwing up during the night,' she replies. 'He thinks he's picked up a bug or something. Maybe something he ate.'

'Oh.'

I'm momentarily stuck for words. The welfare of my employees doesn't feature highly on my list of concerns at six-forty in the morning – except if it might adversely affect my work pattern for the day. And picking up a bug? He's more likely to have picked up one pint too many of John Smiths bitter and is now suffering the consequences.

I digest Beryl's news, stark naked and immune to the freezing air that surrounds me.

'Is he in bed?' I tentatively ask, subconsciously hoping that Pete is furtively lurking behind Beryl's shoulder, prodding and prompting her to carry out his excuses; or that somehow he may telepathically sense my deep concern, propel himself from the bedroom, repent the error of his ways, and volunteer his services for work.

'Last I saw, he was on the loo,' Beryl replies tartly. 'Been up and down all night, bouncing around like Zebedee. Hardly had a wink of sleep myself. Giving me a right headache, he is.'

I'm tempted to ask if she knows the meaning of the word. Has the bloody woman no idea of the headache I've got, that's just got immeasurably worse, thanks to her and her absentee husband?

Knowing the extent of Beryl's power to annihilate opposing forces, I keep my thoughts to myself. But to accept defeat without making some effort to retrieve the situation is unthinkable. After all, Pete won't be the first one to wake up in the morning with a dose of the runs, but still make it into work – albeit with the cheeks of the arse clamped nice and tight and wearing two pairs of underpants.

'No chance he can make it in, Beryl?' I ask in as conciliatory a tone as I can muster. 'I've got a really busy day and it's going to cause me severe problems,' I continue, appealing to his good wife's better nature and authoritarian streak. She's the ultimate power in the household. If she doesn't want him under her feet, he'll be showing up for work as fast as you can say Alka-Seltzer or Immodium.

'Naw, no way, Frank,' she responds sharply. 'The way things are, he wouldn't reach the front door without filling his trousers. I'll see how he gets on later this morning. If he's not any better then, I'm going to call the doc. Pete will ring you this evening to let you know if he's going to be fit for the morning, okay?'

I can hear the challenge in her voice: she's daring me to put up further resistance.

I accept defeat.

'Ah, okay, Beryl. I guess we'll just have to make do,' I reply despondently, also recognising she just might be telling it as it is. Then, as a grudging after-thought – and in a belated attempt to show her my better side – I add, 'Hope he's feeling better later. Give him my regards. Bye for now.'

Placing the phone back on its cradle, I try to absorb the consequences of Beryl's call. Given the problems I've experienced during the course of the week, it's going to be difficult to find a replacement, especially at this short notice. And if I'm not successful, am I prepared to bite the bullet and fill the empty post myself?

I head for the stairway, giving the Windsor chair a baleful look as I side-step around it. 'You're a useless piece of shit,' I tell it, waving my forefinger menacingly. 'Do that again and you're firewood. What do you think of that?'

God help me. Reprimanding a chair. I'm definitely losing the plot.

Chapter three

THE BEDROOM IS an unruly mess, like I'd spent a night in a French tart's boudoir. As testament to my overnight contortions, sheets, blankets and duvet are spread higgledy-piggledy across the mattress. Assorted pieces of clothing lie in untidy heaps around the room, one of my slippers is on top of the wardrobe and my underpants are hanging from a picture hook. To cap it all, a pair of tights is draped over the back of the chair. How the hell did those get there?

Beryl's call has presented me with a quandary. If I can't find a replacement for Pete and have to fill that vacancy myself, that will necessitate wearing the firm's removal uniform. On the other hand, if I can dredge up someone then something more presentable will be required to enable me to meet prospective customers. And that means suit, shirt and tie.

Undecided, I scratch my head and stare blankly at the contents of the wardrobe.

'So, what's it to be, Frank? Uniform or suit?'

My reflection in the full-length mirror regards me thoughtfully, brow furrowed with uncertainty, my ageing body waiting to be spared the agony of any further scrutiny.

My fragile state plays a large part in my decision. I decide on the suit. With a bit of luck, I'll still be able to get someone, even at this short notice. It wouldn't be the first time this has happened and it certainly won't be the last. But if worst comes to worst, I'll have to reallocate the available labour then hope and pray that one reshaped and diminished crew will cope. Three of today's removals are three-man jobs so it will be possible to still provide a service for all four clients – albeit one of them less than perfectly.

But if someone else does a Pete on me then I'm well and truly buggered.

★ ★ ★

A FEW MINUTES later, fully attired, I present myself in front of the wardrobe mirror, turning first to the left and then to the right. I adjust my tie before running a comb through my thinning hair.

'Not bad, Frank. Not bad at all.' My overall appearance shows a marked improvement on earlier. The only blots to my features are the three pieces of toilet paper attached to my chin. These won't be removed until I'm ready to leave.

Satisfied I'll pass muster, I make my way downstairs, this time carefully avoiding contact with the Windsor chair. Although my feet are protected by my size-nine shoes, they don't have steel toecaps. Any further damage could result in the amputation of this particular protrusion.

I enter the kitchen and look around in dismay. And here's me thinking the bedroom was bad. Dirty dishes, glasses, beer tins, empty wine bottles, pots and food leftovers are strewn over the kitchen worktops and filling the kitchen sink. The aftermath of last night's dinner party. It's a disaster zone.

I shrug my shoulders in resignation. With a bit of luck, I'll be able to get home early to sort it out. If not, there's always tomorrow.

My stomach rumbles and groans, crying out for breakfast; anything to help repair the damage caused by last night's gluttony. Trying to ignore the scene around me, I slap two slices of brown bread into the toaster and prepare a mug of tea.

I can't help but reflect on Pete's absence and that labour component of the business which, whilst essential to operations, can cause me such a disproportionate degree of stress: the employment of casual staff.

Unfortunately, the flexibility which gives me freedom to employ them only as and when needed, also works against me. Most will have other irons in the fire. They certainly won't be sitting by the phone waiting for the likes of Francis Frederick to indulge them with a call when the notion takes him. Or, like this morning, when he's desperate. And given that eight casuals are already booked in, that's certainly going to lengthen the odds.

But despite everything, I'm trying to be positive. My first task will be to identify a casual who isn't already booked in and might be willing to come in at short notice.

'It's your only option, Frank,' I declare loudly to the empty room, not very convincingly. 'Or is it?'

I'm kidding myself. There is that other solution to the problem, the one I've already considered and discarded as a non-starter: to put myself forward for shifting duty. A simple answer to a simple problem.

Mug in hand, I begin to pace aimlessly round my tiny kitchen, totally engrossed in my labour problem.

'So, what's it to be, Frank? To work, or not to work, that's the question?' I ask myself a second time, knowing full well the answer. Hungover as I am, the thought of being at the coal face today doesn't fill me with any great enthusiasm. It would also mean that Alice would also have to rearrange client appointments. And cancelling appointments doesn't go down well with punters, not at such short notice. Not when they'll have likely planned their day around my anticipated arrival.

I continue to sup my tea while vacantly staring through the kitchen window into the darkness beyond. But *this being that sort of day*, I've neglected my toast.

The thick, choking smell of acrid fumes makes me aware something is amiss. Turning my head, I see a dense plume of smoke wafting from the toaster. A moment later, two slices of burnt, blackened cow-pats eject onto my kitchen worktop.

Four seconds after that, a shrieking, high-pitched whistle assails my eardrums as the smoke alarm is activated. Turning sharply towards the source of the bedlam, my elbow nudges my mug of half-drunk tea. This teeters on the edge of the table then smashes onto the vinyl flooring, fragmenting into smithereens.

A pitiful moan, akin to a keening, escapes my lips and I'm rooted to the spot until the alarm suddenly ceases.

What my neighbour's going to make of this, I hate to think. First my nightmare. And now this. She'll think I've gone stark, staring mad. 'God help you, Sally.'

I listen intently for signs of activity from next door but silence reigns. With luck, she'll have stayed away from home last night, knowing that a dinner party was planned.

I slowly raise myself from the chair and survey the scene.

'Jesus, Frank! What a bloody shambles.'

If Jane were here, she'd help me out. But she's not. Nor will she be round later. And given the state of the house and those unexplained tights upstairs, maybe that's a blessing. So it's up to me to put things right.

But not this morning; not when those phone calls have to be made and labour secured. And although it hasn't been a good start to the day, there's still a fighting chance to get the train back on the tracks.

'Come on Frank. Get your arse out of joint. It's time to rock and roll.'

Did I really say that? *Moi*? Rock and roll. At my age? And in my condition? Unlikely. Roll under a rock and die, the way I'm feeling.

Chapter four

RESIGNED TO THE TASK ahead, I sit down at my bureau and extract my casual-employee records. This register is as important to me as the Red Book was to Chairman Mao. I'd be well up the creek without it.

Consistent with my lack of enthusiasm for paperwork, the register is simple, consisting of three pages of A4-sized paper, stapled together in the top-left corner. The pages are crumpled and well-thumbed due to continual usage. Every line on each page contains the name and telephone number of a casual, in handwriting that is pretty illegible to anyone but myself. Casuals having come and gone since the list was last updated, many names have a line drawn through them.

'Okay, Frank, crunch time.' My eyes anxiously scan page one. It only takes a moment to establish that, of seven casuals currently listed as available, four are already booked to come in, two are committed to one of my competitors and one is today appearing at the county court in Slough on a charge of drunk and disorderly.

Disappointed, I thumb quickly to page two. 'Don't panic, Frank,' I tell myself as I begin to panic. 'If at first …'

A rapid assessment tells me that, of six casuals theoretically available, three are already booked, one is unavailable due to a broken leg and the other two have been unobtainable for a couple of weeks. They're a lost cause for now.

The inevitability of not finding someone to replace Pete is taking a hold of me, and it's impossible to rid myself of that inner dread about the day ahead.

I burp as my stomach attempts to regurgitate last night's curry. A vile, acidic taste remains in my mouth. And it's horrible, like I've just brought up the cat's breakfast.

I thumb over to page three. Three remaining names give me cause for hope: Morris, Kev and Arnold. The last grapes from the vine.

'Okay, Frank. You're still in with a fighting chance.'

But which of these lads would I prefer to use? Who's my best bet to get out of bed on a freezing Monday morning? And who's most likely to want the work?

'Morris,' I proclaim to myself, more in hope than expectation. 'Morris is the man.'

Morris is a painter and decorator, married with four or five kids. This being winter-time, he doesn't get sufficient work to keep him fully occupied so is thankful for whatever work I can place his way. A reliable bloke he's been when I've needed him, and a conscientious worker, so a good lad to have as a casual. Unfortunately, he wasn't answering his phone last week. I'm hopeful that he might now be back in the groove.

I quickly dial the number in front of me, then sit back expectantly.

After a few anxious moments, my optimism is rewarded.

'Hello. Who's that?' The tone is aggressive, Morris not happy to be disturbed from his slumbers at such an early hour.

'It's me, Morris. Frank. Frank from A to Z. Sorry for ringing so early. I tried to reach you last week, but you weren't answering your phone. I know it's short notice, but any chance of you coming in today?'

There is a momentary silence from the other end. I hold my breath and cross my fingers whilst my stomach rumbles in anticipation. Could my luck be about to turn?

'Oh, shit, Frank. You got me out of bed. I was well away in Noddyland. What, today you want me? Today, this morning? For a removal?'

Now Morris may be tops at painting and decorating, but when it comes to eligibility for entry into Mensa, you might say he's a few pence short of a full shilling.

'Aye, if you can Morris,' I reply encouragingly. 'I really could do with your experience. I can get one of the vans to pick you up. That's if you need a bit of time for breakfast and to get ready. What do you say?' This offer is made in the knowledge that Morris's form of transport, when not on painting duty, is his rusty, ten-year-old Raleigh cycle. He also faces the prospect of a four-mile cycle ride. Subconsciously, I'm attempting to close the door to any doubts that might be revolving in his mind about commuting.

There is a brief period of silence during which I'm on tenterhooks.

'I've got no other work on today,' he eventually replies, disgruntled. 'But I need to have a word with the missus. I don't know if she's anything planned. She's still in her kip. Hold on, I'll be back in a minute.'

With that, he puts the phone down while I mentally resort to prayer.

Please God, please don't let this be shopping day. Please let the kids be up and about, ready for school and not off sick for the day. Please let Mary be desperately short of a pound or two in her pocket and recognise the financial benefits of a day's work by willing hubby, Morris. Please God, please dear God, please, please don't let me down.

Hypocritical, I know, to talk to Him up there. The last time I was in church and gave Him my support was years ago, probably at someone's funeral or wedding. But this is an emergency.

Three or four tense minutes elapse, during which I've ample time to reprise my misfortunes of the day.

My reverie is abruptly terminated.

'Hi, Frank, it's Morris again.'

As if I didn't know who it bloody was.

'Afraid I can't come in, Frank. Got to go to a funeral. The wife's sister's hubby. I'd forgotten about it. Don't know how, because we spent all of last week over at their place trying to sort things out. That's why you couldn't reach me. And to be honest, I really don't want to go today, 'cause I didn't even like the rat-bag, but it's for the missus and her sister, you know what I mean. I've got to make the effort.'

This news hits me like I've been punched in the stomach. All my best hopes shot to hell, just like that! It's as much as I can do not to break down in tears. And as for my prayers... *Well, thanks a lot, Mate.*

'Sorry to hear that, Morris.' I try to sound as if I mean it, but in my mind I berate Mary's sister's silly sod of a husband for pegging out when needed least. Selfish, I know, but getting my crews out on the road comes top of my priorities. Not for me, sensitivity related to the occasion.

But I'm not prepared to give up, not yet. If nothing else, I'm a trier. And I've a thick skin.

'The missus couldn't go alone, could she?' I suggest, desperately trying to think of a carrot which might be acceptable to him and his dearly beloved. 'It would be worth a ten-hour wage packet, if you can make it in – and there'd probably be a cash bonus at the end of the day.' I'm hoping that the confirmation of a likely fifty-five pound payout plus a bonus, might bring Morris and his missus to the sensible conclusion that flexibility must be the order of the day. Morris doesn't need to know that this bonus has just materialised in the last few seconds; or that it'll only be a fiver.

I should be so lucky!

'No way, Frank. The missus would never let me forget it. I'd be in the dog house, honest. Talking about dogs, she's not too happy with me as it is. Thinks I'm a right arsehole. I didn't take our new puppy dog for a walk yesterday when I was supposed to. Did its business all over our carpet. On top of that, she's peed off I've just wakened her. She had a bad night last night, what with her sister leaning on her and the funeral coming up. It would be more than my life is worth to even think of broaching the subject again. See what I mean, Frank? Sorry, some other time maybe.'

'Okay, Morris. I understand.'

Like hell I do. The way I'm feeling, if I could get a hold of his bloody dog at this moment, I'd stick a cork up its backside. And another larger one up Mary's.

No point in making Morris aware of my true feelings, though. 'I thought it was worth a try,' I say. 'Hope you didn't mind my asking?' This is me remembering I have to keep him sweet for another occasion. 'Trust all goes well at the funeral. Speak to you again. Sorry again about the early call. Cheers.'

Deflated, I put the phone down then glance at my watch. 'Bloody hell,' I exclaim involuntarily. It's fast approaching seven-fifteen.

It so happens I'm one of those conscientious bosses who believes in getting into work before the workforce arrives. It sets a good example to the staff. It also gives me time to clear the answering machine and sort out last-minute hiccups. The fact that I take a couple of hours off for lunch or sod off home in the middle of the afternoon is neither here nor there as far as they're concerned. What they don't know won't hurt either of us.

Referring again to my casual labour list, I commence dialling my second-choice number and listen absently to the ringing tones.

Kev, the intended recipient of my call, is a young lad of eighteen who lives with his parents on a council estate, just a few minutes' cycle ride from my premises. Despite being encouraged by the local Job Centre to take up each and every Youth Training Programme under offer, he's been unable to secure full-time employment. This could be because he dresses like an eco-warrior, with his nostril and one ear adorned with small gold-plated rings. Personally, I doubt if he has any desire to work on a regular basis. Despite that, I've had no cause to complain on the few occasions he has clocked in. Unfortunately, he doesn't always turn up when he says he will, which is why he's at the bottom of my list. Kept on file for emergencies.

Impatiently listening to the ringing tones, I refer to my watch, becoming more restless as the seconds tick by.

'Who the hell's that?'

I'm startled by the raucous voice at the other end. A woman's voice, not one I recognise. It's loud enough to make me momentarily withdraw the receiver from my ear.

'Err, could I speak to Kev, please?'

'Bev? Did you say Bev? There's no Bev here,' the gruff voice snorts down the line. 'You must have the wrong number, mate. Who is it, anyway? What d'ya want at this bleeding time of the morning?'

'No, not Bev. Kev, it's Kevin I want to speak to. Kevin Crabtree. This is Frank Tipple from A to Z Removals. Kev's worked for me in the past and I'm wondering if he'd like a day's work. Sorry if I've got you out of bed.'

'Kevin! Oh, it's Kevin you want. Why didn't you say so? Jesus Christ, as if I haven't got enough on my plate. Kevin, you say? Work today? What, that lazy little sod? That'll be a surprise. He was out on the piss last night. Don't even know whether he came home or not. Who'd you say you were, mate? Where are you from?'

I draw a deep breath and count to five. I'm tempted to request that this unappealing member of the female race makes an immediate appointment to see her doctor and instigate an ear wash. Instead, I reply lamely. 'Frank, Frank Tipple from the removal company. Kev, Kevin's done some work for me in the past.' I now try a different tack. 'Can I speak to him, please?'

'Hold on, mate. I'll see if he's in his bedroom.'

I wearily rub my fingers across my forehead. A few moments later, the sound of shouting, muted by distance, echoes down the line as Mrs Crabtree attempts to make contact with the fruit from her tree.

'Kevin, Kevin, are you up there, you little tosser?'

Silence. A few precious seconds pass as I listen intently for a response, my ear pressed tightly against the receiver. More shouting can be heard from afar, fainter this time.

'Kevin, if you're up there, would you get your arse out of bed? There's some bloke on the phone. Sounds a bit of a wanker, if you ask me. Jesus! I can't get a bloody moment's peace in this sodding house.'

I'm assuming this dear lady is Kev's mum. It's obvious she's not aware that her not-so dulcet tones are reverberating down the line. I try hard not to let her instant and unjustified appraisal of my character get to me.

More seconds elapse. My watch is again telling me it's time to go.

The distinct noise of a door being opened then closed resonates in the background, quickly followed by the sounds of shuffling footsteps. Someone else is now standing close to the phone.

'Who the hell is ringing at this hour, Vera?' A reedy male voice. Doesn't sound like Kev, though.

I hear another noise which, to my experienced ear, sounds like a loud fart, followed by further shuffling steps.

'Christ, Ernie.' Ma Kev's voice again. Vera, I guess. 'Did you have to do that right under my nose? That's bloody gross. And it's a bloke from the removal company, if you must know. He wants Kevin.'

'From where? A removal company?' Male voice again. Must be Ernie with the wind problem. 'What's he doing ringing at this time of the morning? And what's he want? We don't need a fucking removal company. Tell 'im to piss off.'

Nice one, Ernie, I'm thinking. *You sure know how to talk to a lady. Keep taking the charm pills.*

'I know we don't need a removal company, you stupid old fart. I didn't say the guy was coming to move us. Why can't you keep your fat ears open and your big mouth shut? The wanker wants Kevin about some work. Now do something useful for a change and see if he's in bed. And for Christ's sake, put some trousers on. You're doing my head in walking around with that wrinkled worm dangling between your legs.'

Listening to this dialogue, I feel I've been transported to another planet. Are they so stupid they don't realise I can hear every word? Or do they not give a toss?

I hear a slowly receding but incoherent muttering from the other end. Then silence. And more silence.

Frustrated, I'm beginning to give up all hope when…

'Who's that?'

Great! It's Kev, in all his glory.

'Hi, Kev. It's me, Frank, from the removal company. Sorry for getting you out of bed so early, but one of my lads has phoned in sick and I need a replacement urgently. Could you come in today to help me out?'

'Today? What day's today?' Kev asks, his voice thick with sleep.

'It's Monday, Kev,' I reply, biting my tongue. *You know, the day after Sunday and the one before Tuesday.*

'Monday, Kev,' I repeat. 'And it's not a bad day at that. If you come in today, I could probably give you another day's work on Friday. I'll also pay cash, if you want.'

I'm hoping that my offer of cash, plus a second day's work on Friday, will clinch Kev's services.

There's an uncomfortable moment of silence while Kev engages his brain. Ernie's reedy voice can still be heard muttering in the background, interspersed with hacking coughs, those of a heavy smoker. Thankfully, Vera seems to have removed herself from my sonar system. I'm grateful for small mercies.

'Yeah. Okay, Frankie. I've got nothing else on today and I could be doing with the dosh. What time do you want me in? I haven't had any breakfast.'

An overwhelming wave of emotion sweeps through me. If Kev had been standing right in front of me, I'd have embraced him in open arms, given him a big Russian kiss (both cheeks), told him what a grand service he was doing for the furtherance of the British economy and, to boot, what a dear, pleasant, loveable mum and dad he had.

Instead, I nonchalantly reply, 'Eight o'clock if you can, Kev. I've got a busy day today, and all the other lads are coming in at that time. Okay?'

'Sure thing, Frankie. I'll be as fast as I can.'

'Good man. And don't go changing your mind. I'm relying on you.' I place the phone on its cradle and, for a brief moment, savour the feeling of normality which seeps through my system. On the spur of the moment, I press the palms of my hands together in supplication and proffer a quick prayer.

Dear God, thank you for your cooperation. Your earlier omission regarding Morris is forgiven. You may now stand down. And I owe you one.

In my relief that the fish has taken the bait, I've neglected to offer Kev the opportunity of a pick-up from home. He now has forty minutes to wash, toilet, get dressed, have breakfast and transport himself to the yard.

Energised, I retrieve my briefcase, switch on the answering machine and limp smartly to the front door, in the process collecting my three-in-one waterproof jacket from the hall coat-rack. As long as Kev doesn't have second thoughts and throw a last-minute wobbly, I've now got a full complement of staff.

Provided everybody else turns up.

Chapter five

I STEP OUTSIDE the front door to a mind-numbing gale-force wind. This rages round the corner of the house, taking my breath away and nearly sweeping me off my feet. Vapour trails of grey mist spew from my mouth like sulphurous fumes, to rapidly disperse into the surrounding gloom. The path, pavement and garden are covered with the white sheen of a heavy overnight frost, glinting in the subdued light of the street lamp like a constellation of small stars.

I grimace. It's a typical, depressing winter's morning. And snow has been forecast. The outlook couldn't be worse. And I'm neither physically nor mentally equipped to cope.

The cold penetrates my outer clothing and a shudder runs through my body. I cast my eyes to the heavens, hoping for divine intervention.

I should be so lucky. It's unlikely *any* shaft of light – even one produced by Him above – could penetrate this mass of black clouds. There's no telling what they contain. But it doesn't look promising. Fingers crossed those silly buggers at the Bracknell Met Office have got their forecast wrong; analysed the incorrect meteorological charts or stuck their fingertips out the wrong windows.

Disgruntled, I ease myself behind the wheel, slip the automatic gear shift into Drive and manoeuvre away from the kerb, briefly braking as a sheet of newspaper blows across the windscreen then disappears over the top of the car.

The radio is pre-programmed to Radio 2. I've now got ten minutes to relax in the company of Sarah Kennedy. Not an intellectually challenging start to the day, but one which suits me fine at this early point: undemanding chatter and light music to soothe the body and soul.

Approximately twelve minutes later – to the sound of Elvis telling me I 'ain't nothin' but a hound dog' – I turn off the main road and into the narrow country lane leading to my business premises. The rain starts to fall, small drops striking the windscreen then erupting into a full-blown rainstorm. The ferocious wind lashes it against the glass, temporarily obscuring my view of the outside world.

'Brilliant, Frank,' I mutter disconsolately, turning on my wipers and peering bleakly through the windscreen. 'The last thing you wanted to see. Can those bloody forecasters not get anything right?'

Recurrent, negative feelings have once again taken hold of me. Employees, rain, freezing temperatures and Monday mornings are definitely not an inspiring mix. If I were a betting man, I'd stake a few quid that someone else is not going to turn up. Possibly Kev, when he sticks his head out the front door and sees what's what. Or James, another of my younger casuals. But as Pete has shown, it could be anybody.

Switching my wipers to full speed, I throw caution to the wind and speed up the lane, before finally pulling to a stop in front of my yard gate. As the engine slowly ticks over, Judy Garland tries her best to convince me that 'Happy days are here again'. It's going to take a lot of convincing. And right now, I've got other things on my mind.

Sitting motionless, I take a long, critical look at the entrance gate, closed and securely locked. It's a monster, weighing a ton, forged and built by the Frank Spencer of craftsmanship. The entrance to Hell couldn't be more forbidding. And to open it in these conditions will be like pushing a steamroller up a steep hill. I'm certainly not looking forward to tackling the big bastard on a day like this.

Hoping for a sudden break in the wind and rain, my thoughts turn to what lies beyond the gate. Not my usual life-has-been-good-to-me thoughts; nor my regular chirpy-chappy thoughts. These are my dark, brooding, morose is-this-the-best-that-life's-got-to-offer? thoughts.

★　★　★

FIVE YEARS AGO it was when I first saw what lay beyond the entrance.

With a deep recession in the housing market – and the lease on my operating centre coming to an end – I'd been searching for an alternative, reduced-cost base. When a local estate agent sent me a blurb describing the property, it appeared – on paper, at least – to be the solution to my quest. But when I arrived at the open gate to await the arrival of the agent's representative, it crossed my mind that the silly sods had given me the wrong address and sent me to a piece of wasteland.

In coming to that conclusion, I was both right and wrong. The large, dilapidated sign erected to the left of the entrance confirmed that this was where I was supposed to be. 'COMMERCIAL PREMISES FOR RENT,' it shouted out in large letters. 'ONE ACRE OF LAND INCLUDING ADMINISTRATION CENTRE. SUITABLE FOR CAR STORAGE, TRANSPORT OR BUILDERS' FIRM. RENT NEGOTIABLE.'

But it was a piece of wasteland, a so-called brownfield site. The size and shape of a football pitch, it was bounded on one side by an electricity sub-station, to the rear by a ten-feet-high wooden fence and to the other side by an embankment carrying the busy Reading-to-London commuter rail traffic. In the short time that I waited for the agent's representative to arrive, half a dozen trains thundered back and forth, making it difficult to think.

My first impressions were not good. I remember thinking that the premises would be more appropriate to Steptoe and Son, rather than a Pickfords of the future, as was my ambition at the time. And it didn't get any better. Looking further down the site and seeing the administration centre tucked into the rear corner, my first thought was that a railway carriage had come off the tracks, rolled down the embankment and been left there to rot.

It turned out to be a Portakabin, twenty feet long by ten feet wide, with a small office, a tiny storage and kitchen area and an even smaller toilet facility. That was the administration centre. As euphemistic a title as one could find in any estate agent's information leaflet. Whoever dreamed that up should have been flogged to death for abusing the Queen's English in such a blatant manner.

It wasn't even a new Portakabin. A closer inspection confirmed that the outside paint was chipped and faded, the windows were single-paned and poorly fitting, and the internal fittings and fixtures might have been the products of an archaeological dig.

It felt like my visit had been well and truly wasted. And at that point, I nearly turned around and drove away. But thankfully I didn't. And that was entirely due to the arrival of the gorgeous young lady whom the agent sent to show me around.

A Miss Temple, as I recall, using her maiden name for business purposes. Not that I was aware of that at the time. If truth be known, I'd have been more than happy to worship at the altar of that particular temple any time. She had the perfumed, sexual scent of the predator stamped all over her.

I really fancied my chances. And looking back, it's difficult to remember what caused this blanket of dewy-eyed mist to descend on me. It could have been the seductive swing of her pert little bottom as she weaved her way to the front door. Or the flash of tanned thighs under her short skirt as she stepped over the threshold. It could even have been the deep valley of cleavage which she exposed as she stooped in the office, ostensibly to pick up a paperclip. But more likely than any of these, it was probably the moment she provocatively positioned herself in the front doorway, creating the near contact of our two forms as I squeezed through. Another half inch and contact would have occurred, causing me to lose all sense of propriety. It was as much as I could do not to clamp my sweaty hands over those magnificent protuberances there and then. Fortunately, common sense prevailed. By a nipple's width!

What a mug I was. And things haven't changed much. She certainly managed to pull the wool over my lascivious eyes.

Fortunately, I didn't make any silly, presumptuous moves. And just as well. A police friend told me later that she was married to a Chinese restaurateur, suspected of being connected with the Triads. Not somebody to trifle with. Any wrong moves then and my head could have ended up on the chopping block, my penis in the sausage mixer and my testicles served up as hors d'oeuvres in one of his restaurants.

But that's something I didn't know at the time. When we had completed our short tour of the administration centre, I was so enamoured by her charms and her physical attributes that, on driving away from the premises, my mind was in a fog and I'd only a very vague recollection of what was on offer.

Yet, here's the funny thing: in spite of everything, the premises have proven to be more than satisfactory for all our operational needs. More importantly, there's been no adverse reaction from customers. On the contrary, over the years I've been here, they've shown commendable common sense in not equating the quality of the premises to the excellence of the service. Many a recommendation I've now got in my files from satisfied householders, business owners and estate agents alike to vouch for that. Confirmation once again that clothing doth not the man maketh.

★ ★ ★

I'M JOLTED FROM my reminiscences by Sarah Kennedy with another time check. Seven-forty-five.

Shit! The staff will be arriving for work in the next few minutes and there are last-minute things to be done.

But I can't do these until I get into the office. And I can't get into the office until I get into the yard. And I can't get into the yard until that bloody gate is open. And that means getting out of the car. But there's no let-up to the wind or rain. So I don't feel like getting out of the car. Stalemate!

Resigned to the inevitable, I switch Sarah off and make my way across the rain-soaked turf. The rain spatters against the corrugated gate with a noise like a machine gun. Within seconds my head is soaked and rivers of frigid water stream off my jacket onto the exposed legs of my trousers.

Somewhere in the adjoining trees, a magpie emits a high-pitched squawk, as if laughing at my plight. It better be careful, though. If I get a hold of it, I'll put my foot on its stupid neck. That'll soon take the wind out of its windpipe. That's the sort of mood I'm in.

Cursing and swearing – and becoming more and more bedraggled – I undo the lock then slowly release the latch bar securing the gate to the post. Digging my heels in to give me additional leverage, I tuck my shoulder tight against the corrugated sheeting. 'Now move, you cantankerous big bastard.'

Holding on grimly as the gate threatens to push me arse-over-heels, it eventually latches on to its fixing-bracket. My fingers are red, raw and numb, my nose is dripping inside and out, and my hair lies flat and soggy on my head like a wet dishcloth.

Frazzled, I quickly reinstate myself within the comfort zone of my car then drive carefully through the yard gate. The car suspension bumps and grinds over the uneven surface and past the ghostly outlines of my four removal vans. These are lined up adjoining the electricity station, the stark outlines silhouetted against the early morning skyline. Although the colours are not at this point apparent, all are paint-sprayed in the firm's livery of blue, the company name boldly emblazoned along the front, sides and back in large white capital letters.

I pull to a stop, extract myself then make my way carefully round the side of the Portakabin. In the darkness, I fail to see the large pool directly outside the front door. My right foot is immersed in the water. A profanity escapes my lips as I immediately step back onto relatively dry ground. Brilliant! I've now got a soggy foot to match my damaged toe. Perhaps Vera's analysis was a little too close for comfort. What was it she called me?

'She called you a bloody wanker, Frank, that's what,' I shout at the front door, juggling with the keyring like a cack-handed clown at the circus.

And the way things stand at the moment that sums me up nicely: Frank Tipple Esquire – King of the Willy-Wankers.

Chapter six

I STEP INTO THE sheltered threshold of the Portakabin, thankful to be out of the rain.

It's pitch black. With no light switch in the narrow hallway, I'm rooted to the spot. If I didn't know better, I could be at the bottom of a mine shaft. But there's no point in complaining to the landlord. There's more chance of him sending me a Christmas card than rectifying this deficiency – the miserable dipstick! And I'm certainly not prepared to spend my hard-earned money upgrading his premises. Not when the bugger could send me packing at any time. What's needed here is a miner's head lamp. But thanks to Maggie, where am I going to find a miner, let alone his lamp, in this day and age? It would be hard enough to find a mine.

I shake the excess rain off my clothing like a freshly bathed puppy then, as my eyes adjust to the dark, gingerly feel my way up the narrow passage, past the hatch window in the partition wall and into the office. The indistinct outlines of the office furniture are barely identifiable in the chinks of light now filtering through the two exterior windows.

I flick on the light switch positioned just inside the door. The room is bathed in the welcoming glow of the 100-watt bulb hanging from the ceiling. Although sufficiently strong to cast a subdued light into the hall corridor, its beam barely penetrates the two exterior windows. But from outside, this single bulb must beckon like a lighthouse. Hopefully, all this morning's staff will be safely drawn to its comforting glow like energetic little moths.

The glass panes in the curtainless windows are covered with a thin layer of ice, obscuring the view to the outside world. Why I don't leave the heating switched on overnight and weekends during cold spells, I'd find hard to explain. That would certainly stop me feeling like a penguin entering its pen. But I don't. And I do know why: there's a thrifty trait in me which continually counts the cost. *Look after the pennies and the pounds will look after themselves.* That's what Ma Tipple used to tell us kids as she handed over our six-penny-bit pocket money at the end of each week. And good advice it was. But then again, she never had to stand in this ice box. She might have thought different then.

That said, she'd have been chuffed to see me do my bit to reduce my carbon footprint. Although exactly what that is, I'm not certain. Can't be a big one, that's for sure. Not with the administration centre as small as it is and me with only size-nine feet. But if turning off the heaters helps prevent the Antarctic from defrosting then I'm all for it. But not to the point where my balls break off and my little willy cracks. That's masochism of the highest order.

I switch the two electric wall heaters to full power then take a moment to appraise my surroundings.

This small room is the hub and heartbeat of A to Z Removals.

Pinned to the right-hand wall is a large graphic chart, providing an instant guide to the progress made by A to Z Removals over the past fifteen years. Resembling an artist's impression of a mountain range, the separate sales and profit lines trace a matching furrow of peaks and troughs – fortunately more of the former than the latter. The respective blue and green lines confirm the steady progress made over the years, despite recessional pressures and stiff competition. Whenever the business goes through a sticky patch, or when I suffer one of my low points – and today could be one of those – this graph gives me some measure of reassurance that it's all worth the effort and that my initial investment was well spent.

Unfortunately, there has been little investment in the furniture. Each piece contains many a scratch and dent as testament to the number of knocks received over many years' usage.

Directly under the hatch window is a small cupboard, measuring five feet long and four feet high. Next to it is a grey four-drawer metal filing cabinet. Both items are crammed to bursting with paperwork vital to the day-to-day running of the business and to meet the ever-demanding requirements of the authorities. All in all, they must hold the equivalent of one small forest. How many carbon footprints have been trod in the manufacture of the paper held there, or how much the sea levels across the world have been increased as a result, I've no idea. Nor do I much care, when it's the government's fault in the first place, lumbering us with their excessive legislative demands.

The remaining space is taken up by two desks, each with one chair. Alice's desk is situated under the window to my left. Given that she handles at least 96 per cent of the administrative output of the firm, her desk is double pedestal and bigger that mine. Her desktop equipment includes a Silver-Reed electric typewriter and an electric calculating machine. If the latter was any older, it would contain a wind-up facility. In addition, she has a telephone, a plastic pen-and-pencil holder and a stacked trio of red plastic letter-trays, each tray full of paperwork. There is no computer to be seen anywhere in the office, demonstrating my unwillingness to adopt modern communication and administration technology.

My single pedestal desk is positioned under the other window, directly facing the front entrance. The only pieces of equipment are a telephone and an answering machine – both items an ongoing but necessary irritant and a regular conveyor of the positive, the negative and the indifferent. The desk also contains a plastic pen-and-pencil holder and one red plastic tray. This contains my appointments for today, arranged by Alice over the course of last week.

The view from my window gives me the ability to see any comings and goings. If the visitor is someone I don't particularly want to see – a salesman, an awkward customer, a Jehovah's Witness or my landlord's agent come to renegotiate rental terms – then I'll be out of my chair and in the toilet before you can say Jack Robinson, leaving a beleaguered Alice to hold the fort.

But it's the arrival of staff that's my key interest at the moment, the first of whom drives through the gates as I watch. Moving close to the window, I rub a small circle in the frozen pane and peer myopically through the clouded, rain-streaked glass. I recognise the faint outline of Herbie's old Vauxhall Nova, as he parks inside the gate. He is immediately followed by Billy in his battered Ford Fiesta. That's two major concerns off my mind. At the very least, I've got my two main men. Both guaranteed to be in the yard and ready for work on the dot of eight am, clocking-in time. With no proper canteen or waiting room facility, they're happy to sit out there – whatever the conditions – until it's time to report for work.

Mind you, it helps that I'm not unionised. But bugger me if I'm going to let them tell me what can and can't be done. Not when it's my business and when I'm the one taking all the risks: putting up the money, risking the loss of my home as collateral for punitive bank loans, and, in times of recession, worrying myself sick, trying to keep us all afloat. In any case, the lads are perfectly capable of ganging up on me as it is, without having some socialist, card-carrying comrade organising them to revolt while skimming a portion of their hard-earned dosh to fund his not-so-comradely lifestyle.

With the thought of the Red Flag predictably getting me hot under the collar, I glance at the office clock. Only eight minutes to go before kick-off.

'Time to check those phone messages, Frankie babe.'

I settle into the chair by my desk, make myself comfortable then stare morosely at the answering machine. Ominously, its intermittent flickering red light is indicating that four messages have been left over the weekend. Are my worst fears about to be realised? Is someone else about to spring a last-minute sickie on me?

Stirring myself into action, I pull my message pad from the top-right drawer, select a ballpoint pen from the plastic holder then tentatively press Message mode. The small cassette begins to revolve and I wait apprehensively for the first message to disgorge. The uncertainty of what's to come is creating knots in my stomach. It's make-or-break time.

Chapter seven

THE MACHINE SPEWS out its first message.

'Hi. This is Angus McIntosh. Yae moved us last week and I hae to say I'm nae too happy aboot it. We've discovered a few damages and wannae make a claim. Can yae send us a claim form, so's we can gae it sorted? Yae can gae me oer the weekend and Monday.'

I listen to this short but pointed message, first with relief that it's not one of the lads reporting sick, then with dismay.

A damage claim. Not what I want to hear first thing on a Monday morning. On autopilot, I list McIntosh's address and telephone number on my pad then press the Pause button as I assess the implications of his call.

Mr McIntosh was one of last Thursday's removals. A young Scottish bloke, from what I remember. And now he's putting in a claim. And not just for one item. He's indicated there've been a few damages. Yet none of the lads said anything to me when they came in on Friday. Herbie was the foreman on that job. He'd have been aware if anything had gone wrong. And I'm sure he'd have mentioned something.

The impact of McIntosh's message causes a small tremor to pass through my body. Any claim of unknown proportions has the immediate effect of causing an instantaneous bout of depression. And that's mainly due to the excess the insurance company have built into my Goods-in-Transit policy. And a hefty excess it is: three hundred and fifty pounds, despite my having an exemplary claims record. It's extortion, pure and simple. Makes the taxman seem like the fairy godmother. But I've got to live with it. Hard as my brokers have tried, this policy is the best deal they've been able to negotiate. And it certainly wouldn't be prudent to operate without one.

'Shit. Nothing can be done about you right this moment, Mister Tosh.' Not the most eloquent manner to address the situation, but the best I can muster under the circumstances.

I resolve to ring him later, to determine what all the fuss is about. But first it will be necessary to have a quiet word in Herbie's ear and find out what he's got to say for himself.

The dual effects of electric heaters and McIntosh's call have brought me out in a hot flush. I remove my three-in-one jacket and sling it carelessly over the back of the chair then, for the second time, press the Play button. With low expectations of what's to come, I again listen intently, pen poised ready for action.

'Hello, Mr Tipple. Mrs Arnett here. You moved us last Tuesday...'

Here we go again. The negative side of my character in the ascendancy, I squirm in my chair as Mrs Arnett delivers the rest of her message:

'Just to let you know that your boxes are ready for collection. Can you tell me when you can pick them up? Oh, and thanks to your men for a really good job. All went well and we were very pleased with the care and courtesy shown by your crew. Will you thank Herbie in particular? He worked really hard. My number is...'

Listening to this message, a smug expression replaces the wrinkles of concern. *A really good job*, she said. Bless you, Mrs Arnett. And good on you, Herbie.

My basic belief in the better nature of the human race is nearly restored. Perhaps life is worth living, after all. Mustn't forget to pass on the message to Herbie and his crew, though. A bit of praise from the customer goes a long way. Helps the lads to realise the importance of the work they're undertaking and the appreciation of a job well done. Goodness knows, they certainly get the brickbats thrown at them when things go wrong.

Message number three has started. Any positive vibes deriving from the last call are quickly dispelled.

'Is that you, you thick Irish bastard?'

I recognise the slurred voice immediately. Cyril Tomkins, one of my regular casuals. Until recently that is, when he developed too keen a liking for the hard stuff. A couple of months ago he turned up for work rat-arsed. I packed him off home with a flea in his ear and also took the sensible decision to exclude him from all future employment. And the silly sod's held it against me ever since.

There follows a succession of derogatory comments, laced with an impressive range of obscenities and accompanied by the raucous sound of heavy metal music in the background. Listening to his diatribe, it never fails to amaze me how a drunk – especially a totally inarticulate one like Cyril – can sound so utterly imbecilic. And I should know. Last night's performance of mine would have provided ready confirmation of that.

I impatiently drum my fingers on the desktop, willing the message to end. There's a pause while Cyril plumbs the depths of his intellect for a final wounding comment. I don't have long to wait.

'Piss on the lot of you. Wanker!' *Click*. End of message.

Thank you, Cyril. Thank you very much. And may you have a nice day, too.

I try to put the content of this latest appraisal to the back of my mind. *Wanker, indeed*. First Ma Kev, now Cyril. One more strike and I'm definitely going to have to reassess myself.

Things are definitely warming up, in more ways than one. A mix of melted ice and condensation runs down the inside of the windows and my armpits are beginning to sweat. As message number four commences, I remove my inner coat and throw it over the back of Alice's chair. Is this the message I don't want to hear?

'Hi Frank, Jane here! It's seven thirty and I've just got up. Didn't want to disturb you at home. Hope you were able to get out of bed and into work this morning. When I left last night, you looked the worse for wear. By the way, everybody enjoyed your bank-robber impersonation, but can I please have my tights back. Also, hope you don't mind my asking, but what was that you put in the vindaloo? You said you were going to use a hot spice, but I didn't think it would remove the lining from my stomach. Only joking, Frank. Anyway, thanks for a good party. Trust you've survived okay. See you tomorrow. Love you, bye for now.'

Bless her. Always concerned for my welfare. What would I do without her? She's got a lot to put up with, what with my drunken antics and my culinary experiments. Don't remember doing the bank-robber impersonation, though. Hope Jane wasn't wearing those tights prior to my efforts to entertain. If so,

I've no idea how they got from her hips to my head.

Relieved that my fears regarding absenteeism have been groundless, I erase the preceding messages then peer anxiously through the window to see what's happening outside. Although visibility has improved, my view of the front entrance is still impaired. Additional cars are now parked alongside the embankment next to Herbie and Billy and a number of bodies have collected by the front gate, seemingly oblivious to the falling rain. But I still don't know if I've got a complete team.

Pressing my face against the window, I attempt to do a headcount while identifying who's who. I make it eight, but it's difficult to be sure. The assortment of bodies keeps circulating like a herd of sheep in a small paddock. It's also impossible to see whether anyone has remained in their car.

With only a few minutes to go before clocking-in time, a growing apprehension is taking hold of me. If I'm right about the eight heads, that leaves me three under par. And that will mean one customer with no removal van and crew.

The consequences of that don't bear thinking about. That customer won't be able to move out and the incoming party to the chain won't be able to move in. If another removal company can't be found, both families will have to be put up in a hotel until it's all sorted out. And how long will that take? Jesus! There'll be overnight hotel expenses to pay, plus any extra costs the incoming remover has to face, plus anything else the solicitors can swing my way due to the stress caused to both customers. Add the solicitors' bills and it would be a bloody disaster.

All this speculation is compounding my misgivings. Kev and James are my major concern this morning.

But there's nothing to be done at this late stage. Another few moments and I'll know exactly what the score is.

Hopefully, par for the course!

Chapter eight

STEELING MYSELF for what's likely to be my most stressful period of the day, I stare gloomily through the window at the shadowy figures milling around the entrance. On cue, as if sensing my concerns, they slowly start to make their way towards the Portakabin, carefully skirting the water-filled potholes.

Observing their approach, I can't help but smile. This straggling column reminds me of a herd of cattle heading for the milking yard. It's as much as I can do not to open the window, cup my hands round my mouth and emit a succession of loud *moos*. Haven't got the nerve to do it, though. Don't want the staff to think I'm a smart-arse. More to the point, one or two have got no sense of humour. There's a risk that someone will get the hump and take off on me. I can't afford to lose anyone else this morning, as a result of my childish antics.

As they wend their erratic path down the yard, I'm still desperately trying to get a fix on the number of heads. But with the poor light and the positions of the men interchanging by the second, it's well nigh impossible. As the pack draws closer, the chatter of voices can be clearly heard, the noise becoming increasingly vociferous as they reach the front door. Herbie, the senior man in the organisation and my top gun, is in pole position. His size eights will be the first footsteps over the threshold not one second earlier than eight am. It's like he's got a clocking mechanism built into his shoes. That's Herbie for you. But I'm happy enough just to see him and the rest of the troops arrive on time.

The mass of bodies begins to fill the narrow entrance, but with no light in the hall and so many crammed into the confined space either side of the hatch window, it's impossible to determine how many have arrived.

The discordant sounds of chit-chat and banter are successfully drowning out all external sounds, the raw and raucous dialogue interspersed with a series of belches and farts. To add to the general pollution, wafts of grey smoke begin to seep through the partially opened hatch window. So much for my attempts to make the office a smoke-free zone.

If truth be known, I'd ban all smoking in the office entrance and also in the vans, but Herbie has warned me this wouldn't be well received by the lads. In his opinion – and his is an opinion to be valued – the likely outcome would be a walkout. And that's a risk I can't afford to take. Power to the working class.

My lack of conviction in the matter can be justified in five ways. One, I can't be in all of the vans all of the time, monitoring what's going on. Two, there's no provision within the Portakabin for a smoking area. Three, on a day like today, one wouldn't even send the mother-in-law outside for a smoke. Four, any smoke that does penetrate the office can normally be quickly dispersed once the lads have gone. And five, it's a small concession on my part, costing me nothing. So one I can readily afford to concede.

I've therefore learned to turn a blind eye to Health and Safety directives, grit my teeth and recognise that the tax from one man's smoke will likely pay for another man's hip replacement. In another couple of years it could well be Frankie who's the recipient of that hip, thanks to Herbie and the lads.

Resigned to whatever the roll call holds in store for me, I rise from my chair and move towards the hatch window. 'Morning, lads!' I cry out cheerfully, disguising my real feelings in true theatrical style. I fight to be heard over the noise. 'Hope everybody's fit and well, 'cause we've got a busy day ahead. I just need to check everybody's in, then we'll get you on your way.'

It would be wrong to assume I'm now faced with an orderly set of men, giving me their undivided attention, eagerly and attentively waiting for the next pearls of wisdom to emanate from my lips. The fact of the matter is: this isn't the army, I'm not the regimental sergeant major-type, and a lot of these guys are certainly not soldier material. Some of them have never been taught to respect authority – certainly not in the manner one would've expected in days long gone by. And as the majority don't have permanent contracts of employment – with nothing much to lose – they've no reason to kow-tow to anyone. And that includes Francis Frederick Fidel Foster. But I've learnt to live with it.

I'm therefore fighting against an ever-continuing explosion of repartee and banter as I attempt to bring some order into the morning's events. Everybody wants to be a Morecambe and Wise. But if they're happy, I'm happy, more or less.

'Okay, lads, settle down. And can you give me a bit of quiet, for Christ's sake.'

My labour rota for the day is attached to a clipboard hanging above the hatch window. As I remove it, there is a brief lull in the noise levels then the babble of voices recommences. Trying to ignore the renewed bedlam, I refer to the roster then, without further ado, commence the roll call. My pen is dramatically poised in mid-air, ready to place a corresponding tick against each name as necessary. This action yet again reaffirms my thespian credentials, intended to reaffirm my command of the situation.

'Herbie and Billy, present and correct,' I cry out at the top of my voice, at the same time ticking twice on my clipboard with an extravagant flourish of my pen. My head halfway through the hatch window, I feel the need to bring the troops up to speed with the labour situation. 'By the way, lads, Pete's off ill today, so I've got a bit of re-adjusting to do.'

'Is that why you've always got a hand down your trouser front?' This piece of wit comes from Charlie, who reckons he's a bit of a wag.

'Oh, very funny, Charlie,' I respond, not in the mood for humour – especially not this morning. 'Let's see if you're still laughing come seven this evening, given the job you've been allocated.'

This response draws good-natured banter from someone else down the end of the hall. I've got to be careful, though. Charlie's one of those blokes happy to have a jibe at someone else's expense, but not so keen when it comes to taking a bit of his own medicine. Also, he's not aware of his forthcoming additional responsibility as my substitute driver and foreman. I can't afford to get him off on the wrong foot.

'Alright then,' I continue, ignoring the heckling. 'Charlie's in. Good to see you, Charlie. What would I do without you?'

'Fred? Stephen? Speedy? Jim?' I now call out in quick order, trying to make my voice heard above the babble. Four affirmative grunts are returned from deep in the hallway and four further extravagant ticks are placed to the side of the names.

I refer again to the roster. 'John? OK, I see you.' *Tick.*

Eight up, three to go.

Still apprehensive, I crane my neck around the edge of the hatch. 'All right, I can see you, Albert.' Albert is another of my regulars. He's standing somewhere in the second row dutifully raising his arm to be noticed, two fingers formed in a recognisable V-sign. Too thick-skinned to take personal offence, I ignore the gesture, tick and press on. 'James?'

There's no immediate answer. The only sound is the continuous hubbub of voices, followed by loud guffaws from the end of the corridor. Someone's either cracked a joke or broken wind.

'James?' I call out again, louder this time, a hint of panic in my voice. My head turns from left to right as I scour the hallway. Apart from Kev, James is the only other irregular casual due in today.

The noise in the hallway has momentarily ceased as heads seek the object of my concern.

'James? Has anyone bloody well seen James?' I holler hysterically, my frustration getting the better of me. A few eyes regard me with what could be concern, but is more likely to be pity.

'Yeah, he was here a few minutes ago. I think he's gone for a pee.' This is Billy, who at long last deigns to supply the relevant information. Why couldn't he have told me when I first asked? The bastard, probably enjoying my discomfort.

Billy is my second-in-command, after Herbie. At six-feet three-inches in his socks, fifteen stones, ex-heavyweight boxer and ugly with it, he's not one to be trifled with. Causes *me* no problems, though. He's like a big pussycat in my hands, most of the time.

There are a few moments of relative silence whilst ciggies are puffed and I draw breath. Speedy and John, now standing directly outside the hatch window, are regarding me with smug, self-satisfied expressions on their faces. Nodding his head in my direction, Speedy cups his hand over his mouth, sniggers and makes some remark to John – obviously not meant to be overheard by me – at which point John creases up with a burst of laughter.

'Want to share the joke, Speedy?' I shout through the hatch window, needled but trying hard not to show it.

'Naw. Nothing to interest you, Frank,' Speedy replies, a large smirk on his face. He sneaks a quick sidelong glance at John and Speedy, who turn away, but not before I see the grin on their smug faces.

As the obvious butt of their joke, I'm irritated that they've got no apparent respect for my position. But reason prevails and I say nothing. At least the silly sods are smiling and not standing around with faces like a horse's arse.

With the confirmation of James's attendance, my optimism is renewed. Beecher's Brook has just been jumped, the final furlong is about to be ridden and the winning post is now in sight. Just Kev to book in and we're all set for the off.

'Is Kev there?' I enquire tentatively, anxiously scanning the sea of faces. Blank looks are returned by Speedy and John. They're the only ones now directly facing the hatch. The rest continue to ignore me. As if that's not enough to irritate me, someone has closed the entrance door. A grey pall of smog is lying heavy in the stale air.

Increasingly annoyed, I try again, this time shouting at the top of my voice, my patience and contorted smile long gone. 'Have any of you silly buggers seen Kev? You know, Kev, the young guy with the shaved head and the ring through his nose. And could somebody open that bloody door before we all frigging choke to death?'

'No, Frank, no sign of him!' That's from Herbie who has pushed his way down the hallway and is now standing closest to the door. He opens the door and flips his dead fag-end across the yard. A refreshing gust of air blows down the hallway and through the hatch window.

Shit! Fallen at the last hurdle. Yet Kev seemed keen enough to get his hands on some ready cash. I'd have bet a couple of quid he'd show up. Maybe he's looked out the window after my call, seen the rain, and decided to go back to bed.

'Okay, lads. Everybody's in but Kev, but we can make do without him. Time to get this show on the road.'

I tell this little porky with my tongue stuck firmly in my cheek – and without Herbie, at this stage of the game, knowing he's one crew member light. I'm not about to tell him though. What he doesn't know won't hurt him, not until later, when his arms and legs fall off.

Without further ado, I remove the four work-sheets from the top of the cupboard and rapidly allocate foremen and crews to their respective removals. Each of these work-sheets is the foreman's bible for the day. It contains the all-important collection and delivery addresses, the estimated cubic capacity of the load, the major items of furniture to be removed along with the cost of the removal, enabling the foreman to pick up the requisite cheque or cash from the customer on completion of the job.

Charlie takes the news about his additional responsibilities in relative good humour. Herbie is the last to be given his instructions. He quickly peruses his job sheet. 'What's this then, Frank? A five-bedroom house, a load of over two thousand cubic feet, the packing to do and you're only sending two of us?' He looks at me suspiciously. Not for nothing has he been with me for fifteen years.

'No problem, Herbie,' I reply, lying through my back teeth but not batting an eyelid. 'Looks worse than it is. I'm sure you and Jim will be as right as rain on this one. Yes, easy-peasy but if you do run into any problems, I'll get you an extra pair of hands for tomorrow, okay? In fact, if any of the other lads finish early today, I'll send them round as well.'

Not a hope in hell. I hold my breath as Herbie reflects on this for a few moments. He looks long and hard at the job sheet, looks at Jim then – with Jim not showing undue concern – looks back at me. After a further perusal of the sheet, long furrows stretching across his brow, he turns on his heel and heads out the door towards his van with Jim in tow.

The hallway quickly empties as the crews straggle towards their allocated vans. They leave behind a stale smell of cigarette smoke and body odours. Herbie, Billy, Charlie, Speedy, Jim, Fred, John, Stephen and Albert are all presented smartly in the company uniform. James is the odd man out, wearing an assortment of clothing which appears to have been purchased at a jumble sale. But he's presentable.

Herbie has just climbed into his van and I've returned to my desk, when I see Kev shoot through the entrance gate on his bicycle, narrowly missing Billy as he drives out of the yard.

'Hallelujah! Glory and praise be to the gods,' I cry out, rising from my chair and jumping a foot in the air. Hypocritical, I know. But if one's got to express one's feelings every now and then, why not to Mr Big? It's never too late to try and win a few Brownie points.

I quickly exit the office door and position myself in the hallway entrance, shielding myself from the continual downfall of rain. Charlie and Speedy are impatiently waiting in their respective parking positions. They're blocked in until Herbie goes. 'Hold your horses,' I shout across the yard to Herbie, as he prepares for departure. 'I've got some reinforcements for you.'

I turn to watch Kev's approach, my spirits renewed. Twenty yards from the front door he skids around the water-filled potholes then performs an impressive wheelie before bringing the front wheel back to earth and sliding to a halt outside the door.

'All right, Frankie,' he says, as he dismounts then turns to lean his bike against the Portakabin wall. My eyes are drawn to the stripes of wet mud etched on his clothing from bum to neck. The silly sod's got no mudguard on his bike.

I look at him askance. He's wearing a black T-shirt, torn at the neck, the emblazoned words I'M A LITTLE BOY WITH A BIG DICK only partly covered by a worn bomber jacket. As if the mud stains aren't bad enough in their own right, his jeans are faded and frayed, pock-marked with patches of oil and paint and with sizeable holes at the knees. To cap it all, literally, a sodden bobble hat is perched on his head like an upturned bird's nest. He's a wet, bedraggled, soiled and sorry-looking specimen of manhood; a living embodiment of a life lived in the slow lane. His nose ring glints in the early morning light and his face is covered in dark stubble. If the local farmer sees this specimen, he'll want to stick him on a pole in the middle of a wheat field. And I definitely don't want my client to face him turned out like this. They'll be thinking he's come straight from the council's waste tip.

But I don't have the luxury of turning him away. And Herbie isn't going to give a sod how he looks. He's now got his extra pair of hands. That's all that will matter to him. Especially when he realises the extent of his duties.

'Hi, Frankie. Sorry I'm late,' Kev says as he steps inside the door, rain running off him in miniature waterfalls. His bomber jacket hangs on his skinny frame like a wet sponge and his knobbly knees show through the holes in his frayed and soggy jeans.

Apart from James, Kev is the only other casual I haven't as yet got round to supplying with the company uniform. In common with all new casuals, they have to show their worth and loyalty for at least eight weeks of regular work before I'm prepared to splash out the necessary funds. And as no-one has ever turned up previously looking like a scarecrow, the lack of uniform hasn't been a problem. But Kev's appearance is not an image likely to enhance customer confidence or the reputation of A to Z Removals. He can't go out in this state.

I've got to do something to spruce him up.

'Hold tight for a minute, Kev,' I instruct him, hurrying back into the storage section of the Portakabin. Frantically rummaging through the shelving in the large storage cupboard, I pull out two used uniforms and three worn T-shirts returned by previous employees, and hold the trousers up for inspection.

Neither set is the right size for Kev. They're going to hang on him like a marquee. But they're all I've got, and they'll be a marked improvement on what he's wearing at the moment.

I select one pair of trousers and a T-shirt and return to the hallway where Kev is still patiently waiting for his job allocation.

'Good man, Kev,' I say, pretending that the soggy mass now standing in front of me is of the human variety. 'Good to see you, better late than never. You're with Herbie and Jim; they're in the van waiting.

'But listen, before you go, do us all a favour and change into this gear. You're a bit muddy up the backside and you're liable to muck up the customer's furniture if you sit down on their best chaise longue. They'll be a bit big, but should be fine if you use that belt of yours. Oh, and put this T-shirt on. It'll make you look more like a professional removal man. And thanks for coming in at short notice. Are you alright for Friday?'

Receiving an affirmative from Kev on all fronts, I wait expectantly in the hallway whilst he goes into the storage area to change. Herbie, Charlie and Speedy are chafing at the bit as they sit in their vans, a cloud of smoke filling each cab.

After a couple of minutes, Kev reappears, the firm's T-shirt now replacing his torn black one and the blue trousers hanging around his backside and legs like two large windsocks. But all in all, he's now looking a lot more presentable.

With his arrival and makeover, an enormous weight has been lifted off my shoulders. In keeping with my upbeat mood, I give him a friendly pat on the arm. 'Right then, Kev. Off you go. Herbie will explain what the score is. If I'm not here when you come back today, I'll leave your wages in the office with Alice. You can pick them up tomorrow or Friday, whichever you prefer.'

With this final instruction and show of benevolence, Kev leaves the confines of the hallway while I return to the warmth of the office.

I watch through the side window as Kev makes his way to the van. As he reaches the cab, he exchanges words with Herbie who first appears bemused, then flabbergasted, and finally agitated. *He's sussed you out, Frank.*

There follows a considerable amount of frantic arm-waving and general pointing, before Kev finally climbs up into the van alongside Jim. Herbie gives me a long quizzical look through the van window then mouths something indecipherable before finally turning on the ignition. Pretending that nothing is amiss, I give him an encouraging thumbs-up. Without further ado, he puts his foot on the accelerator and departs, two fingers extended from the window, and a plume of thick, grey exhaust fumes hanging in the air.

The way is now clear for the remaining two vans to leave. Herbie, Jim and Kev are quickly followed through the entrance by Charlie and his crew mates, Fred and John. Then Speedy finally moves off, Albert and James comfortably sitting in the passenger seat. All three vans disappear from view, leaving behind large churned-up tracks of mud on the surface of the yard.

Staring through the window, my mind momentarily wanders to Speedy. Not his real name, but one that's stuck with him for as long as I can remember. And whoever landed that moniker on him must have had a sense of humour. Normally the last one out of the yard and the last back in, that's Speedy. Never takes one minute to do something when he can take two. A reliable bloke though, very experienced and takes a pride in doing a good job, so I can't really complain when his removals take longer than they should.

Turning away from the window, I suddenly remember I've forgotten to tell Herbie about Mrs Arnett's 'Well done!' message and to ask him about the damage claim from McIntosh. Now I'm going to have to talk to Tosh without ascertaining all the facts. Bugger!

Pushing McIntosh's claim to the back of my mind, my thoughts turn to the day ahead. Considering my earlier setbacks, I'm now filled with a burst of optimism. Despite all my totally unnecessary fears, four complete crews have presented themselves for duty, four households will shortly be serviced, and four fat cheques will soon be winging their way in my direction. *Let the cash tills ring and the customers sing and may all my troubles be behind me.*

Unable to contain myself, I spontaneously break into song: *'Pack up your troubles in your old kit bag and smile, smile, smile…'*

Overcome with this dose of positive thinking, it didn't occur to me that the sentiments expressed in this old war ditty would, for me, turn out to be as irrelevant as a thin ray of sunshine in an Artic winter.

Chapter nine

THE HECTIC BUSTLE of the last ten minutes has been replaced with a silence you could cut with a knife. The tranquillity is broken only by the chattering of magpies, the distant hum of early morning traffic drifting over from the A4 and the pitter-patter of the rain hitting the roof.

Outside, the early winter dawn is slowly and inexorably pushing the night sky into oblivion. The black outline of the electricity substation, surrounded by its menacing array of grids and pylons, can now be clearly identified on the far side of the premises. Contrasting starkly with this man-made monstrosity, the shrubbery and trees by the front entrance have taken on a more recognisable hue, the earlier black and grey shades noticeably softened and a hint of the natural green and light-brown foliage of the evergreens now visible. The leafless branches of the larger trees are clearly silhouetted against the stormy sky. Buffeted by the strong winds, the branches are creaking at the junction with the trunks. Thankfully, none are close enough to demolish the Portakabin itself. That would really make my day.

The surface of the yard is now covered with large pools of water and scarred with mud tracks gouged into the soft earth by the tyres of the vans. Without a marked improvement in the weather, these are certainly going to deteriorate over the course of the week. God help the customer who visits the premises. They're not going to be overly impressed, especially if they've just put their vehicle through the car wash. On the plus side, those furrows could be ideal for planting potatoes come spring time.

I turn my gaze upwards, watching the never-ending mass of clouds scurry across the slate-grey sky, propelled by the strong winds. Whether we're going to end up with more rain or snow, well, that's anyone's guess. But however it turns out, God help the lads, trying to cope. It'll be a small miracle if all four crews return without incurring some damage.

As I stare vacantly through the window, the rain suddenly ceases, like someone has closed the tap of a garden sprinkler. A few moments later, a break appears in the clouds and a shaft of sunlight settles over the top of the embankment, clearly delineating the line between land and sky. The ray of sunshine rapidly traverses down the side of the embankment, settles across the roofs of the parked cars then intermeshes with the electricity pylons and grids before disappearing out of sight towards the A4.

This unexpected ray of sunshine – gone as quickly as it arrived – is a sight for sore eyes. A natural-born optimist, I'm wondering if this could presage the metaphorical dawning of a new day, a sign of better times ahead.

The memory of my early-morning trials and tribulations has begun to fade, seeming now to be the product of my hyperactive imagination or an unmemorable dream. And although the temperature outside is still low enough to freeze the balls of a brass monkey, the office itself has now warmed up sufficiently to contribute to my sense of well-being.

I cross the hall into the kitchen and fill the kettle in preparation for my most important uplift of the morning. With Alice not due to appear on duty for another half-hour, and with no customers likely to call or telephone before our normal office opening time of nine o'clock, I've thirty precious minutes or so to put my feet up, relax, and exorcise any remaining gremlins in my system.

A few minutes later, I return to the welcome warmth of the office to enjoy my first caffeine-induced fix of the day.

I carefully tip my chair back on its rear legs then position my legs comfortably along the top of the desk. Balanced precariously and with both hands cupped in a warm, loving embrace around my mug, the hot, luxuriating liquid of my coffee caresses my throat and trickles towards my grateful stomach.

An inner glow of peace filters through my consciousness and my mind begins to wander along well-trodden avenues of inconsequential thought.

The strident ringing tone of the telephone on my desk shakes me from my reverie, causing me to nearly tip over backwards.

'Aw, bollocks,' I cry out in distress, awkwardly withdrawing my legs and banging my mug down onto the desktop more sharply than intended. Coffee slurps over the edge of the mug and pools across the surface of the desk. But the mug itself stays stable and intact. I'm thankful for small mercies.

I hurriedly reach for the phone. 'A to Z Removals,' I answer brusquely, annoyed that my first break of the day has been interrupted before it's started. No *Good morning, how can I help?* as per my normal telephone answering manner.

'Good morning. Is that Mr Tipple? Miss McLaughlin here.'

On hearing the soft, precise voice oozing down the line, the cogs in my brain slowly grind as my alcohol-infused cells attempt to place the lady in my mind. The cogs eventually shift into second gear and the connection is made.

Miss McLaughlin. I might have known she'd be calling. This was as predictable as a baby born with an uncontrollable sewerage system.

Miss McLaughlin is one of today's scheduled removals. And how could I have forgotten her? About fifty-five-years old, going on ninety, she's a retired school headmistress, pedantic and with the personality of a dead crab. And she's a worrier. Since first making contact, she's been a right thorn in the flesh, what with her frequent, interminable telephone calls and constant need for reassurance, with each contact resulting in a minute dissection of her forthcoming removal beyond the bounds of normal inquisitiveness and reason. All in all, she's been testing the forbearance of Alice and myself to the limit. It seems to me the only question she hasn't asked is whether her removal crew dress to the left or the right. But she may well address the tackle question when the lads arrive this morning.

Billy is foreman for the job, an assignment made only after more deliberation than normal. Despite having a face that makes Shrek look like the fairy prince, he has the best temperament to cope with the onerous idiosyncrasies of this particular lady. Won't allow himself to be irked if she follows him around, fussing, faffing and prattling, which she's more than likely to do. I'm confident he's the right man to ensure her foibles are dealt with in a courteous, calm manner, which is more than I can trust myself to do.

'Yes, Miss McLaughlin. Frank Tipple here. Sorry for keeping you waiting. What can I do for you?'

'Ah yes, Mr Tipple, my removal is today. I'm just checking to see that everything's okay, that the van is coming this morning as arranged.'

'Yes, of course everything's okay,' I respond sharpish-like, exasperated by the totally unnecessary nature of the call and the abortion of my coffee break. 'The crew left about ten minutes ago. They should be with you in about five minutes.' *And God help them.*

'Oh, okay, Mr Tipple. Thanks. I was just a bit worried you might have forgotten me. I haven't heard from you since I last spoke to your office.'

Subconsciously, my index finger furiously and indiscriminately commences to dabble in the small pool of coffee lying inert in the centre of my desk. Small wet lines begin to trace outwards, following an indeterminate pattern now being woven by the magic of my fingertip.

I'm fuming. It was only last Wednesday that Alice confirmed everything was on course. Four days ago. Of course she hasn't heard from us since then. We're not operating a bloody chat line.

It's blatantly obvious that underlying her behaviour is her fear that my removal crew are going to reduce her furniture to firewood, relieve her of her best silver, demolish the walls of her property, defecate in her bath, or trample her beloved cat Polly into a furry mush.

All this despite the fact she's been recommended to us not only by three friends, but also by her estate agent. So why is she putting herself through this angst when she's well aware that our record is second to none? Why can't she accept that and let us get on with the job?

'Hello, Mr Tipple. Are you still there?' The sound of her anxious, prissy voice jolts me from my reverie. Reminding myself of the importance of that cheque I'm expecting later in the day, I exercise my limited diplomatic skills, tried and sorely tested over many years of customer contact.

'Yes, I'm still here, Miss McLaughlin. No need to worry. We certainly haven't forgotten you.' *As if you'll let us!* 'As I say, the lads are on their way and should be with you shortly. You've got my best team coming and I'm sure you'll have an excellent removal.'

I get up from my chair, quickly move towards the internal office door as far as the telephone cable will permit, then open and shut the door as loudly as possible. 'Sorry, Miss McLaughlin, another client has just come in to see me on an urgent matter. I've got to go now. The lads should be with you in five minutes or so. Bye.'

I quickly replace the phone in its cradle then take a deep, long breath. One more little porky-pie to be marked by Him up above, but needs must.

I have a sudden craving for a cigarette. Amazing, considering my last puff of a cancer stick was thirty years ago, making me a staunch member of the anti-smoking brigade. But it's further confirmation of the impact Miss McLaughlin is having on my nervous system.

My attention is drawn to the doodle traced with my coffee slops on the desktop. Two matchstick figures, LS Lowry-type configurations, face each other across the surface of the desk. One is male, the other female. The right arm of the male is held high over the female in a threatening pose. In the clenched fingers of the hand is a large dagger. This is pointing down in the direction of over-large breasts, imposed on the matchstick female frame. Little speckles of coffee (blood?) drip away from both breasts and dagger, before winding their way back to the main puddle of coffee.

'Wonder what the headshrinkers would make of this little lot?' I mutter. Frank Tipple, closet psychopath.

I pull a J cloth from the bottom drawer of my desk and slowly mop up the stains of my assassination attempt, presumably on Miss McLaughlin.

As I sip my remaining coffee and regain my composure, my thoughts turn to customers in general and one indisputable fact: where would I be without them? Without a business and an income, that's what. And in my more objective moments, I'd have to admit that most are as good as gold. Not a peep out of them from beginning to end. Undemanding, honest as the day is long and generous in their understanding of the complexities of the removal operation. Job offered, job accepted, job done. No hassle. Yes, most of them a pleasure to do business with.

But not all. Others, fickle in mood and attitude; demanding, devious, officious and finding fault. Or just plain pedantic, like Miss McLaughlin.

Given her underlying doubt about the quality of the service she might get, it's still a surprise to me that she decided to put her faith in A to Z and not with a more recognisable national outfit. I can only surmise it was the recommendations that swung it our way. From her point of view, a wise move since she'll get as good a removal from my firm as anyone, and better than many. But I'm increasingly doubtful whether it's such a great move for me. If Billy doesn't get things right, this could turn out to be one job I could well have done without.

'Best of luck, Billy boy.' Billy has been duly warned about the client's anxious, fussy nature, but has shown no special concern. He'll treat her no differently to anyone else. And as he'll be turning the corner of her street in a few minutes or so, hopefully that should be the last I'll hear from her.

When will I ever learn?

Chapter ten

BLISSFULLY UNAWARE of the next setback about to darken my day, I listlessly leaf through my work schedule for today.

Alice has arranged four appointments: three removal estimates, followed by a damage assessment. All reasonably close geographically and all set up for this morning, with nothing planned for this afternoon.

Excellent news. It'll give me a chance to get home early and lick my wounds. But I'm not looking forward to that claims assessment. Until it and McIntosh's complaint have been sorted, they're going to cast a blight on my day.

Spreading my legs across the desktop, I drain the remnants of my coffee then gaze blankly through the window. The welcoming shaft of sunlight which flitted across the yard earlier has now been consumed by an accumulation of thick black and grey clouds. On cue, the rain begins to fall, speckling the pools of surface water with bursts of minute eruptions. At the rate it's coming down, I'll need to hire a rowing boat to get the punters in and out of the office.

My thoughts turn back to Mister McIntosh's ominous phone message. A strong gut feeling tells me that Bonny Prince Charlie isn't going to be readily deflected from pursuing A to Z for any deficiency there may have been in our services. And he did say he'd be at home today. So there's no excuse for not calling.

'Right Mr Tosh,' I mutter, resigned to whatever bad news he has in store for me. 'Let's sort out your crappy problem.'

I remove my feet from the desktop, stabilise my chair and dial Tosh's number, nibbling on my fingernail like a mouse on a piece of cheese.

Connection made, a few seconds have elapsed when the telephone on

Alice's desk starts ringing. Startled by the unexpected interruption, I stare open-mouthed at the source of this latest distraction.

I'm caught in a moment of indecision. What to do? Continue to hold for McIntosh or take this incoming call? I definitely can't deal with both; my arms aren't long enough and my mouth isn't programmed to conduct two simultaneous conversations.

But this incoming call could be someone wanting to book their removal. Or it could be a request for a removal estimate, potential future business. Both more important than Tosh's affairs.

I bang my receiver down sharply, push my chair back and move swiftly to Alice's desk. 'A to Z Removals, how can I help you?'

I listen expectantly, but there's no immediate indication that anyone is on the line.

'Hello, A to Z,' I repeat, pressing the phone tightly to my ear. A series of distinctive staccato pips tells me the call is from a public telephone kiosk. Someone's trying to feed coins into the slot.

Who could be trying to reach me from a public telephone box at this time of the morning? Oblivious to the thunder of a passing train and the rattling of the Portakabin window panes, I slump onto Alice's chair, half on, half off the seat.

The pips stop abruptly as the caller finally manages to insert his coins. 'Hi, is that you, Frank?'

Hearing Billy's voice, I immediately relax, taking another sip of coffee. He's letting me know he's arrived safely. It doesn't cross my mind to wonder why he's at a public phone.

'Hi, Billy,' I reply nonchalantly, rearranging my legs across the top of Alice's desk. 'You got there alright then? I suppose she told you she's been on the phone wondering –'

Billy brusquely interrupts my discourse.

'No, Frank,' he says, sounding agitated. 'We haven't got there, there seems to be a problem.'

Anyone who'd chanced to see the expression on my face at that very moment would have thought that Billy had just outed himself, declared his undying love for Stephen and announced that they were eloping to Gretna Green.

Dragging my legs off the desk, I sit upright in the chair, my back ramrod straight like someone's shoved two steel rods up my bottom.

'Billy, what the hell do you mean, you've got a problem? You've only just bloody got there.'

'Well, Frank, we arrived about ten minutes ago but nobody's answering the door,' he answers, sounding vexed. 'We've been all around the house. A neighbour thinks they've gone off to work. I'm phoning from a call box at the end of the road.'

'Jesus Christ, Billy. That can't be right. It was less than ten minutes ago she phoned me to check if you were coming. She's got to be in.'

Something Billy has just said strikes me as a bit odd. 'Hold on a minute, Billy. What do you mean "they've" gone off to work?' I query. 'Is that definitely what the neighbour said? That "they've" gone off? Not she? As far as I know, she lives on her own. Are you sure you've got the right house?'

There is a pregnant pause at the other end followed by some muted, indecipherable response. Billy must feel that such a silly question doesn't warrant a lucid or expansive answer.

I rise up from Alice's chair, the telephone pressed so tight to my ear it's making it tingle. 'Listen, Billy,' I shout, more loudly and aggressively than could be deemed reasonable. 'She's got to be there. No ifs, ands and buts about it. Maybe the doorbell's not working, or she's got her hi-fi or washing machine on and hasn't heard you. Go back and have another try. If there's no answer, go round the back, bang on the windows, do what you have to do. Abseil down the bloody chimney if necessary.

'But before you do anything, first check that you're at the right number and the right bloody house. Have you got that? One way or another, make sure to ring me again to let me know what's happening before I have a bleeding heart attack.'

'Yeah, yeah. Okay, Frank. No need to get your knickers in a twist. But in case she's still not there and I have to come back here, you'll have to phone me back. I've no more loose change. Oh, and you owe me forty pence for this call.'

Crisis points like this make me fervently regret not keeping apace with modern technology in supplying the foremen with mobile phones. But Frankie being Frankie – conservative, a member of the old-school brigade and a bit of a meanie to boot – this is one piece of technology which has been deemed an unnecessary intrusion. Besides which, who in their right mind would wish to irradiate their brain cells in such a manner?

'Okay, don't worry about that, Billy,' I say, trying to keep a grip on my temper and willing myself to modify my language. Completely losing my rag with Billy and swearing like a trooper isn't going to help matters, or set a good example. 'Give me the number of that phone box you're in. And listen, Billy, I don't want to phone McLaughlin and unnecessarily panic her, so I won't do anything more until you contact me. Whatever happens, get back to that phone box as quick as you can. Or better still, call me from McLaughlin's phone once you get in.'

As I jot down the public kiosk telephone number provided by Billy, the pips sound as his money runs out. The phone disconnects.

I'm sitting erect in my chair, perplexed. The realisation is dawning that, with Miss McLaughlin's removal, we seem to be heading up the proverbial creek. And yet she's expecting them to arrive anytime soon. That's what I told her.

Given the nature of the beast, it's impossible to accept that she isn't standing on her front doorstep with the welcome mat out and everything in a state of battle readiness for forthcoming operations. A pound to a penny Billy's the one who's cocked things up. But how? He's got his worksheet and it's got her full address on it. He said he knew where it was.

Rising from the chair, I stand immobile at the side window, totally impervious to what's going on outside. So many negative thoughts are revolving round my mind that my head feels like it's been immersed in a bed of concrete.

Willing one of the telephones to ring, I begin to pace back and forth, on each turn glancing anxiously at the clock. It's now over eight minutes since Billy called. He's had more than enough time to get there by now. So why has he not contacted me? Is the bugger winding me up? My God, if he is, I'll have his guts for garters.

'Okay, Frank. Enough's enough. Ten minutes, you said. Phone the bloody box.' My patience worn to a frazzle, I quickly dial the number supplied by Billy, fidgeting from foot to foot. I should have gone for a pee five minutes ago.

'Hi, Frank, is that you?'

I grit my teeth and say nothing. Who else might be ringing that particular call box at this specific time of the morning?

'I've just got back to the kiosk,' he says, his breath coming in short, laboured pants. 'All this farting about is going to kill me.'

I'm totally unconcerned about the state of Bill's welfare, or his arsehole. 'Enough of the hot air, Billy. And don't be going all wimpish on me. Did you get her or not?'

'Afraid not, Frank,' replies Billy, confirming my worst fears. 'Honest to God, Stephen and I have both tried everything, but there's definitely no one at home. Oh, and I've checked the worksheet. The address is definitely 46 Springfield Road and that's where we are.'

I detect a cocky 'I told you so' inflection to his tone.

'The wife's best friend lives down here,' he says. 'She works at Legoland, just a few minutes down the road from here.'

With an impending crisis on my hands, I can't in all honesty say that the location of Billy's wife's best friend's residence or work-place feature at the top of my list of items for discussion. In fact, one might even question the relevance of that particular piece of information to the business in hand.

I'm just about to give Billy a sharp rebuff when a few of my active brain cells click into gear and a small shaft of realisation magically pushes its way to the forefront of my perceptions.

'What did you just say, Billy?' I query, my voice raised three notches. Dumbfounded, I'm sitting forward on the edge of my seat like there's a six-inch nail sticking into my backside. 'Did you just say "a few minutes from Legoland"?'

I'm finding it difficult to contain my rising annoyance, frustration and relief that this Rubik Cube of a problem may have been solved.

'Are you in Windsor?' I ask tentatively and tersely, already knowing the answer.

'Of course I'm in Windsor, where do you think I am?'

Despite his aggressive tone, I know he doesn't mean to sound offensive – it's just the way he tells 'em, as Frank Carson would have said.

I hold my tongue and take a deep breath. 'Listen Billy, I believe I know what the problem is. But before you go off half-cocked, I need to check my office copy of Miss McLaughlin's estimate, to make sure I'm not getting my addresses mixed up. Hold tight while I get her details out.'

I quickly make my way towards the four-drawer filing cabinet. As I pull out the second drawer, Alice's telephone rings stridently.

Shit! Whoever this is, it's going to take too long to find McLaughlin's details and confirm the outcome with Billy before the caller rings off. And with the house-moving market at its lowest point of the year, I can't afford to lose out on potential business.

Leaving the filing cabinet open, I dash back to my own receiver. 'Listen Billy, I've got another call coming in which might be important. I don't know how long it's going to take, so here's what I want you to do. Now, are you listening carefully, 'cause I'm only going to say zis vonce.'

In my heightened state of agitation, my accent mimics Michelle from the long-running TV comedy *'Allo 'Allo!.*

'While I'm answering this other call, go and double check the address you have on your worksheet. Trust me on this one, Billy. Because I don't think your customer lives in Windsor. But I'm not definite, until I check her copy estimate. I'll give you five minutes, then ring you again. And don't keep me waiting. Your customer is going to go off her rocker if you don't get there soon.'

Without giving Billy the opportunity to debate the merits of my instructions, I replace the receiver, fervently hoping he'll get his finger out and do what I ask.

The other phone has been ringing insistently. Darting back to Alice's desk, I take a deep breath then scoop up the receiver.

'Morning, A to Z Removals. How can I help you?' I enquire courteously, my natural in-built training resurrecting itself.

'Mr Tipple? Miss McLaughlin here again!'

My heart sinks as deep as a torpedoed battleship. Who else could it be? Bloody, bloody, bloody hell. My teeth savage the top of another finger and a small piece of finger nail is projected from my mouth like an Exocet missile, landing on the top of Alice's desk.

'There's no sign of a van yet and I'm starting to get a bit worried,' she says.

'Oh, eh, hello again, Miss McLaughlin,' I reply, trying to sound calm and in control. But my mind is working overtime. How can I extract us from this tricky situation when I'm not certain what's gone wrong?

Various excuses and arguments race amok in my mind, causing a traffic jam. But one factor shines through the confusion like a searchlight: honesty is not the best policy. She's not going to be much impressed if she's informed that Billy might be at the wrong address and nowhere near to commencing her removal.

'No need to worry, Miss McLaughlin. We've had a tiny hiccup regarding the timing,' I stutter, squirming in my chair. 'When you phoned earlier, I forgot to tell you that Billy, the foreman on your job, had to drop off boxes to another customer. This will have delayed him a little bit. I should have mentioned this earlier, but don't worry, he should be with you in another fifteen minutes or so.'

I inject a short forced laugh, which sounds as false to my own ears as it surely must do to anyone else within earshot. *A bit like a hyena on heat*, I'm thinking.

Fortunately for me, my assurances are accepted. I hang up, my brain feeling like it's been pickled in a vat of alcohol. Beads of perspiration trickle down my back and under my armpits. The combination of booze and curry from last night is doing me no favours at all. I'm a bloody mess.

Come on, Frank. Pull yourself together. Find that bloody estimate quick and check that bloody address. Moving quickly to the open filing cabinet, I extract the thick file containing copies of all removal estimates provided for last month, filed in alphabetical order. Two minutes later, Miss McLaughlin's copy estimate is in front of me. As I suspected, Billy's not only at the wrong house, he's in the wrong bleeding town. Although relieved that I've got to the bottom of the problem, I'm also peed off. All this last-minute hassle with Miss McLaughlin could have been avoided if the prat had taken the trouble to read his worksheet properly.

Aware that five minutes has passed and he should now be waiting for my return call, I quickly dial the number of the public phone box, trying hard to suppress my growing anger. But there's no answer. I should have told Billy where I thought he'd gone wrong earlier. But I wasn't sure of my facts. He could have ended up going on another wild goose chase.

'Come on, Billy, where the hell are you?' I mutter into the receiver, my frustration reaching boiling point. 'Come on, you knob, answer.'

At long last the receiver is lifted from its cradle. 'Billy, where the bleeding hell have you been, you stupid knobhead?' I shout into the receiver.

'Hello, who is that?'

What's going on? That's not Billy, unless he's had a sex change in the last five minutes. So who the hell is this? And where the hell is Billy?

'Oh, eh, hello,' I stutter, running my hand carelessly through my remaining strands of hair. 'My name's Frank. I'm trying to get through to a bloke who's supposed to be waiting for this call. His name is Billy. Can you see anyone standing outside the phone box?'

There's a silence then, 'There's no-one outside. I've just stepped into the phone box to call my sister. The phone was ringing, so I picked it up and got you. I want to phone my sister, so can you put your phone down and clear the line?' The lady's voice is tremulous and croaking, like she's got something stuck in her throat. An old biddy by the sound of it.

Oh buggerydo! Another twenty minutes wasted, while some old moo rabbits on to her sister with Billy possibly still unaware of his balls-up and Miss McLaughlin doing her nut at Springfield Road.

I have a sudden and desperate need to urinate, but there's no way this old dear can be permitted to prattle on to her sister for another twenty minutes when Billy could be turning up at the call box at any moment. But if I'm to persuade her to wait her turn, she's got to be given a justifiable reason.

My mouth engages on automatic, the words falling over themselves as they exit my lips. 'Excuse me, madam,' I say, adopting my best wheedling tone. 'Under normal circumstances, I'd be pleased to hang up. But I'm afraid this is an emergency. There's supposed to be a bloke waiting there to check that his wife's caesarean has passed off satisfactorily. She's in the maternity hospital. I'm his boss as it happens, but that's not important.

'The point is, the surgeon at the hospital – apparently he's their top man – well, he's just been on the phone to say that his team are experiencing difficulties with the birth. They think it may be sextuplets. Between you and me, I think that Billy – he's the lad who is supposed to be waiting for this call – and his missus have been on this fertilisation business. Whatever they've been up to, it has produced some pretty unexpected results. They've sown the seeds of their own destruction, you might say. Anyway, the surgeon wants Billy to get there as fast as possible. It seems like it could be a life-and-death situation for the little bugg– babies.'

Even to my own ears, I've never heard such a load of old bollocks in my entire life. And I've no way of knowing what the old dear on the other end of the phone is thinking. Nobody could be daft enough to accept this load of cobblers.

I pause for a couple of seconds to allow the full impact of my disclosure to penetrate the lady's ancient brain. My bladder is full to bursting and I briefly consider the practicality of peeing out the window. Impossible, without first clambering onto the desk, then getting down on my knees. The state I'm in, I'd probably tip over and fall out the window. And what's Alice going to think if she drives into the yard and sees a shrivelled inch of male organ poking through the window.

With a full bladder and an empty bollocks-bag, I'm still not certain whether my discourse has provided her with reasonable grounds to abort her planned call. But after a few moments she replies, registering a detectable note of concern. 'What can I do, ducks?' she asks hesitantly. 'My daughter had twins and that was hard enough. But to have six or seven...'

I breathe a sigh of relief. Brilliant. She's gone for it. Now I've got to keep her on the back foot. 'Be a dear, see if there's a big guy with blue trousers hanging around. That will be Billy. I don't know what effect this will have on him.' I inject a tremor into my voice. 'One baby would be bad enough, but to have six or seven at the same time... Well, if anything were to go wrong, I don't know how he'd take it.'

Steady, Frank, you're doing all right so far. No need to go over the top.

I flop onto the chair with my legs crossed.

'Okay. Hold on a minute,' she replies, setting the receiver down.

A few moments pass, during which I inspect my nails. A small speck of blood has appeared at the edge of one fingernail. I mentally chastise myself for acting like a big baby. The sooner Jane supplies me with a dummy-tit the better.

Hearing the phone box door open and close, I draw myself upright in anticipation.

'Hello, it's me again,' she says, her voice rising with a hint of excitement. 'There's someone running up the road. Yes, he has blue trousers on. Hold on, I'll tell him you're on the line.'

The distant humming of passing traffic is broken by the sound of muted voices. With my ear pressed tightly to the receiver, I'm straining to hear the dialogue taking place at the kiosk door. Her words barely audible, the dear lady is advising Billy his boss is on the line. She then offers her commiserations regarding the state of his wife's health and expresses her sincere wishes that all goes well with the births. God bless her maternal instincts. But I don't know what Billy's making of it all. Now if she'd only please put him on the line. My wish is answered.

'Hi, Frank, it's me again,' he says, breathing even more heavily than before. He'll be worn out before his removal's even started.

'Billy, for the love of God, where the hell have you been? You said the phone box was just down the road. You should have been back ages ago. That other call which came through was your customer, asking where the bloody hell you were. She's doing my nut in. Now, did you check the address or not?' I say this knowing full well I'm holding all the aces in the pack. God help Billy if he tries to weasel out of this one.

'Sorry it took so long, Frank. A traffic warden was putting a ticket on the van when I got back there. I had to move it – the van that is. There were double yellow lines everywhere. He wouldn't accept we were about to do a removal, as no-one was there and the van was locked up. Stephen had gone off to get some fags. I've had to park the van further up the road. Sorry about the ticket.'

A parking ticket. Another thirty quid down the drain.

'Never mind that for the moment,' I say testily. 'Now did you, or did you not, check that address?'

'Well, as you know, Frank, we're in Windsor. It seems we should be in Slough,' Billy responds warily. He sounds a bit subdued. And so he might, considering the cock-up he's just made.

I blow my top, shouting louder than necessary into the phone. 'I know you're in bloody Windsor, Billy. I knew you were in bloody Windsor the moment you mentioned Legoland. Can you not bloody read? Do you not think I have enough problems on my plate without having your customer, Mrs Bloody-God-Almighty, Pain-in-the-Ass, Goody-Goody-Two-Shoes McLaughlin breathing down my bloody neck?'

My earlier remonstration to the lads about unnecessary swearing have been forgotten in the heat of the moment.

'Sorry, Frank,' Billy replies contritely. 'As I said, I know Springfield Road 'cause of the wife's best friend. I've been there often. I automatically assumed it was the Windsor Springfield Road we were going to. Sorry. That's all I can say.'

Anybody can make a mistake, yours truly as guilty on that score as anyone else. If someone is prepared to say those magical words 'I'm sorry' and take full responsibility, then I'm not one to push the knife in. I'm nothing if not a pragmatist, and a pretty decent chap to boot, even if I do say so myself.

My pot goes off the boil and the concerns of the last ten or fifteen minutes quickly evaporate. I exhale slowly. 'Right, Billy,' I say. 'What's done is done. There's nothing we can do about that now. Get yourself over to Slough as fast as you can. Get back on the M4, come off at junction five, go underneath the motorway then left towards the Colnbrook bypass. After that, it's first or second on the right.

'Oh, and listen, Billy, I've told your customer that you've been dropping off boxes at another customer's, so don't let me down on that. Don't tell her you went to the wrong address. It'll make us all out to be right wallies.

'And one more thing. Watch what you say to the old dear outside the phone box. She thinks your missus is in hospital expecting a brood of babies, so if she says anything, just nod your head then bugger off quick. And no more bloody parking tickets, please.'

Without further ado, I put the phone down and dash to the toilet. Another minute longer and Alice would have needed a pair of Wellington boots.

Returning to the office three pounds lighter, I lean back in my chair and once more gaze abstractly through the window. Lost in a series of bleak thoughts, I'm ardently hoping that this latest sorry episode with Billy will prove to be a clear line now drawn in the shifting, treacherous sands I've had to navigate thus far.

Then I remember those two damage claims I've got to deal with. I raise my eyes to the ceiling and conjure up a short but fervent brief prayer. *God help me.*

A strident inner voice instantly mocks my hypocritical and temporary conversion to the power of the Almighty.

Help you, Tipple? And why would I want to do that? What have you ever done for Me, except castigate everything I stand for. And now you've got the nerve to ask Me to bail you out when you run up against a measly bit of trouble.

You're nothing but a snivelling, pathetic, intolerant, blasphemous son of Satan. Now piss off before I set the angels of retribution on you. Wanker!

Chapter eleven

FEELING OUT OF SORTS, I retrieve my mug and make my way back to the kitchen. Thanks to Miss McLaughlin and Billy, I never did get the full benefit of that first coffee. Perhaps a fresh one will help put me to rights.

Three minutes later, I slurp the scalding liquid, wallowing in its flavour like a dehydrated hippopotamus at an oasis. Beads of sweat are forming on my forehead – whether from the coffee, the adverse effects of Billy's shenanigans, or the high temperature in the office is hard to tell. As long as it's not the onset of 'flu, I'm not too worried. It's not the first time I've felt like a piece of dog shit.

Delving into my pocket, I pull out a frayed and soiled handkerchief, wincing at its appearance. It looks like it's been used to clean the windscreen of the car. If Jane saw it, she wouldn't be impressed. Nor would my customers. Still, ten years of service from one scrap of cloth can't be bad.

My brow receives a quick wipe before I return it to the safety of my pocket then check to see what the weather's doing. The rain has turned to sleet. Snow could be arriving sooner rather than later.

My thoughts turn back to Billy. Despite his cock-up, I can't help but feel a tinge of remorse for the way I've spoken to him. It's not going to be much fun out there today. Paths and steps will be treacherous and customers are going to be more stressed than usual. The lads are going to need their wits about them to protect the furniture and keep the clients happy. But if anything is to go wrong – like Billy ending up arse-over-heels while carrying Miss McLaughlin's best bit of china – today's the sort of day it's likely to happen.

Poor sods. I hope the customers are in benevolent mood regarding refreshments. That will sustain the morale of the troops and help to keep their concentration on the job.

Taking another welcoming gulp of coffee, I again leaf through my four scheduled appointments. Three of the sheets have a sky-blue background, the fourth white: a colour coding system thoughtfully instigated by Alice to enable me to identify different operational functions within the company.

The sky-blue sheets give me cause for optimism. These are requests for removal estimates. They'll give me the opportunity to turn on the Tipple charm and exercise my selling skills, finely honed over many years. If I play my cards right and impress the customers, they could sow the seeds of future business. They could also go some way to keeping my bank balance in the black and my bank manager in the pink.

The only details contained on the sheets are the name and address of each client and the date and time of the appointment. On completion of the assessments, I'll have added all the necessary information to enable me to price up each removal. If and when we are contracted to undertake the removal, the worksheet will then pass into the hands of the removal foreman.

Alice has scheduled the first three appointments within a tight time frame: the first for nine-thirty, the second at ten, and the third at ten-thirty. They're all local, which means time won't be wasted travelling or hanging about between calls. It should also enable me to spend fifteen to twenty minutes face to face with each customer to discuss their removal arrangements and field any queries.

There should then be time to return to the office, check with Alice on any further developments, and grab a quick bite at the shopping centre cafe before my fourth scheduled visit. Then, when that unwelcome business is out of the way, go home. Easy-peasy.

The thought of food causes my tummy to rumble, not surprisingly given my meagre breakfast. My stomach's giving me notice that a fry-up would go a long way to putting me to rights.

I turn my attention to the fourth sheet lying in front of me. Knowing that this particular appointment has been in the offing does nothing to diminish the gloomy effect it still has on me. The white background immediately identifies its purpose, confirmed by the simple heading at the top of the sheet in red capital letters: CLAIM. Below the main heading, Alice has typed the name and address of the customer: a Mr Crinkley, now resident in Bracknell. Directly underneath, she has recorded the briefest description relating to the alleged damage: 'Settee damaged.' That could mean anything.

Given the circumstances surrounding the removal and Herbie's insistence that nothing was damaged, this is one claim I'm particularly not looking forward to assessing.

'Methinks you've got a rainbow claim on your hands, Frank,' was how he cryptically responded when he heard that Crinkley had put in a claim.

Recalling the origin of this expression, a wry smile creases my lips. It was the first time I'd heard this expression and incomprehension was etched on my face.

'Christ, Frank,' he then said, as he looked me straight in the eye. 'Did your old woman not teach you anything? A rainbow: that arch thing in the sky with all the colours in it. That's what the customer reckons he's sitting under. He's expecting to find a nice pot of gold – at your expense. But there's no way we did the damage. The leg on that table was damaged before we even moved it or he did it himself after we left. The guy's a grease-ball.'

And so it turned out. It was the remnants of dried glue still attached to the broken leg which gave the game away. It had been repaired at some time in the past. And the customer must have been aware of it. As far as I'm concerned, that was as mischievous a claim as I'd ever met.

From that day onward, the 'rainbow' classification became official A to Z jargon, to classify claims bearing no relation to objectivity or reality, and invariably leading to a total and irrevocable breakdown of relations between Tipple and customer. Judging from Herbie's report, Crinkley's claim could be such a one. It has all the ingredients of a witch's brew.

Although the claim was made a number of weeks ago, it's only now that Alice has been able to arrange a mutually agreeable date for us to meet. And today's the day, at twelve o'clock to be exact.

A twelve-noon appointment. My childhood memory of Gary Cooper's shoot-out in *High Noon* springs to mind. There could be something symbolic about the timing of this particular appointment. It's not difficult to envisage a metaphorical spillage of blood and guts during the course of our meeting. Whether it will be Crinkley's or mine, we'll have to wait and see.

My deliberations are momentarily interrupted as two trains pass simultaneously on the embankment. The Portakabin shakes to its foundation and the windows rattle, buffeted by the velocity of the displaced wind. As both trains pass, I close my eyes and lightly massage my brow. One small marble seems to be trundling round the inside of my head and another bigger one round my stomach. Even a proper lunch may not be sufficient to cure these ills. Especially with the Crinkley and McIntosh's claims to deal with.

Try as I might to put them to the back of my mind, they keep dominating my thoughts. 'And why's that, Frank? Why do they wind you up so easily?' I ask rhetorically, moodily addressing the wall of the Portakabin, impervious to the fact I'm once again having a one-way conversation with an inanimate object.

Taking a moment to consider a rational response to my own question, I scratch the back of my head before delivering my conclusions. 'You know bleeding well why,' I mutter to my blurred reflection in the windowpane, an exaggerated scowl crossing my features. 'It's the compensation culture, that's what. That pernicious disease that's pervading society with its take-what-you-can-and-bugger-everybody-else philosophy.'

To emphasise my strong feelings on the matter, I give the desk a smack with the palm of my hand then, for good measure and in a fit of pique, deliver a kick to the bottom. Had anyone observed this mini drama, they would surely have believed a madman had escaped the asylum. Anyone except Jane, that is. She'd have recognised my outburst and behaviour for what it was: one of my grumpy-old-man moments.

The mere thought of this growing blight on our everyday life has darkened my mood and my benign scowl has morphed into a malignant and grotesque mask of contempt. Certain of my own moral rectitude on the matter, I've climbed onto my metaphorical high horse. The cheeks of my arse are precariously straddling the shiny leather saddle, my feet are less-than-securely positioned in the stirrups, and my quivering thighs are squeezed tightly against the horse's muscular flanks. My mount is steaming, chafing at the bit and raring to go.

It's the Americans I blame. As if foisting McDonald's, Sylvester Stallone and 'Have-a-nice-day!' on us hasn't been enough to test our goodwill to the limit, their greedy, ambulance-chasing lawyers have now successfully shipped their no-win, no-fee, sue-and-be-damned culture over to good old Blighty, and, in the process, infected the minds and attitudes of a significant proportion of the population – some of which are my customers, quite prepared to take me to the cleaners if they think they can get away with it.

Only some, admittedly, but a devious minority who believe that, because they've paid A to Z Removals a premium to insure their goods and chattels, this then automatically gives them the green light to seek redress for damage – irrespective of whether this was caused by the negligence of the A to Z Removals' workforce or not, and with scant regard for the adverse effect this might have on the reputation of my crew or the firm.

Whenever I unburden myself on Jane – sweet, innocent and honest Jane, who would never knowingly pull a fast one on anybody – she cannot accept that some people have the morality of an ant. She also can't understand why I should get so wound up when my insurers are there to take the brunt of any dispute and assess each and every claim.

But that would be too simple a solution for the bowler-hat brigade. The truth is they've no interest in getting involved until a claim exceeds my three hundred and fifty pound excess. As the majority fall within that limit, that means that I'm the one who has to do the initial donkey work, distinguish the genuine claim from the suspect one, assess the extent of liability, and negotiate a settlement package agreeable to all parties, inevitably, on the odd occasion, making an ass of myself. *Heee-haw! Heee-haw!*

Although it is in my own interest to take responsibility for the actions of my staff, one would need the wisdom of Solomon to secure a safe passage through the whole bloody rigmarole. It would be laughable if the implications weren't so serious. Because even Jane could see that the process involves a conflict of interest, sufficient to induce a weeping and gnashing of teeth. Customers like Crinkley and McIntosh, having contracted A to Z to carry out their removal in the belief that any subsequent claim will be assessed by an independent party, instead find that Francis Frederick Foster Fidel Tipple, defendant in the matter, has not only assumed the role of investigator, but is also judge and jury. Is it any wonder I get myself in such a state?

Outside, heavy snowflakes are now falling, tossed in eddies by the whirling wind. Such is the density of the snow, the entrance to the yard and the electricity sub-station are barely visible. It won't be long before a fine white blanket covers the entire surroundings.

Inevitably, my thoughts return to Mr McIntosh's telephone message. I can't ignore it and hope it'll go away. It has to be dealt with. And as my ma would be saying were she here now: 'Francis, lad,' she'd trumpet, her forefinger waving in the air and her head nodding side to side like a wise old bird. 'There's no time like the present. So don't you be putting off until tomorrow what you can readily do today.'

With a prolonged theatrical sigh, I pick up the telephone receiver like I'm handling a live stick of dynamite.

Chapter twelve

I DIAL THE NUMBER supplied by McIntosh then listen apprehensively to the ringing tones. I'm praying that no-one will be at home and that his complaint won't have to be addressed until the crew have given me their take on the matter. He might even have had second thoughts about registering a claim. *Who am I kidding?* With not just one, but a few damages, it's highly unlikely Tosh is going to let this rest, particularly if his claim is hunky-dory.

I check the time. Nine am. Only seventy minutes on duty, during which I've been basted, braised, boiled, baked, bruised and buggered. It's going to be a long morning.

Waiting impatiently for a reply, I extract a pencil from the pen holder then begin to gnaw the well-chewed end. Anything to keep my fingers out of my mouth.

'McIntosh here.'

The end of the pencil breaks off in my gritted teeth. I eject a sliver of wood from the side of my mouth and pull myself together. 'Ah, good morning, Mr McIntosh,' I reply, steeling myself for whatever barbs he chooses to shoot my way. 'Frank Tipple from A to Z. You left a message on our answering machine. How can I help you?'

'Oh, yes, Mr Tipple, I've bin waiting for yaer call all weekend,' he responds brusquely. His voice has all the serenity of a chicken being throttled for Christmas. 'You did'nae happen to call a wee bit earlier this morning, did yae? Someone phoned when I wae in the bathroom, but thae phone went dead just afore I gae tae it?'

His accent sounds to my untrained ear like he's been reared in the Glasgow

Gorbals. Not that I'm an expert on Scottish dialects. But there's certainly no mistaking where he was born and spent the greatest proportion of his life.

'Phoned earlier? No, that wasn't me,' I lie unnecessarily. Obviously he hasn't dialled 1471, otherwise my off-the-cuff whopper would be seen for what it is.

Not content with telling one porky, I embroider it with another. 'To be honest, Mr McIntosh, I've been busy getting my crews off. Six jobs on today, there's a lot of people wanting our services. Guess it's the excellent reputation we have. Anyway, I thought it best to contact you before you go to work.'

Why I feel the need to upgrade the number of removals, or why I'm compelled to suggest the punters have been lining up at my door, I'd be hard pressed to explain. Jane would tell me it's one of those unattractive Tipple defence mechanisms, designed to pre-empt any negative comments I'm anticipating from the mouth of Tosh concerning the quality of our service.

'I'm nae gaeing to work,' he now responds impatiently. 'And, if thae truth be known, neither am I tae interested in hae many jobs yae hae today. What I am interested in is thae fact I've haed to take thae day off tae try and sort thae mess following Friday's removal. Yaer men hae caused quite a bit of damage and I'll need a claim form. Can yae put one in thae post immediately?'

His tone is icy and hostile, like the weather outside. And I'm not much taken with his surly response. After all, what's he got to beef about? A pound to a penny he hasn't stubbed his big toe, activated his smoke alarm, broken his breakfast mug or had two cow-pats for breakfast.

'Oh, sorry to hear you've had some problems, Mr McIntosh,' I reply, injecting all the consideration I can falsely muster. Hypocritical I know, because at this moment I'm feeling more sorry for myself than for this miserable little bugger. 'Of course, I'll need to come and see the damaged items. As you're probably aware, it's not possible to submit a claim to our insurers until I've first assessed the damage. Can you give me some indication what the problem is?'

'What dae yae mean, yae cannae put my claim through tae yaer insurers?' The grating sound of his raised voice reverberates down the telephone line, causing me to momentarily withdraw the phone from my ear.

I'm taken aback by the hostility of his response. As feared, this communication is not going to be simple or reasoned. 'Well, Mr McIntosh,' I reply hesitantly. 'There are procedures–'

'Listen tae me, Mr Tipple,' he interrupts, his voice raised three decibels.

'Dinnae start giving me a load of flannel about procedures. I've paid thae insurance premium yae charged, and a substantial sum it was, I would remind yae. Now that yaer guys hae caused sae damage, I wannae make a claim. Nae, whae's the problem? Yae dae hae an insurance policy, dinnae yae?'

Nettled both by his aggressive attitude and the slur on my integrity, my own hackles begin to rise. No way is anybody going to talk to me like I've just rolled out of a sewerage pipe, especially not someone who needs to take an elocution course as a matter of some urgency.

My inner voice is telling me to keep my high horse secure in the paddock and get a firm grip on the reins. And that voice is right to admonish me. I take a long deep breath then exhale slowly before replying. 'Of course I've gae, got an insurance policy, Mr McIntosh. But, as I'm sure you realise I can't accept any old claim without first determining the nature and extent of the items damaged. It will also be necessary to confirm that our crew have indeed been negligent. You know what I mean?'

On my part, I'd have thought that this was a reasonable line of argument to take.

'Nae, Mr Tipple, I dinnae know what yae mean,' he bellows. 'In fact, whae yae are saying makes nae sense whaesoever. And let me tell yae, I'm nae having it.' The decibel level has moved up another two notches, his strong Scottish accent becoming more pronounced.

A vivid picture of Tosh appears in my mind: he is standing by his phone with a Tam O'Shanter perched on top of an unruly mop of ginger hair, a tartan flush spreading over his countenance, a cloud of steam rising from under his kilt, and a sporran bouncing up and down between his legs like a hyperactive paint brush.

A brief smile creases my face.

His voice goes up another decibel as he works himself into a lather. 'If yae think yae're going to squirm yaer way oot of this, yae've gae another think coming. Dae I make maeself clear?'

This is going to be worse than I thought. But no way am I going to put up with this nonsense. My request is perfectly reasonable and if McTavish here continues down his current path with this hoity-toity attitude, he's going to find his bloody claim dealt with a lot faster than he ever anticipated.

It's only with a supreme effort on my part that I'm managing to retain any semblance of civility. 'Excuse me, Mr McIntosh, but I don't believe it's necessary to adopt that tone of voice. And I must say, your attitude leaves a lot to be desired. I've no intention of giving you a load of flannel, as you so quaintly put it. And I certainly haven't indicated at any stage of our brief conversation that I'm not treating your call with anything other than serious intent.

'On the contrary, what I have done is respond promptly to your message, I've politely requested some fuller details of your complaint, and now, in order to fully assess the nature of the damages, I'm simply requesting the opportunity to come down and see you, and the damages, face to face. At that point, and only at that point, can I then objectively decide on any further action that needs to be taken. I can't be any fairer than that. It's a reasonable request to make, don't you think?'

'Nae, I dinnae think that, I dinnae think that at all.'

I've no idea what he is thinking, but I know what's going through my mind: if this little haggis carries on in this vein when we come face to face, he'll end up playing his bagpipes through his backside.

I prepare myself for the further slings and arrows he's about to fire by withdrawing the telephone six inches from my ear. As anticipated, a cacophony of noise explodes down the line.

'What I think is this, Mr Tipple, seeing as yae wannae talk about reason – and I think this is a very reasonable thing tae ask – whae's thae point in me paying an insurance premium if I cannae make a claim when damage is caused to my goods? Are yae trying to tell me my goods hav'nae bin damaged? Are yae trying tae tell me thae I'm telling yae my goods are damaged when thae're not? Is that wae yae're trying to be reasonable about? Is thae it?'

Enough's enough. It's time to bring out the big guns and remind Tosh of the A to Z terms and conditions of removal. And what a formidable barrier of defences they are. Twenty-eight in total. And I know each and every clause off by heart.

'No, Mr McIntosh, that's not what I'm saying. It may well be that my lads have been guilty of damaging some of your effects, but that's not the point. If you would please listen, what I'm saying is that under the terms and conditions we agreed to do your removal, I – not the insurers, but I, Francis Tipple – must be given the opportunity to assess any damage claim before it can be referred on.' *And before I dip my hand into my three hundred and fifty pound excess.*

'What dae yae mean, terms and conditions,' he shouts into my ear, his bagpipes fully loaded. 'What terms and conditions are yae talking about? I know naething aboot terms and conditions. It's thae first I've heard aboot them.'

I knew it: the silly bugger hasn't bothered to read the terms and conditions set out on the back of his estimate.

My throat is as parched as a camel's backside. I take a quick swig of coffee before enunciating my reply slowly and precisely, like I'm talking to a child. It also helps me to keep some control over my emotions.

'Mr McIntosh, the estimate that we sent you: do you happen to have it close to hand?'

'Estimate? Nae, of course I havnae,' he yells, his bagpipes expelling air as fast as he can refill them. 'I've just moved house, in case yae hae forgotten. And whae's thae estimate gae to do with anything in any case? Is this another red herring yae're throwing at me?'

'Well, now that you happen to ask, Mr McIntosh, I'll be more than happy to oblige you,' I reply, lacing my raised voice with a healthy dose of sarcasm. 'No, it's not a red herring I'm throwing at you; nor is it a cod, a mackerel, or any other kind of fish. So if you would do what I ask, I believe you'll be doing us both a considerable service.

'Now, will you please find the estimate we sent you? I assure you this is very relevant to our discussion.'

My reply is delivered at such a pitch that Tosh and I will soon be able to communicate directly without the assistance of BT.

There is the briefest moment of silence whilst Tosh gives due consideration to my request. His response is muted: 'Ach, all right, but I'm definitely nae happy with thae way this is being handled. Yae understand, Mister Tipple?'

So saying, he bangs the receiver down. I luxuriate in the blessed silence. My only concern is how long it's going to take him to find the estimate. I've got to be heading off soon to keep those appointments.

At this juncture, Alice, my sixty-eight-year-old secretary, drives through the entrance gates in her twelve-year-old Ford Fiesta. In her indomitable manner, she shows no concern for the safety of herself or her car, but steers straight through the biggest pothole in the yard, causing a shower of rain, sleet, snow and mud to cascade from the wheels. The car veers sharply to the left then jerks to a violent stop, the front bumper resting against the embankment edge.

As a testament to her driving skills, various dents and depressions can be clearly seen along the length of the car. This damage, according to Alice, is the fault of the builders who constructed her single garage six inches narrower than standard garage width. Hey presto: bang, scrape and wallop as she attempts to manoeuvre her Fiesta in and out.

Bernie, her hubby, has another tale to tell: it's his firmly held belief that the garage is standard size and that Alice wouldn't be able to ride a bicycle onto a roll-on roll-off ferry without making contact with some part of the ship entrance. Shame, though, as I do worry about her, especially driving around on a morning like this. But I don't believe Bernie loses any sleep over it. So why I do, I don't know, unless it's the thought of having to replace her if she writes herself off.

Awaiting Tosh's return to the telephone I'm keeping one eye on the clock, the other on Alice. She's having a real struggle to prise herself out of the car. Not an easy manoeuvre for an older woman to perform in normal circumstances, and certainly not in these extreme weather conditions.

After a brief struggle, she finally succeeds in propelling her body from the interior into an upright position. She then rocks precariously on her spindly legs while attempting to lock the car door, hold onto her handbag and raise her umbrella.

Mission completed, she slowly proceeds down the yard, with her white plastic mackintosh ballooning around her like a windsock. With every step, she's wrestling to prevent the umbrella from turning inside out while keeping her footing secure on the snow-covered surface. Her footwork – a shimmy here and a shimmy there – is impressive to observe in one so old. But her progress against the wind figures somewhere in the three-feet-forward, two-feet-back category. At the rate she's going, she won't reach the office door until lunchtime.

Tosh finally returns to the phone. Averting my gaze from Alice's erratic progress, I concentrate on the matter in hand.

'Are yae still there?' he asks, his voice grumpy and bad-tempered.

'Yes, I'm still here, Mr McIntosh.' *But if you don't smarten up a bit, not for much longer.*

'I cannae find thae bloody estimate, nae at all surprising considering thae state yaer removal lads left us in. In any case, we haen't bin able to unpack everything. Yae havenae forgotten we just moved house last Friday. Now, can yae stop being obstructive and send me a bloody claim form?'

'No, Mr McIntosh, I've already explained why I can't send you a claim form. And no, I haven't forgotten that you've just moved house. As I've already clearly indicated, what I want before anything else is to assess the damages. And that's final. So it's up to you to accept that or not.

'But if you do want me to come to see you, I suggest you find that estimate, as this would be to our mutual benefit. Because on the reverse side of the estimate, you will find a total of twenty-eight conditions under which we were prepared to undertake your removal, all written in the Queen's English, which most people with a modicum of common sense are able to understand. These terms and conditions apply to each and every client that we agree to move.'

I hear Alice eventually entering the office behind me. Ignoring her, I continue to point out to Tosh the error of his ways, all pretence of civility long since gone.

'Now Mr McIntosh, if you would care to read through those terms and conditions – specifically referring to clause fourteen, subsection three – you will see that your removal contractor reserves the right to inspect any alleged damages with a view to determining liability and negligence. I'm now confirming that I intend to exercise this right.'

As Alice would be quick to confirm, I can be an officious sod when minded, a real legal beagle when the protection of my own human rights is concerned. And until I've concluded a full and thorough investigation of his claim, I'm not prepared to accept anything he tells me as gospel. Innocent until proven guilty.

While I've been updating Tosh on our contractual arrangements, there's been a constant rustling of paperwork over the telephone line. It strikes me that Tosh might have found his estimate copy and is beavering his way through the terms and conditions trying to find the relevant clause. Recognising that he's not yet sufficiently primed, I press home my advantage.

'Now it so happens, Mr McIntosh, that even though I'm extremely busy today, I'm prepared to re-organise my schedule and make a special trip to see you – at around two this afternoon, in fact. It's the only possible slot available in today's busy schedule. *Apart from my home comforts.*

'Or perhaps you'd prefer me to leave the matter with you, to give you time to consider all aspects of your claim in relation to those terms and conditions?'

Although I'm not optimistic, this last option is worth trying. Once he's perused those conditions and realised the limits of our liability, it's conceivable he might just realise his damages don't fall within the scope of our contract.

All that can be heard is the continued rustling of papers, suddenly followed by a sharp crack, like something falling onto the floor and smashing. Whatever it is, it causes Tosh to swear yet again, unaware or beyond caring that I can hear him. I make a mental note to ensure he doesn't add the offending item to his list of claims. After a few seconds of silence, he comes on line, more agitated than before.

'Listen to me, Mr Tipple, since yaer people moved me, I've haed naething bae trouble, and I'm telling yae, I'm nae happy about thae whole business and thae way yae're dealing with it. But I suppose if yae hae tae come, I've nae much choice in thae matter. But when yae dae come, I'll wannae some quick action. Two o'clock then.' Having had the last word on the matter, Tosh puts the phone down.

I'm not just needled, I'm seething. There's nothing that winds me up more than somebody putting the phone down without so much as 'I'll see you later' or 'By your leave'. But if Tosh wants to play hard-ball, that's okay by me. Two can play at that game. Customer or not, there's no way I'm going to turn the other cheek, not unless it's the cheeks of my backside. A little moonie on my part might go a long way to taking the wind out of his bagpipes.

Despite the disagreeable tone of our conversation, my inner voice is still reminding me of the need to remain impartial regarding the forthcoming assessment. But the chances of that state of mind continuing beyond two o'clock this afternoon are slim.

Swivelling round, I watch as Alice removes her mac. In the absence of any coat hooks, she drapes it across the top of the filing cabinet. Small rivulets of sleet and snow slide off the mac, down the edge of the cabinet and onto the carpet.

She peers at me owlishly through the spattered lenses of her gold-framed spectacles, her grey curly hair sitting haphazardly on her head like a well-worn tea cosy. Looking at her slender frame – a five-feet-two-inch pipe-cleaner with arms and legs – I'm amazed that the force of the wind under her opened umbrella didn't airlift her onto the top of a tree.

Having heard the tail end of my conversation with McIntosh, she gives me a long, quizzical look, but says nothing. I recognise that look well. *Who are you upsetting now, Frank?*

'Morning, Alice. That was Mr McIntosh, whom we moved on Friday,' I advise her, feeling the need to unburden myself. 'He maintains the lads have caused some damages, although no-one said anything to me. I assume you haven't been told anything.'

'Hardly likely, Frank, seeing as I'd left the office on Friday long before the crews got back, and you haven't given them my home phone number, have you?'

'Oh, right, Alice. Of course, silly, stupid me. Anyway, I've got to go and see him later. He sounds like he might be a cantakerous sod – a fellow countryman of yours, as it happens.'

This last comment sounds like I'm blaming Alice and the entire Scottish race for the whole sorry business. 'Not that that's got anything to do with it,' I add belatedly.

Alice has been in my employment for nearly twelve years now. She knows me, my moods, my strengths and my weaknesses more than anyone else. Although she only ever intended to take on part-time employment, she works a forty-hour week. And she's worth every penny.

There's nothing she can't turn her hand to. Typing, word-processing, bookkeeping, wages, general administration: she can do it all. Having started work at sixteen, she's had more than enough time to build up her considerable wealth of practical experience. Why she doesn't retire, go home and put her feet up, is a mystery. Well, actually it's not. Alice doesn't hide a firmly held belief that twenty-four hours a day sharing life with Bernie (who has now been retired for over eight years) would not be advantageous to the longer-term good of Alice. 'The bugger would just get under my feet all day long,' is how she explained the situation. Tough as an old boot she is, and sharp as a whistle. In Bernie's shoes, I'd be more than happy with the present domestic arrangements. And there's no doubt in my mind who's commander-in-chief in that particular household.

When the lads were first introduced to Alice, they were gob-smacked that I hadn't retained the services of a young dolly-bird to warm the cockles of my heart on a cold and desolate winter's morning. But they would think that. Their brains are tucked down the front of their trousers. And they don't have the responsibility for running a business and paying the bills. Because what young, modern bimbo – with dyed-blonde hair, legs up to her breast bones and tits the size of turtle shells – would have the necessary basic education or training to perform all the tasks Alice can undertake? Or be prepared to tolerate the limitations of these office facilities?

One other factor helped to keep my feet on the ground: a sixty-eight-year-old secretary would be unlikely to surprise me by announcing a forthcoming pregnancy then demand maternity leave on full pay and with job guaranteed. Positive age discrimination. Bring it on, baby.

★ ★ ★

ALICE HAS BEGUN to prepare her desk in readiness for the day ahead. If she has taken offence with my earlier comment about Tosh's origins and character, she refrains from replying, confirming that such ill-advised and subjective comments are not deserving of recognition.

'It's a terrible morning, Frank,' she says taking off her glasses and cleaning the lenses. 'The battery was low and the car wouldn't start, so Bernie had to get out of bed to put the jump-leads on. Then there was so much traffic on the road. Not a good start to the week, one way or another.'

'I know how you feel, Alice,' I respond meekly, not wishing to burden Alice with my earlier setbacks. 'It hasn't been a good start to the week. But things can only get better.'

She says nothing further, but continues to stand watching me with that same quizzical expression on her face. I'm beginning to wonder whether I've done or said anything else to upset her when she asks, 'Have you been attempting to top yourself this morning?'

With no idea of what she's talking about, and not being much in the mood for irrelevant conversation, I regard her blankly.

A smile creases the corners of her mouth. 'Your tissues,' she says, pointing at my face. 'You've got three bits of toilet tissue stuck to your face? Looks like you've been trying to commit *hari-kiri*.'

I put my hand up to my chin and feel the small hardened pieces of toilet tissue. 'Oh bloody hell, Alice, I wondered what you were on about. No wonder the lads were giving me funny looks this morning. They must think I'm a bloody idiot. Thanks.'

Retreating to the kitchen, I carefully remove the offending pieces. Observing my face in the mirror, I'm pleased to note the tissue has served its purpose. No transfusion will be needed today.

I return to the office. 'Thanks again, Alice. Oh, by the way, Pete's wife phoned to say he wouldn't be in today, so make sure he's docked a day's pay at the end of the week. I had to get Kev in at short notice. I'll be settling up with him in cash but you'll still need to put it through the books.

'I'm also going to meet McIntosh at two o'clock, so don't make any more appointments unless it's absolutely urgent. To be honest, Alice, I've had a bad start to the day. I'll probably knock off early, to recharge the batteries for tomorrow.'

Showing her maturity and years of experience in dealing with the vagaries of management, Alice presents the back of her head then busies herself rummaging through her handbag. Whether she's taken my comments to heart is hard to tell. She's probably got enough of her own problems without pretending to be concerned about mine.

'Listen, Alice, I'm going to have to get off now. After these three estimates, I'll try to get back to the office before going to see Crinkley. Don't forget to take a note about Pete's pay. And can you ring Mrs Arnett? She wants her empty packing boxes picked up.

'Oh, and one more thing. Can you extract our copy of McIntosh's estimate and leave it on my desk. I'll need that when I see him. Okay, Alice, that's all for now. See you later. Hope you'll be kept busy.'

Alice reassures me she's been listening, by noting my instructions on her message pad. She then ignores me again, sits down at her desk, momentarily views the desolation outside, then removes the cover from her ten-year-old Silver Reed electric typewriter. She emits a loud sigh, designed to remind me, yet again, of her aversion to using equipment from a bygone age.

I pull on my pinstripe coat followed by my three-in-one winter jacket, then tuck my four appointment sheets into my presentation binder. With a sense of relief, I leave the warmth of the Portakabin. This marks the end of phase one of my working day. Hopefully a new, more productive phase is about to begin.

If only. At that point, it hadn't sunk in that my crystal ball was undergoing a serious malfunction.

Chapter thirteen

I LEAVE THE WARMTH of the Portakabin and step outside into the bitter cold, careful to avoid the cause of my earlier misfortune. Although it's no longer raining, the pool of water seems to be growing by the minute. And there couldn't be a worse place for it to develop, dead to rights at the front door. Any bigger and we'll need to swim across it. How Alice, at her age and in her condition, managed to cross it without doing the splits is a mystery. If I give the landlord a ring, he might put down some concrete, build a small bridge, or lay on a supply of wellington boots.

Some hope. I'm more likely to get hit by an asteroid than receive a free bucket of sand and cement or a few four-by-fours from that miserable sod. He's that sort of landlord.

Zigzagging my way gingerly over the slushy white surface towards the car, I clear a thin layer of snow from the windscreen then gratefully install myself within the relative comfort of the interior. Tears are welling up in my eyes. If the lads saw this, they'd think I'm a big girl's blouse – not that I'm ashamed to shed a tear or two given the appropriate occasion. Like when a customer's cheque bounces. Or I receive notification of a claim. Or a tax demand arrives from the Inland Revenue.

The outline of Alice's woolly mop of hair is visible through the window as she applies herself industriously to her work. Not that there's much to do today, this being a quiet time of the year. Her latest Mills and Boon tale of romance and intrigue will be out of her bottom drawer in an hour or so, helping to while away the time.

And I've got no problem with that, as she'll do what needs to be done.

Hopefully, there'll be a few telephone calls from prospective customers and maybe a couple of bookings to keep her reasonably busy. If she gets bored she may be tempted to run the vacuum over the carpet. But that would be a first. She's made it perfectly clear that cleaning up after Bernie is far and beyond the call of duty.

Aware of those precious seeds of future business waiting to be sowed, I slip the gear selector into drive-mode and manoeuvre the car across the bumpy, soggy surface onto the lane. In the background, Terry Wogan is preparing the great British public for the day ahead. Although he's not one of my favourite presenters, Radio 2 provides my preferred choice of music, taking me back to the heady fifties and sixties.

I head towards Maidenhead Bridge and the Windsor bypass. The main road is reasonably clear of snow, with only the edges showing evidence of the recent blizzard. The traffic is also sparse, given the time of day. The school run will have run its course and those four-wheel drives with their pretentious my-car-is-bigger-than-your-car drivers should now be safely parked out of harm's way. There'll also be plenty of our public servants who will have skived off for the day, suffering from an obscure and ill-defined bug which will have magically cleared by tomorrow.

Smouldering over a long-held grump about the inequality of pay, pension entitlement and general working conditions between public and private sectors, I pass over Maidenhead Bridge, glancing briefly to my left. Coincidentally, a passenger train is slowly traversing the red brick arches of Brunel's historic bridge, sited a couple of hundred yards upstream. This same train will be shaking the windows of the office and rattling Alice's false teeth within the next fifteen seconds. This thought momentarily brings the tiniest hint of a smile to my face, one of the few that will grace my face today.

With nothing else to occupy my mind – and with Abba reminding me that 'Money, money, money, it's a rich man's world' (not a world I'm likely to inhabit) – I begin to recall the adverse chain of events which has assailed me since awakening from my nightmare.

It's Monday, the first day of my working week, yet here I am, already wanting to clock off and go home.

'Some chance,' I mutter to the windscreen. Not with a one-man business to run, the mortgage to pay and food to be put on the table. On this note – and with the apt sound of the Carpenters' 'Rainy days and Mondays' replacing Abba and Wogan for the next three minutes – my thoughts turn to the cheques which Billy, Charlie and Speedy will be bringing back later.

My mood instantly changes for the better. Those cheques are rays of sunshine which serve to lighten my darkest moments.

A couple of months after meeting Jane, she asked what had kept me in the removal business over so many years. Was it for the love of it? she asked, all sweet and innocent. The thought crossed my mind she might be losing her marbles, or was trying to wind me up. But no, she was serious.

Momentarily at a loss for words, I had to take two long sups of my *Pinot Noir* whilst collecting my thoughts for an appropriate response. 'Work for the love of it?' I stuttered hysterically, trying vainly to keep some semblance of control but unable to stop the tears streaming down my cheeks. 'You've got to be joking, Jane.'

From the look she gave me, it was obvious she wasn't joking but she did regret that she'd asked the question. 'So, what then?' she queried with considerable exasperation, thinking I was taking the mickey. 'If it's not that, smart-arse, what gives you the motivation?'

That was one of the easiest questions I'm ever likely to have to answer. 'It's the lolly, Jane. Yes, indeed, the lolly, loot, dosh, money – call it what you will. It's those beautiful cheques which drop through my door at the end of the day and which enable this poor, miserable sinner to pay the bills and maintain a pauper's standard of living. They are my *raison-d'etre* for working.' Given my theatrical tendencies, the pauper element was overplayed somewhat.

That being as it may, if Jane had pressed me on the job satisfaction aspect of it all, I'd have had to admit to a sense of pride each time my vans trundle out of the yard. Or when the customers ring to confirm a job well done. Or when my updated sales graph affirms steady progress. Well, it wouldn't be natural not to have some feeling of pride.

In tune with my thoughts, the melodic sound of Dire Straits' 'Money for Nothing' floats across the airwaves.

'Aren't they the lucky ones?' I mutter to the windscreen before wisely concentrating on my first appointment. This customer, a Mr Watson, will need to be convinced that A to Z Removals should be his preferred choice and that he can entrust me with the care of his valued belongings.

Having already spoken to Alice on the telephone, he will have formed some initial impressions of our firm and our service. And first impressions are important. Fortunately for me, Alice has an extremely pleasant and efficient telephone manner, so I'm confident that her initial telephone discussion with Mr Watson will have been positive and may well have smoothed my path.

That said, this will be the first opportunity Mr Watson has had to meet Mister Shifter himself, in person. It will be his impression of me which will prove critical in determining whether he decides to use A to Z Removals. If I turn up looking like something the cat dragged in, then proceed to give him a lot of baloney about the nature of our services, it won't be hard to know what's going through his mind: *I'm not going to trust this lying tramp with my best silver tea service.* I'd be the Titanic of removal estimators! *Don't call me, Mr Tipple, I'll call you. Have a nice day.*

Irrespective of what's transpired between Mr Watson and Alice, it's now down to me – Mister Shifter, the front cover and face of A to Z Removals. Not a face that's likely to feature on *Vogue*, but one presentable enough for an old geezer who's suffered an above average accumulation of wear and tear over the years.

Satisfied that I'm mentally and physically prepared for the challenge ahead, I make my final turn into Acacia Avenue then, two hundred yards further on, draw up to the entrance to Mr Watson's residence.

I'm optimistic that this customer will buy into my service, not only due to my appearance but also by the professionalism of my forthcoming presentation.

And why should I think otherwise? I've got the experience. I've got the right image. I've got the charm. And I've got the gift of the gab. What could go wrong?

Chapter fourteen

I STOP AT THE OPEN five-barred gate, check the number on the side of the post then steer slowly towards the front entrance, the car tyres crunching on the gravel.

The lawns are immaculate, the borders filled with a combination of herbaceous plants and winter flowers, all very pleasing to the eye. It's obvious that Mr Watson is a keen gardener. My instinct tells me that he will also have a tidy and methodical approach to life. And he'll likely expect the same high standards of care from his removal company. This may be one call where I have to pull out all the stops, and deploy all my presentational skills to best advantage.

I draw up outside the front door, cut the ignition and retrieve my presentation folder. Bracing myself against the combined elements of wind and cold, I extract myself from the comfort of the car and crunch over the gravel towards five stone steps leading up to the front door. Striving to project an aura of professionalism, I rearrange the contours of my lips upwards then tentatively press the doorbell.

The front door opens, at which stage I fully project a cheery look, the like of which will rarely have been witnessed by my staff.

A shadowy figure fills the centre of the darkened doorway.

'Good morning, Mr Watson,' I exude cheerfully. 'Frank Tipple, from A to Z Removals. You made an appointment for me to see you.'

My first mistake. The person I'm addressing is not male.

When recounting the situation to Jane, she couldn't understand how anyone could be so stupid. 'Tell me this then,' I retorted, miffed at her lack of understanding. 'If you were faced with an indeterminate apparition five feet ten inches tall and three feet wide, with no makeup, hair cropped close to the head, the makings of a light stubble above the top lip, and with a pair of baggy tweed trousers enveloping a backside as rounded and solid as an Armenian shit-house… Well then, don't you think you might also have made that same basic error?'

Jane just looked at me but said nothing. I could tell she wasn't convinced. Or maybe it was my language she didn't like. But then again, she didn't actually get to see the formidable roly-poly standing on the doorstep.

There is a pregnant pause, during which Mrs Watson gives me a long, cool appraisal with frosty eyes. 'Good morning, Mr Tipple,' she finally responds.

Was it my imagination, or did I detect an emphasis on the word 'Mister'? To make me aware that my boob has been recognised, and that her eyesight is better than mine?

'And it wasn't my husband who phoned for the appointment. It was me.'

She spits this information out in a deep, cultured accent, short and clipped enough to slice through a two-inch paving slab.

'Come in,' she snaps, abruptly turning her substantial backside on me as she moves into the hallway. Thankful to be out of the cold, I close the front door behind me. She is facing me, her stance intimidating: arms folded across her substantial breasts, her legs akimbo, her lips pulled tightly together and her eyes boring two holes in my head.

It would seem that this is where initial business is going to be conducted. And here was me thinking she'd offer a cup of hot tea to get things started.

A second person enters the hall from the rear of the house. Seeing me glance behind her, she turns briefly. 'Oh, that's Mr Watson,' she curtly advises, by way of introduction.

She continues speaking, her broad back firmly turned to her dearly betrothed. 'It's okay, Fred dear, I can handle this. You go and finish your breakfast. Right, Mr Tipple, what do you need to know?'

The dismissive manner in which she attempts to banish hubby to the kitchen instinctively makes me glance down the hallway. It wouldn't surprise me to find a shaggy four-legged friend sitting there, tongue hanging out, and tail wagging, waiting for its next command from master.

I'm thinking that this is one domineering lady. And given the manner in which she addresses her husband, I'm already beginning to have reservations about her suitability as a customer. If she treats him like that, what's she going to be like with my removal crew or me, especially if something goes wrong?

Ignoring his wife's instructions, Fred has ambled quietly up the carpeted hallway towards us, wearing what appears to be Mickey Mouse slippers, no less. He stops one foot behind her, peering round her left shoulder. He's a tiny man, about five feet four inches or so. From where I'm standing, only his head is visible, the rest of his body hidden behind her considerable torso.

I'm transfixed by the top of his head. For a man in his late sixties, he's done well to preserve his black, fuzzy hair in its present condition. But then I realise he's wearing a wig, and not a very expensive one at that, if the fit and style are anything to go by. It looks like someone has plonked a black mop on top of his head.

He's said nothing so far and Mrs Watson seems unaware that he's now standing directly behind her. She is impatiently awaiting my response, as frigid as a lesbian in a room with a flock of abbots.

I avert my focus back to the mistress of the house. 'Ah, yes, right then, Mrs Watson. What do I need to know? First, I need to know where you're moving to.'

Her throaty, cut-glass reply slices through the air like an arrow from a highly strung bow. Similar to the arrow that cut Fred down to size a minute ago. 'Cheltenham. To be precise, a small village called Battledown, on the outskirts of Cheltenham.' Her mouth closes into a tight, narrow line.

'And is it a house you're moving into? A bungalow? Or an apartment?' I enquire courteously, back into my stride, my pen scribbling.

'A detached bungalow,' she replies icily, the frostiness clinging to each syllable with the texture of an ice cube. 'Newly built. The painters are in the process of applying the final touches before the new carpets are laid. And there will be no trouble with access for your vans. We have checked with the builders.'

Her well-rehearsed response is spat out in staccato style, like a sergeant major on the parade ground. It wouldn't surprise me to find she has already given this same spiel to half a dozen other removal estimators.

Thankful for the distraction from Fred's wig, I lower my eyes and busily record the information she has just provided.

She watches me closely with a degree of scepticism, her eyes as dull and cheerless as a frozen haddock. Out of the corner of my eye I'm aware of four inches of hair bobbing around behind her broad shoulders. With Jumping Jack Flash hovering around in the background, it's difficult not to let my attention stray from the mistress of the house.

'Right, Mrs Watson,' I say, attempting to project a business-like approach in the face of her curt and abrasive response. 'I need to establish what needs to be moved. Can I suggest we start upstairs?'

Having no good reason to argue the toss, she turns sharply to head for the stairwell. Unaware that her dearly beloved is standing behind her, she plants a size-nine foot on top of Fred's Mickey Mouse foot, causing them both to stumble. As they grapple in a desperate endeavour to stay upright, I fear they're both going to topple onto me. Aware of the sensitivity of my big toe, I step back. I'm not worried about Fred standing on my toe, but if the fourteen stone of Mrs Watson's considerable frame makes contact with this little piggy of mine, then Frankie here is headed for the nearest A&E.

'Jumping Jehovah, Fred,' she cries out venomously, regaining her balance as Fred bounces off the wall. 'I thought I told you to finish your breakfast. What do you think you're doing, standing right on top of me? Have you nothing better to do?'

Uneasy about the incident and her manner in dealing with it – like seeing a naughty child being reprimanded by its parent – I wait expectantly to see if Fred has the bottle to give *Frau* Watson her come-uppance.

'Sorry, dear, just thought I might be able to help,' he replies meekly, his voice creaky and subdued. He stands there with a penitent look on his face, like a chastised puppy. If Mrs Watson had looked at me at that particular moment, she'd have seen disappointment etched all over my features. And here was me hoping Fred might have some balls.

He has taken up position out of harm's way. The words 'little and large' immediately spring to mind; where she has the build of a rugby prop, he has the frame of a featherweight boxer. His studious, intellectual-type face is full-cheeked and rosy, embroidered by a set of heavy, brown-framed glasses which barely disguise a substantial clump of grey eyebrows. He's wearing a loose-fitting pair of brown corduroy trousers, topped by a colourful Fair Isle sweater. This is two sizes too large, falling to within inches of his knees. With the combination of comic slippers, weird looking wig and lack of dress sense, one wouldn't describe him as typical of your modern man. The overall image is one of a mad scientist.

Something else is amiss. His wig has moved and is now slightly askew on his head. But he doesn't seem to be aware of it, nor apparently does his missus. She's still giving him a look which would wither an oak tree from a mile away.

Up to now, he has made no attempt to communicate with me. He's also showing no signs of embarrassment over the manner in which his handler is admonishing him – not that she's finished with him yet.

'Well, don't get in the way, Fred,' she snarls in her clipped tones, her lips curled like a rabid dog. 'I'm perfectly capable of dealing with Mr Tipple without your assistance. Right, Mr Tipple, follow me.'

Tempted to give a smart regimental salute, I instead follow as she pushes past a docile Fred who has to flatten himself against the wall. She waddles smartly up the central staircase, baggy trousers billowing round the uneven but ample contours of her wobbly backside. The light from the landing window is temporarily blocked out as she makes her ascent.

As it happens, I'm one of those who fully support equal rights. But if there's one thing that's hard to stomach, it's the sight of a grown man (or in Fred's case, a garden gnome) subjugated and humiliated by the obstinate and autocratic will of his wife – particularly when, in all likelihood, she plighted her troth, promising to love, honour and respect the pathetic little sod. So much for nuptial promises. The Pankhursts and Germaine Greer have a lot to answer for.

Despite her attitude, business is business. It won't do to let personal feelings overcome the need to drum up much-needed work. I stop at the halfway point on the stairwell and take time to look closely at the walls. These have been decorated recently, with not a mark to be seen. I can't see her taking kindly to having the paintwork defaced, even if she is moving out. I make a quick note on my worksheet.

When I reach the top of the central stairway, she is awaiting my arrival, making no attempt to disguise her impatience.

Tough. I've got a job to do, and I'm going to do it properly. And if that means she has to wait, so be it.

Glancing along the corridors running to either side of the stairwell, I can see five doors. Three or four of these will be bedrooms, one a bathroom and one possibly an airing cupboard. But they'll all need to be checked.

Without further reference to me, Mrs Watson turns along the landing and into a sizeable bedroom. The main items of furniture consist of three chests of drawers, a dressing table, a row of built-in wardrobes and twin beds. One small bedside lamp adorns the single night table situated between the two beds. The furniture is top quality and no personal chattels or possessions are visible apart from one small radio clock perched on the dressing table. This is obviously a guest room.

'The main bedroom, Mr Tipple,' advises Mrs Watson, contradicting my presumption. She waddles across the room and stops in front of the front window, casting a large shadow across the nearest bed.

How could I be so stupid, thinking Fred would want to share a double bed with his size-twenty spouse? It would be like sleeping with a baby rhinoceros. At the first amorous intention on her part, the breath would be squeezed out of him faster than air from a pricked balloon. At the very thought, my lips contort into a needless smirk. To observe Fred and his missus getting their act together would be like watching the coupling of a rowing boat with the Queen Mary.

Mrs Watson has turned to face me, her eyebrows raised, visually questioning my next move. I quickly and sensibly rearrange my expression to one of more serious intent.

'Are you taking all the free-standing furniture with you?' I ask.

'Yes.' This clipped reply is delivered along with a look that says: *'And what else do you think we're going to do with it, you stupid tit?'*

Ignoring the sneer, I note the relevant items on my worksheet. 'And will you be packing your own personal effects, or is that something you would also like me to quote for?'

'No, we will do our own packing, thank you.'

I could have sworn that Mrs Watson spoke without moving her lips, then realise the voice has come from behind me. Lo and behold, Fred has followed us up the stairs, the stair carpet masking the sound of his footsteps. He is now standing just inside the bedroom door, peering owlishly through his glasses in our general direction, the wig still perched haphazardly on top of his head.

Despite having my enquiry answered by Fred, I've lost all confidence in his ability to have any meaningful input into the decision-making process. Instinctively, I turn back towards Mrs Watson, curious as to her reaction. To pack or not to pack? Could this be the moment that Fred asserts himself and starts to wag his own tail, causing me to reappraise my earlier judgement? Or is this modern-day Delilah to slay Samson once again with another masterful display of female chauvinism, leaving his entrails trailing grotesquely from every orifice of his body?

I don't have long to wait. Fred has been silly enough to precipitously stick his head over the top of the parapet.

'Fred, dear.' The manner and the nano-second in which this use of his name shoots from her mouth, in no way softened by the 'dear' appendage, tells me instantly Fred is about to suffer another arrow straight between the eyes.

'Mr Tipple's question was addressed to me and I believe I'm better equipped to answer it. And did I not make it clear that I would deal with him?'

As this caustic humiliation of Fred is delivered, I could swear that fumes emerge from Mrs Watson's nostrils like the dragon she is. And I fear further punishment is about to come.

Sure enough, she fires a clipped, icy and poisonous broadside with her Gatling-gun tongue, unconcerned at my presence, and totally insensitive to any embarrassment she might be causing Fred. 'Fred, dear,' she spouts, giving him a look that would melt an iceberg. 'There is no way I have time to undertake packing, what with organising all aspects of this removal, plus the housework, garden and shopping. And you know you're not capable of doing much.'

I'm not sure if this *coup de grace* is meant to reflect Fred's physical condition and mental well-being, or is simply a clear demonstration to both Fred and me who's in charge.

Despite strong doubts that Fred might still wish to exercise some opinion on the matter, I look over my shoulder for a possible riposte. There is. And I should've known what it would be.

'Okay, Priscilla dear, I just thought it would reduce our costs,' he replies, duly repentant, and not at all fazed by her domineering attitude.

That's three times our little Mickey Mouse Fred has been knocked to the canvas. But at least he's still in the ring, though not putting up much of a scrap. And there'll be no need for hospital treatment, providing he keeps ducking and diving.

Fred has obviously got nothing further to add. He continues to ignore my presence and stands there, arms folded, calmly waiting for further developments.

Deeply saddened by the demise of Fred (yet again), I check the contents of the furniture. Only one wardrobe and one chest of drawers have been allocated to Fred for his personal possessions. The other three wardrobes and chest of drawers contain his wife's belongings – all appearing to my untutored eye to contain top-of-the-range goods with upmarket labels. I guess that once she leaves the front gate, she'll need the best camouflage available. Not that it'll make much difference, as mutton is still mutton, no matter how it's served on a plate.

All their personal effects are stacked and stored in a neat and orderly fashion. The packing by the crew will need to be carried out with the same attention to order and detail. Priscilla won't take kindly to having Fred's socks, singlets and boxer shorts tossed topsy-turvy into a box alongside her bras and knickers.

I make a further annotation on my worksheet to this effect then, after a quick check of the en-suite bathroom, return to her presence. Confirming that I've seen what needs to be seen, I pretend to tick a box on my worksheet as a demonstration of my professionalism.

She's not impressed. With a barely suppressed tut-tutting and an accompanying shake of the head, she turns her back then sweeps past poor Fred once again, the displacement of air rocking him on his heels. Dismissing him as a lost cause, I work my way into her slipstream and tamely follow her along the landing.

The relevant items of furniture and personal effects to be packed and moved in each room are noted, each notation again burnished with exaggerated flourishes of my pen. All the while, the forbidding presence of Mrs Watson continues to hover behind me silently like an overweight Buddha, but without the accompanying serenity.

We move on to the landing, in time to see Fred disappear into the bathroom. Whatever the reason, he's decided to take no further interest in the proceedings. Wise man.

Anticipating my next move, Priscilla begins to head towards the top of the stairs. But I'm not finished up here. There's one further important area to check, so the old bat is going to have to wait.

'Excuse me, Mrs Watson,' I call, stopping her in her tracks. 'Is there anything in the loft?'

She turns round, her expression questioning the necessity of such a stupid question. 'Yes,' she responds curtly, but fails to elaborate. Silence descends as we look up at the trapdoor.

'Well, can you give me some idea of what's up there?' I prompt her, standing my ground. By rights, I should be having a look for myself, but the thought of climbing a ladder and rifling through a dusty, cold loft doesn't fill me with enthusiasm. There's also the danger that she might want to come up with me.

Jesus. The thought that I might have to share the ceiling joists with Priscilla causes me to break out in a sweat.

Thankfully, entering the loft is not something she plans to do. She brusquely assures me there are only twenty to thirty assorted boxes of miscellaneous goods. I decide to accept what I'm being told in good faith. Silly, because it wouldn't be the first time I've been caught short in that regard.

'Will you want us to get the goods down?' I ask, ignoring my own doubts.

'No, Mr Tipple, my husband will do that.'

Considering her earlier comments, I'm surprised she believes Fred capable of completing this onerous task successfully. Given his physique, I wouldn't have thought he'd have the strength to climb up the loft ladder, never mind carry twenty or thirty boxes down again. But if she expects Fred to do it, that's it. I just hope he doesn't injure his crown jewels by slipping between the joists or falling out the trapdoor.

Priscilla decides the time is ripe to move proceedings on. 'Right, Mr Tipple, that's all upstairs. Downstairs now, lounge first.' This, rattled out in parade-ground style, make me wonder if she might have spent some time in the army. It doesn't take a lot of imagination to see her bullying her troops around the barracks.

The more I'm exposed to this butch, hard-nosed lady, the less enthusiastic I feel about her suitability as a customer. With her unforgiving and dictatorial attitude, this is a removal which could end up being more trouble than it's worth. But as work is scarce at this time of the year, it's too early to jettison any potential boost to my income.

Her posterior has already begun to rumble down the stairs ahead of me, each stair creaking under her weight as we go. Reaching the entrance hall, she opens a door to our left and we enter the sitting room.

As I begin the process of annotating the main items of furniture, Priscilla takes up a position in the middle of the room and adopts a stance like she's ready to engage in a bout of sumo wrestling.

Disconcerting as her behaviour is, I ignore her and continue to do what needs to be done. She may think I'm wasting her time, but this record is important. And it's as much in her interest as mine that I get it right.

I move towards the back section of the lounge. Priscilla revolves on her heels like she's on a turn-table in a microwave oven. She follows my progress closely but continues to say nothing, which suits me fine.

My assessment of the sitting room is concluded. Mrs Watson is now standing by the door, watching me like I'm about to slip one of her valuable paintings down the front of my trousers. 'Thank you, Mrs Watson. That's all I need here,' I say sickly sweetly, completing my notations with another flourish of my pen, less extravagantly than earlier given my reduced zeal for the task.

Without further ado, she leads me out of the room. Fred has disappeared from the scene; probably still upstairs, searching for a spare set of balls.

'The dining room.' She announces this with a grunt like a baby piglet. Communication completed, she resets her mouth into a humourless thin line, the small clumps of grey stubble on her top lip accentuated by the dim light.

It crosses my mind that it's been a long time since a customer treated me with such a lack of hospitality. Yet she's the one who requested my presence. So why's she's treating me like I've brought the plague into her household?

Steeling myself, I recommence my long-established routine, taking particular interest in the contents of two six-by-four-foot display units. Each unit is crammed to capacity with toy cars. There must be a hundred – of varying shapes, designs, sizes and colours – all neatly displayed. Who would have thought that Fred would keep a toy car collection at his age? Or that Priscilla would agree to display them? Maybe she does have a heart and soul after all.

My eyebrows rise as I move closer to view the collection. While the task of packing the cars doesn't concern me greatly – after all, they are just toys – each will need to be individually wrapped. And that's going to take a packer considerable additional time that needs to be costed.

I'm about to ask her if she might prefer to perform this duty, in view of the extra charge I'll have to make, when Fred makes a further unexpected reappearance. He shuffles into the room, his head down and his hands occupied as he attempts to adjust the zip of his trouser fly. He seems to be unaware that something is protruding from the gap and causing the problem. I think it's his shirt, but if it's his willy-winky, that'll be painful. But there's no way I'm going to help reunite his manhood with the rest of his scrotum. His missus can do that when I've gone. She might even enjoy inflicting further pain on him.

Pretending nothing untoward has occurred, I turn my attention back to the display cabinets.

'This is a very interesting collection of toy cars, Mrs Watson,' I comment hypocritically, inwardly wondering why a mature couple would be bothered to keep such childish pleasures on full display.

She regards me with a look of contempt. 'They are not *toy* cars, Mr Tipple. They are classic model cars. And I must tell you, they're collector's items, very much sought after and of great value.' A small drop of spittle settles on the stubble of her top lip and glistens in the light like a tarnished pearl.

Me and my big mouth. But model cars, toy cars: they all look the same to me. Despite my self-justification on the matter, it's obvious I've pressed the wrong button. So much for my self-proclaimed professional expertise.

'Of course, Mrs Watson,' I acknowledge quickly, trying to appear suitably chastised. I don't have any problems grovelling when necessary. And if it works for Fred, it should work for me. 'I should have known that, Mrs Watson. Yes, of course, model cars. They must be extremely valuable. But have no fear, they'll get the best of treatment from A to Z.'

Hoping I've recovered my status as a professional estimator, I now feel the need to add the personal touch.

'Do they belong to your children?' I ask, in all innocence.

Mrs Watson regards me balefully from behind frosty eyes. 'No, Mr Tipple', she replies tartly. 'I would have thought it apparent as you completed your inspection that my husband and I do not have children.'

Silly me, how could I have possibly thought that the conception of children could ever have featured on Mrs Watson's list of things to do? Or that Fred would have the necessary equipment to assist in that endeavour.

'They are, in fact, my husband's collection,' she continues coldly, her diction sharp as a guillotine. 'And he will want extra special care taken. That's if we decide to use your company, of course. Each one is an original and pretty much irreplaceable. Isn't that correct, dear?'

Involuntarily, I turn to look at Fred, who has managed to stow his tackle safely. He is now sitting at the dining table, idly leafing through a Delia Smith cookbook.

Not bothering to look up from his cookery book, he says nothing but simply nods his head vigorously in the affirmative. In the process, the wig once again moves slightly, lodging a quarter of an inch towards the back of his head. An additional rim of unweathered pink skin is now clearly visible. I'm thinking that one more nod from Fred and that hairpiece is going to end up on the floor. Neither Fred nor Priscilla appear to be aware of this latest development. Hair today, gone tomorrow.

'Don't worry, Mrs Watson,' I respond, mustering as much authority into my voice as possible. 'You can be assured that my packers will take the utmost care. They're all fully qualified for this specialist work.'

Having completed my assessment of the dining room, I try to steer us in the direction of fresh territory. 'Perhaps we can look in the kitchen now.'

As I pass Fred, I'm sorely tempted to reach down and reposition his wig. Instead, leaving him to the wisdom of Delia and shepherd's pie, I follow Priscilla into an extensive kitchen. In keeping with the rest of the house, everything is sparkling clean, a minimal amount of clutter on the worktops. Mr Muscle obviously struts his stuff in here on a regular basis.

With Mrs Watson in close attendance, I'm opening the cupboards to assess the extent of the packing to be done when the misshapen top of Fred's head appears round the doorway. He's like a lost sheep, the way he's wandering round the house.

'Would you like a cup of tea, Mr Tipple?' Hearing the unexpected sound of Fred's voice – and delighted that the source of this particular request should emanate from his lips and not those of his overbearing wife – I'm momentarily struck dumb.

God, I thought nobody was ever going to ask. And yes, Fred, I could murder a cup, bless you. Mine's a white with two sugars, and perhaps a couple of chocolate biscuits to keep me going.

I'm just about to give Fred the verbal thumbs-up when the lady of the house decides to intervene in her own indomitable manner.

'I don't know why you are asking Mr Tipple that, Fred dear. I'm sure Mr Tipple is far too busy to idle his time away drinking tea. Isn't that so, Mr Tipple?'

I'm pissed off. The old bat could at least have let me decide for myself.

Biting my tongue, I find myself hypocritically and pathetically nodding my head in the affirmative. Just like Fred. 'Yes indeed, Mrs Watson. Nine customers to fit in this morning,' I say, gilding the lily somewhat. 'I can't afford to doddle. A lot of people keen to use our services. But I do appreciate the offer, Mr Watson,' I add, addressing Fred. Despite his lack of gumption, at least he did ask. And he deserves all the support he can get.

'Right then, Mr Tipple,' Mrs Watson continues triumphantly, having again successfully demonstrated the power of positive thinking. 'That's the house done. Can we now move on to the garden and garage? And can you please speed things up? We have an appointment to see our solicitor at eleven o'clock and we can't afford to be late.'

Yes sir, no sir, three bags full, sir.

Having girded her loins, she turns to hubby, then calls out her next command. 'Fred, stay indoors. I can handle it. You know you've been suffering from the cold recently.'

He's more likely to suffer a loss of his hairpiece. One strong gust and that wig will surely end up on the roof. It would make an ideal nest for some deserving bird.

Giving Fred up as a lost cause, I follow Mrs Watson around the garage and garden, compiling my notes in a lacklustre manner. Any enthusiasm and bonhomie I may have had has now been dissipated by Priscilla's frosty, unfriendly, officious demeanour and her treatment of Fred. Much as I hate to admit it, she's successfully knocked the stuffing out of me. It's becoming increasingly clear why Fred is the shadow of the man he is, God help him.

Our tour of the external parameters of her property completed, we return, shivering, to the warmth of the kitchen. As we enter the kitchen, my eyeballs nearly pop out of my head. Fred's wig is now covering the teapot in the middle of the kitchen table.

A dual-purpose wig and tea cosy. Whatever next? But is the wig intended to keep the teapot warm, or is the teapot heating up the wig in readiness for Fred's forthcoming trip to the solicitor? Whatever, he appears to be completely unfazed by the incongruity of the situation.

I don't know whether to laugh or cry. I've seen a lot of things in my day, but this has got be a first. If only I had a hidden camera. Because Jane will never believe me. She'll think I'm having one of my theatrical turns.

Although Priscilla can't have failed to notice, she's showing no signs of discomfort or embarrassment at Fred's pot- and wig-warming technique. Perhaps it's normal procedure on a winter's day.

'Is that all the information you need, Mr Tipple?' she asks tersely, observing me closely through narrowed eyelids and drumming her fingers loudly on the worktop.

'Yes, er, thank you, Mrs Watson,' I stammer, attempting to pull my jaw up from the floor. 'That's me finished, so unless there's any more information you'd like, I'll say goodbye to you and Mick– Mr Watson for now. Thank you for your time. It's been a most interesting experience.'

'Your quotation will be in the post this afternoon and, whatever your decision, I trust that all goes well on removal day.' *But if it's a windy day, don't forget to superglue that wig to Fred's head.* 'If you've any further queries, please don't hesitate to contact us.'

She gives me a long, hard look, her pale eyes the colour of flint. 'Have no fear, Mr Tipple. If there's anything I need to know, you can be certain I'll ask. Make no mistake about it. And be sure to forward full details of your insurance policy.'

With nothing further to be said, and with my tail tucked behind my legs, I exit via the kitchen door. This is closed behind me without further comment.

I stand immobile, taking in the refreshing air and allowing the cold wind to sweep around me unabated. I feel like I've just endured the tenth round of a closely fought prize fight. It certainly hasn't been a visit to raise my expectations of a successful outcome. And having to deal with Priscilla following any possible fall-out from the removal could cause me a considerable amount of prolonged heartache.

As for Fred? Well, despite everything, my heart goes out to him. Having to live with her day in, day out, would be enough to bring most men to their knees.

Chapter fifteen

I ESCAPE the claustrophobic, suffocating presence of Mrs Watson, feeling like I've been granted a reprieve from a life sentence in prison. What I've just witnessed is a marriage blessed in hell; an apocalypse of the first order. Is it any wonder Jane and I are reluctant to formalise our partnership?

Quickly making my way back to the car, I collapse into its protective interior and turn on the ignition. A refreshing blast of cold air from the vents helps to blow away the choking cloak of Priscilla's oppression. With one last admiring glance at the lawns, I pull out into Acacia Avenue then begin to look for a suitable parking place. It's imperative that all elements of the Watson's removal are reassessed while the details are fresh in my mind. Various factors need to be considered: the overall cubic capacity of the load; the quality of the goods; the number of crew required at Windsor and Battledown; the time required to complete the operation; diesel costs; and finally, any unusual risk factors peculiar to the job. Relative to its importance, this task has the grandiose title of Client Risk Assessment Process, more commonly referred to by the lads as Frank's CRAP. Only when I have finished my CRAP can my charge be finalised.

I pass a row of large Victorian properties, all long-since converted into offices or flats. The front of each building has small parking areas, but with no vacant spaces, I drive on slowly.

After another forty yards, a bus stop appears on my left. Not an ideal stopping point but the best I'm likely to find before I reach the motorway. I pull into the lay-by directly in front of the bus shelter. Two of the glass partitions have been vandalised, the smashed fragments strewn on the ground.

Wanton destruction, in the Queen's own backyard. Not that Her Majesty is likely to experience this mindless destruction first-hand, living as she does in her fairy-tale world of castles and palaces. If it was possible to petition her on the matter, I'd have her proclaim a royal decree that the yobbos causing such mayhem should have their strutting, arrogant, indolent little arses transported to the army barracks at Windsor, where they might contribute something useful towards the development of Her Majesty's kingdom. And if the army wouldn't have them, I'd haul the stocks out of the Windsor Castle dungeons and stick their useless, scrawny necks through the apertures for a week – giving us poor, downtrodden plebs the chance to heave a few rotten eggs or kitchen knives at the gormless miscreants.

This long-term grump causing me to seethe, I cast my eyes towards the shelter. Within the remaining partitions, two elderly ladies are huddled together on a short bench. Their arms are entwined as they snuggle up for warmth. Thin plastic mackintoshes flap loosely around their thick woollen overcoats, the hoods pulled over elderly, grey-topped heads. Their faces are ashen, wrinkled with age and a life of penury. Each is tightly gripping a leather handbag strapped to a small two-wheeled trolley.

They are watching me closely, possibly thinking I'm going to offer them a lift. Or suspicious I'm an old geezer on the pull. They could also resent the fact that I'm temporarily blocking the access for the next bus. On reflection, that's probably their main concern, and I'd probably feel the same in their position.

As if reading my thoughts, one of the ladies says something to her friend then detaches herself and gingerly shuffles across the slushy pavement to the side of the car. She leans over and peers owlishly through the snow-smeared passenger window, tapping the glass lightly with her gloved knuckles. Resigned to what is coming, I lean over and wind down the window, leaving no more than a six-inch gap. I don't want to lose the heat building up in the car.

Her elderly pixie face is a mass of wrinkles and filled with concern. 'Excuse me, ducks,' she says in a hoarse whisper, barely heard above the sound of wind and engine. 'Do you know this is a bus stop? You shouldn't be stopping here.'

Despite the uncharitable thoughts running through my mind, I recognise that a reasonable question has been asked of me. And having been brought up by Ma Tipple to show respect for senior citizens – I'll be one myself in another few years – it's with considerable understanding and patience that I reply reassuringly: 'Yes dear, I know it's a bus stop. But don't worry. I'll only be here for a couple of ticks. I'll be well gone by the time the bus gets here.'

I give her my sweetest smile then quickly rewind the window. The old dear, clearly unconvinced, watches me closely for a moment then slowly returns to the bench. Once seated, she glues herself to her friend. There follows some animated conversation, with considerable head-nodding and finger-pointing in my direction.

This little matter having been peacefully and diplomatically settled to my thinking, I now ignore them. The engine of the car continues to turn over, the heater blowing a comforting blast of warm air around my ankles and drowning out the external noises of passing traffic.

I place my presentation folder on my lap and busily commence to scribble further notes on the back of my worksheet. Without this record, my memory of individual clients and the main factors relating to each removal would quickly fade. But notes or not, Priscilla Watson is not a customer I'm likely to forget. This could be one removal where my hapless foreman and crew stagger home in disarray, broken and shattered. And if she gets a sight of what I'm scribbling, I've little doubt she'll have me up before the beak on a charge of defamation of character.

There's no doubt in my mind that she has a low threshold of tolerance. If one dinner plate is broken, she'll expect a completely new dinner service. Any blemish to the walls and she'll demand a full redecoration throughout the house. Any soiling of her new carpet at Battledown, however minimal, and she will, at best, insist on carpet cleaners of repute; at worst, a replacement carpet. The slightest scratch, indentation or mark caused will be instantly detected and produced as evidence of my crew's total incompetence. As for the model cards, well, I can imagine her reaction if we so much as cause the paint to be stripped off any single piece of Fred's collection. I certainly wouldn't want to be the one to meet her with him blubbing over his bent MG Sprite, or a wheel missing from his Aston Martin. Fred might well suffer a nervous breakdown. And that could be two of us.

This old battleaxe has not only put the frighteners on Fred, she and her moustache are certainly scaring the hell out of me.

A shiver runs through the entire length of my body. Whether this is due to my CRAP, or because I'm coming down with some additional ailment, I can't be sure. Although my stomach is still causing me discomfort, I'm consoled by the thought there's been no repetition of my earlier headache. My toe is also on the mend, so things seem to be looking up.

Immersed in my thoughts, I've been unaware of the increasingly poor weather conditions, the passing traffic and the two elderly ladies still sheltering within the damaged bus shelter. As I raise my eyes from the worksheet, it's quite clear from their general demeanour they're still not happy that I'm occupying the bus stop, but that's what old age can do to rational thought.

Attempting to reassure them, I give them a brief acknowledgement with a royal wave of my hand, then, in best Winston Churchill manner, extend two fingers into the air to indicate my estimated time of departure: *two more minutes and I'll be off.* In performing this well-intended gesture, I fail to recognise that this action might be misinterpreted. Instead, in all innocence, I begin to audibly talk myself through the costing elements of the Watsons' removal.

'Right then, Frank, let's see what we have here,' I instruct myself, concentrating deeply and absorbing all the information I've collated over the previous minutes.

A minute later, drawing on the experience gleaned over many years of agonising about costs and profits, I finalise my charges. 'One thousand seven and fifty hundred pounds,' I cry out triumphantly, noting the total with an especially extravagant flourish of my pen. Three hundred and eighty more than I'd charge a normal customer.

Satisfied I've reached the right conclusion, I address myself once more. 'Is that your final answer, Frank?' I ask, looking at my reflection in the car mirror.

'Yes, final answer,' I reply triumphantly, like I've won a million pounds on *Who Wants To Be A Millionaire*. I underline the final charge with two further flourishes.

A couple of days later, when explaining to Jane the measures I'd taken with regard to this pricing, she professed to be surprised. Not only did she feel I was being a mite avaricious, but she didn't think it was good business practice to overcharge customers, possibly deterring them and their friends from considering me in the future.

That may well have been a sensible point, but as I tried to tell her, this being the bottom line, I wasn't convinced it would be in my best interests to take on this particular job, considering my instincts about Priscilla.

'Do I really want the potential aggro?' I asked her rhetorically. 'And do I want to put in three days of hard graft only to find her putting the screws on me, with the possibility of a minimal reward at the end of it? It's not as if I'm desperate for the money. And in any case, there's a strong possibility my competitors will also be covering their backs and adopt the same approach.'

Jane wasn't convinced. But if Priscilla does receive a more competitive quote, then the best of British luck to whichever company gets the job. Assuming the unlucky crew are supplied in advance with flak jackets and hard hats, they could well survive the ordeal. Whether Fred and his wig will, well that's another matter.

My CRAP now complete, I'm startled by a long, loud blast. I sit erect in my seat and turn my head to the right. A bus has pulled up adjacent to my door, the interior lights shining brightly through the surrounding gloom. Bollocks! I didn't see or hear that coming.

I cast a bewildered look upwards, disconcerted by the convoluted, snarling face of the bus driver as he looks down at me. He gives his horn another going-over, a look of pure rage on his face sufficient to crack the glass separating us. Mouthing in my direction, his lips are contorted into a grotesque shape, the words inaudible. But there's no mistaking his message.

The automatic bus door opens and he rises in his seat. For a moment I fear a direct, embarrassing confrontation is about to occur. Instead, a youngish passenger, with a rucksack on his back and carrying a small bouquet of flowers, steps down from the bus, only just managing to squeeze between the bus and the front wing of my car. He gives me a dirty look before proceeding along the pavement towards the hospital.

The passengers occupying the nearside seats are peering down from along the length of the bus, enjoying the spectacle.

'Shit, shit, and shit,' I mutter, desperately securing my seat belt. The sooner I'm out of here the better, before this mad bull decides to leave the comfort of his cab and give me what for.

Fortunately for me, the driver has left sufficient space towards the front of the lay-by to enable me to pull out. I reach for the gear selector, hurriedly slip the gear into drive mode and apply my foot to the throttle pedal. As the car eases forward, I'm dumbfounded when, with a long blast of the horn and a final shake of his fist, the automatic door closes and the driver suddenly accelerates. I jam on the brakes as the front of the bus nearly hits my front wing. As it passes, the remaining passengers peer down, some smirking, others with a 'you stupid sod' look on their faces. I'm left parked in the lay-by, totally gob-smacked.

Realising I've had a close shave – ramming the bus and having a physical or verbal assault from the gorilla in the bus – I find my hands shaking. But that's the least of my worries. The driver has left without the two old dears. Either he didn't seen them because they were huddled in the corner of the shelter, or his line of vision was blocked by the car. And even if they saw the bus coming – which is unlikely as their eyes were fixed on me – they wouldn't have been able to get their trolleys through the gap between bus and car.

Don't worry, I told them, *I'll be out of here in a tick.* No doubt spoken with the same silly, smug and patronising expression that gets Jane really wound up. But I didn't think for one moment I'd still be here when the bus arrived. Or that the driver mightn't see them. And now these elderly ladies will have to hang around in the freezing cold for another half hour, waiting for the next bus. Bugger, bugger and bugger.

I glance in the rear-view mirror. One of the old dears is standing forlornly at the side of the road, her arms futilely raised after the departing bus. The other old lady has fixed her sights on me, murder etched all over her wizened features. As I watch, she starts to perform a soft-shoe shuffle towards the car, dragging her trolley behind her.

Hells bells! She looks mad enough to clout me across the head with her handbag. At the very least, I'm going to be on the receiving end of an unwelcome level of acerbity.

Pretending not to notice the shuffling approach of the steaming lady and her trolley, I press my foot down on the accelerator. The car shoots onto the main road, rear wheels skidding on the wet, snowy surface. In my rear-view mirror the rapidly diminishing forms of the ladies are left stranded in the murky gloom like two lost souls. Mouths agape, they look miserable, forlorn, cold and exceedingly angry as they watch my getaway.

My guilt at the part I've played in their plight is assuaged by the thought that, should they suffer from hypothermia whilst waiting for the next bus, the King Edward Hospital is just round the corner. Any emergency treatment should be quickly and readily available.

On that positive note, I switch on the radio then turn onto the Windsor link road towards the M4 and Slough. Wogan the wonder boy has departed the airwaves, replaced by the jocular inanities of Ken Bruce. There's time to put the chaos of the last few moments behind me and wind down in Ken's wacky company before engaging with my next client.

Five minutes later, with Jose Feliciano doing his best to 'Light My Fire', I leave the motorway then cross the Three Tuns intersection onto the Farnham Road. As I'm in danger of being late for my next appointment (a Mr Fettucini, according to the worksheet), I ignore the worsening conditions and put my foot down. Following my indiscretions at the Watsons, I don't want to jeopardize my chances of securing this job.

I'm blithely unaware that the seeds that I'm hoping to plant in Mr Fettucini's mind with regard to securing his removal contract will be blown away faster than I can sow them.

Chapter sixteen

I'M DRIVING THROUGH a full-blown snow storm, my eyes glued to the road and my speed faster than is sensible for the conditions.

Bloody weather. And it doesn't take a rocket scientist to work out who's to blame. It's those Yankee Doodle Dandies, polluting the atmosphere with their gas-guzzling cars and their materialistic need for every sodding aid to an over-indulgent life.

But they're not the only ones. It's also those little people from the land of fried rice, with their coal-fired chimneys and billions of little bottoms spouting pollution into the atmosphere.

I switch the wiper blades to full speed and turn on the headlights as Ken Bruce announces his next choice of record: Art Garfunkel with 'Always Look on the Bright Side of Life'.

I pull a face. It's easy for Art to pontificate, with a few million dollars in the bank. But what about the poor downtrodden workers, struggling to pay utility bills? It's not easy for us lot to look on the bright side. Not with every man and his dog squeezing us for every last penny we've got and screwing us at every available opportunity. I'd bet a pound to a penny my landlord is singing along with Art at this very moment, the bastard.

In a mean mood, I switch off Art and his stupid jingle then turn into the council estate where my next two customers live.

Driving into the centre of the estate, I'm reminded how uniform, drab and lifeless it is, with street after street of grey, pebble-dashed, semi-detached houses sitting between austere, high-rise flats reaching to the sky like layers of windowed concrete coal-bunkers. But a removal is still a removal, no matter where it's conducted. And despite its limitations, this estate has been a good revenue producer for A to Z Removals over many years. In my book, Mr Fettucini's money will be as good as the lord of the manor's, even if he does blow his nose on the back of his sleeve. And his CRAP should be low and at the other end of the CRAP spectrum from Priscilla.

As I pull up in front of his house, I'm well aware that jumping to conclusions is not to be recommended, irrespective of past experience. The fact is, I don't know what awaits me behind Mr Fettucini's doors. The man may turn out to be a member of the aristocracy, albeit fallen on hard times. I might also discover a veritable treasure trove of antiques and artefacts.

I retrieve my presentation folder from the passenger seat and make my way up the snow-covered footpath. The exterior of the building is in a reasonable condition, except for one cracked pane of glass in the downstairs window. The fact that it hasn't been replaced confirms my suspicions about what I'm likely to find within.

Arriving at the door, I adjust my features and expose my dentures then knock briskly. In response, a dog begins barking ferociously. And it's a noisy brute.

Listening to the racket, I can't be sure whether the noise is emanating from inside or outside the house. Wherever it is, I hope it's under control. Even with tails a-wagging, it's difficult to know whether the four-legged buggers are going to bite your leg off or lick you to death. But this one doesn't sound like a licker.

I stand facing the front door like a lost sheep, quickstepping from foot to foot endeavouring to keep warm, then listen intently as I hear a loud shouted command to the dog, this sprinkled with a few F-words. This exhortation has the desired effect and silence reigns.

I'm preparing for Mr Fettucini to open the door when, without warning and shocking me to the core, an enormous rottweiler suddenly launches itself against the inside of the cracked window, barking madly and exposing a set of shark-like molars.

The effect of the dog's unexpected appearance and aggressive behaviour causes me to involuntarily step back. Dancing on its hind legs, its front paws ferociously scrabble at the glass, a slimy stream of slobber dribbling from its foaming mouth.

Now I know how the pane got cracked. And it's not going to take much for the rest of it to come crashing down. Jesus! If that raving brute comes through the window, I'm up shit creek. It'll have my testicles off in no time at all. I just hope that bloody pane is going to hold firm. But there's no way I'm going in there if he doesn't chain the brute up.

With the door still unopened, I knock more loudly, eyes nervously fixed on both the dog and the crack in the glass.

I've only to wait a few more seconds before the door opens and I get my first sight of Mr Fettucini. My smile falters, the dog is briefly forgotten and my earlier presumptions of Fettucini switch from aristocracy to Mafia.

A pair of shifty eyes regards me balefully from under two considerable expanses of beefy black eyebrows. A roll-up cigarette hangs loosely from the corner of a thin-lipped mouth, the smoke wafting up and inwards into his hallway.

The person whom I'm assuming to be Mr Fettucini is in his late-forties, about five feet ten and stocky. And he looks a right hoodlum. Straight off the set of *The Godfather*. A neck as thick as the thigh of a prize bull provides ample support for a turnip-shaped head, this topped with a crew-cut. His close-set eyes look out over a large pug nose, which is covered with a series of small blue veins.

His enormous biceps and muscled forearms – smothered with tattoos, mainly of tits and bums – strain the fabric of a tatty, short-sleeved black T-shirt. Conversely, his fat belly is enclosed in shell-suit bottoms, the size of a small tent and expansive enough to house a troop of Boy Scouts. The thin fabric does little to disguise the fact that he isn't wearing underpants. If I didn't know otherwise, I'd think he had a police truncheon and two tennis balls tucked down his trousers.

He is seemingly unconcerned about the antics of the rottweiler, which continues to bellow and claw frantically at the window.

'Yeah?' Mr Mass now grunts from the corner of his mouth, his head tilted back, his lips drawn tightly round the runt of his cigarette, his piggy eyes questioning the reason for my very existence. This is definitely a different type of welcome from the one experienced at the Watsons, but equally off-putting. *And good morning to you, Mr Fettucini!*

I try to ignore the brusqueness of the welcome. 'Mr Fettucini?' I query timidly then introduce myself. 'Frank Tipple from A to Z Removals. I have an appointment to see you.'

'Oh, yeah, right, mate,' he grunts, before removing the fag-end then flicking it over my head and into the snow. He then pulls a small metal tin from the pocket of his shell-bottoms, extracts a pinch of loose tobacco and cigarette paper and rolls up a tiny, scraggly-looking cigarette.

My first impressions are not good. The man's a big, fat, ignorant sod. Not a very charitable opinion to apply to a prospective customer, but what the hell. He hasn't the good grace to invite me in and out of the bleeding cold. Not that this big piece of blubber is likely to be feeling the cold.

It's only with difficulty that I'm keeping my professional cool and saying nothing smart. In any case, this isn't a customer one would choose to tangle with, especially with that bloody rottweiler in there. And despite his attitude, there could still be a profitable job to be had at the end of the day.

The end of the roll-up flares as it finally ignites. He takes a long drag then blows out a stream of smoke. 'Okay, mate, have you got a price for me?' he asks truculently, a small piece of tobacco stuck to his upper lip.

A price for him? How can I have a price for him when I haven't even got through the bloody door?

Despite the stupidity of the question, my response is intended to convey understanding, warmth and cheer, feelings which will hopefully be reciprocated by Mr Fettucini. 'No, sorry, Mr Fettucini, I can't give you a price until I've assessed your removal. Perhaps I could come in and get a few basic details from you, then maybe you could show me around?'

If I expected a sensible response to my proposition, I'm very much mistaken.

With his roll-up cigarette burning away rapidly at the corner of his mouth, he gives me that drop-dead look that that makes me think that a large snot is hanging from my nose.

'What do you mean, come in, assess my removal?' he snarls, tiny specks of spit and tobacco shooting from his mouth. 'Why do you think I'd want you to do that? You've got to be having a fucking laugh.'

His form adopts an even more belligerent pose, his fat belly wobbling like a giant jelly fish. The rottweiler continues to paw at the window, trails of slobber running down the glass.

I don't know what to think or say. Why would he ask for a quote and then not be prepared to show me around his home? Perhaps, like Billy, I'm at the wrong house. Maybe this isn't Fettucini. Bemused, I find my voice. 'It is Mr Fettucini I'm speaking to?'

'Yeah, who do you think I bleeding am? Tommy Cooper?' Having gained some pleasure from his own particular brand of sarcasm, his lips contort into an attempt at a smile, but instead makes him look more like his rabid dog. This has moved away from the window but is continuing to exercise the power of its vocal cords from somewhere within the house.

I purse my own lips into a tight smile. Anything to humour the ugly tosser. 'I understand from my secretary that you requested an estimate for your forthcoming removal?' I respond, 'but before I can give you an estimate, I need to establish how much furniture and personal effects need removing.'

Mr Pasta now regards me like I've just invited him to become president of the Gay Rights Association. 'You can forget all that fucking crap, mate. And your daft bird has got it wrong. I'm not moving. It's a safe that needs to be moved, up to Hammersmith. All I wanted was a price for the job.'

As I receive this pertinent piece of news, I mentally note to give Alice a bollocking for not fully briefing me. What Fettucini doesn't know is that the removal of safes is not something I agree to undertake very often nor with any degree of enthusiasm.

If it's one of those little ones that two lads can lift manually and slip on a two-wheeled trolley, then no problem. There could still be a morning's work in it. But if it's a Chubb one-ton chunk of solid steel, then I'm happy to leave that to the experts. Better no safe than sorry. Francis Tipple's personal code of Health and Safety.

'Oh yes, of course, right. I'm sorry, Mr Fettucini, my secretary didn't advise me it was just a safe you wanted moving. Can I have a look at it, please?' Looking at the shady character standing in front of me, I can't help but wonder what valuables he might hold to warrant possession of a safe. And why does he need a safe with that monster prowling round the house?

He shoots me a look of sheer venom, his fag hanging from the corner of his down-turned thin lips like a piece of rabbit turd.

'Look at it? Fuck that,' he snarls, spitting his aggression like a tom-cat on heat. 'I've told you already, mate: all I want is a price. Understand? Now, are you going to give me a fucking price or not?'

I'm taken aback by his tone and foul language. 'I'm sorry, Mr Fettucini. I'm afraid it's not as simple as that. Before I can give you a price, I need to know a few facts about the safe. Which floor is it on? How big is it? Will two men be able to lift it? Does it...'

My line of questioning comes to an abrupt stop as he heaves his bulk over the doorstep, bringing the extremity of his belly to within touching distance of my own. Hypnotised, I stare fearfully into the pupils of his shifty eyes as he removes the shrivelled remains of his roll-up then blows a waft of cigarette smoke directly into my face.

'Listen to me, mate, and listen real fucking good,' he growls, gesticulating wildly, the glowing tip of his cigarette inches from my face.

'If you think I'm showing you where I keep my fucking safe, just so you and your Irish mates can come here one night and nick it when I'm down at the fucking pub enjoying a few pints of ale, then you got another fucking think coming. Now fuck off back to the peat bog where you came from before I set the fucking dog on you.'

With that, he turns on his heel, and the door is closed in my face. As if to confirm that the meeting is concluded, the rottweiler reappears and resumes its abuse of the window.

I'm in a state of shock. I've just received a verbal mugging, the first time in twenty or so years I've been on the receiving end of a reception and language like that. At least six of the F-word, all contained within a short sentence. Even Charlie or Billy could never match that, no matter how provoked they were.

Thank you very much, Mr Fettucini, I'm thinking. *That was very gratifying. It's been a pleasure to do business with you. But, next time you're planning to move anything, don't call me, I'll call you, you shifty-eyed, fat-assed, pot-bellied descendant of an Italian turd.*

Gaining some satisfaction from mentally giving Fettucini his come-uppance, I skate down the pathway, totally oblivious to the danger underfoot. I collapse into the car seat, throwing my presentation folder with Fettucini's uncompleted worksheet onto the passenger seat.

The car windows are now entombed within an inch of snow, my vision of the outside world totally obscured. Trying to compose myself, I turn on the ignition and wipers then close my eyes, letting my body and mind slowly recover from Fettucini's onslaught. He's certainly the nastiest piece of work

I've had to deal with in a long, long time. Thank you, Alice, thank you very much. Can't wait for the next one.

I can't help but wonder what contraband he might be hoarding in his safe. From the look of the man, plus his bloody-minded attitude, I'd bet a thousand to one that it hasn't been lawfully gained.

I momentarily consider passing on my suspicions to the local fuzz, anonymously, of course. I could also give the RSPCA a ring and warn them about that bloody dog of his. If nothing else, it would at least give me some form of redress for my wasted time and the unnecessary stress he's caused.

Common sense prevails. If I grass on Fettucini and he subsequently receives a visit from the local bobby within the next twenty-four hours, sure as hell he's going to put two and two together. And guess what? Frankie's name comes rolling out of his hat. Two weeks later, having been easily traced, Frankie boy finds himself laid up with a broken arm, fractured leg, bent ribs, two black eyes, no teeth, and suffering an irretrievable breakdown, or on his way to the mortuary in a cardboard coffin.

With my eyes closed and my imagination running riot, I visualise the headlines and copy appearing on the front page of Friday's *Maidenhead Advertiser*:

Removal proprietor grasses on client and gets himself well and truly mowed. Police have recovered a number of body parts, strewn randomly around the Berkshire countryside. Whilst a formal identification has yet to take place, a set of dentures found near one of the parts is believed to be those of missing local removal boss, Francis Tipple. Sources close to the investigation report that Mr Tipple recently assisted police in recovering a large stash of bullion from the home of a local gangster, well-known to the police, with previous convictions for robbery and aggravated assault. Further enquiries are ongoing.

The images in my mind are too vivid for my liking. 'Forget it, Frank,' I advise myself, opening my eyes to the real world. 'The dickhead's not worth the aggro. On your bike, and fast as you can, mate.'

So saying, I pull myself upright and prepare for take-off. It's definitely turned out to be one of those days. And it's not over yet. If I'd had any sense,

I'd have stayed in bed and let everybody else get on with it.

'It's too bloody late for that now, Frank!' I admonish myself. 'You've started, so you'll have to finish.' Spoken just like the man on *Mastermind*.

I try to take a leaf out of Mr Garfunkel's song book and look on the bright side. After all, I've now got two good tales to recount at my next dinner party: Fred with his wig, Mickey Mouse slippers and roly-poly missus; and now Fettucini. If I perfect a little routine beforehand, there should be something to milk from both experiences, as long as I don't go overboard with the bad language or sequester Jane's tights to do another bullion-heist impersonation.

Feeling more upbeat than I'd have thought possible two minutes ago, I quickly check the address of my next client, Mrs Oglethorpe, who lives just a few blocks from my present location.

This removal estimate has been requested directly by the council on Mrs Oglethorpe's behalf. As they will be picking up the tab, it gives me good reason to be optimistic. This call should not only be straightforward, but the outcome should be more positive than at Fettucini's. After all, lightning never strikes in the same place twice. Everybody knows that.

Chapter seventeen

I WEND MY WAY through the snow-covered streets, my mind back on the mishaps that have befallen me this morning. If only there was some light at the end of the tunnel. Not blooming likely, with visits to Crinkley and McIntosh looming on the horizon.

At times like this, when I'm bewailing my fate because the whole world appears to be ganged up against me, Jane always feels it necessary to remind me why I've got no just cause to feel that way.

'For goodness sakes, Frank,' she'll say.

Those four words tell me that a bollocking is about to be delivered. Sure enough, a sharp rebuke invariably follows. 'Get a grip on yourself and stop thinking every man and his dog has got you in their sights,' she'll continue, always concluding her reproof in exactly the same manner: 'And just for once, why can't you think of all those poor people in Africa, much worse off than you are. Be truly thankful for what you've got.'

When she scolds me like I've been a naughty boy, she sounds more and more like my ma, catching me with my hand in the biscuit tin.

She's right, of course. Because I'm not too badly off. There are good days when the sun shines and when customers are affable and considerate; when I've no labour problems; when my CRAPs are excellent and my estimates productive; when removal bookings flow over the phone; when fat, profitable cheques slip through the door; when my bank manager smiles when he sees me. And days when I'm physically and mentally in good shape. One way or another, I'm fervently hoping that this next appointment will prove to be the turning point.

According to information gleaned by Alice, Mrs Oglethorpe is an elderly lady living on her own, her husband having passed away and her daughter having long flown the nest. The housing department is transferring her from her three-bedroom semi into a one-bed, ground-floor flat, to make the bigger house available for a family. Alice has highlighted one further comment on the worksheet: Mrs Oglethorpe is a bit deaf.

Thus warned, I turn off the ignition, tuck my presentation folder under my arm, and make my way up the short path. Mindful of Alice's advice, I take a firm hold of the large, shining brass knocker fixed to the centre of the white PVC door and give it a thorough hammering. I then huddle on the doorstep, attempting to get some basic shelter from the whirling maelstrom of snow.

With no answer forthcoming, I vent my increasing frustration on the door.

'Come on, Mrs Oglethorpe. Be a good girl and open the bloody door so that Icicle Man can enter.' Small streams of vapour shoot from my mouth. In an effort to improve circulation, I lift my legs up and down rapidly while beating my arms together. It doesn't do anything but make me feel foolish.

Increasingly impatient, I move towards the front window. A lace curtain prevents me from seeing inside so I smack the pane robustly with my bare knuckles before returning to stare blankly at the closed door. With no sign that my window-knocking routine has done the trick, I'm temporarily at a loss as to what to do. Is she in or out?

I decide to try the back door. She may be at the rear of the house – too far from the front to hear the knocker, especially if she's no hearing-aid.

Feeling more optimistic, I make my way cautiously round the side, nearly losing my footing on a small area of ice that's formed beside a cracked drainage pipe. If Mrs Oglethorpe uses this path over the next few days, she could end up performing a Torville and Dean routine, skating all the way to Wexham Park Hospital.

Unlike the PVC front door, the kitchen door is constructed of wood. A large glass panel has been set in the top half of the door but my view inside is obscured by condensation and a net curtain.

I repeat my knuckle-banging routine. At the same time, in an endeavour to create the maximum noise possible, the wooden panel at the bottom of the door receives an unwarranted kicking.

Too late, I remember my stubbed toe of this morning. As my injured toe makes contact with the wood panel, a searing current of pain propels its way upward. Involuntarily, I emit a long drawn-out howl, sounding like a Red Indian on the warpath. 'A-a-a-r-r-g-h!' I cry out in distress. 'You stupid, frigging wanker. Shit, bollocks and buggery-do.'

Bouncing up and down on my good leg like Zebedee from *The Magic Roundabout*, I hobble round in a small circle, my brain refusing to disengage from the damage caused by this latest assault on its foot soldier.

As I perform my one-legged dance routine, a frail, faint voice floats through the pane in the kitchen door. 'Keep your hair on. I can hear you, I'm not deaf.'

Thankful that my latest effort to raise Mrs Oglethorpe has been rewarded – at considerable further cost to my health – I stop prancing and turn to face the door. The net curtain is pushed aside and a small, round, lived-in face, with the crown of her head topped by a mop of curly white hair, peers myopically through the condensation.

'Mrs Oglethorpe?' I question loudly through the glass, trying to ignore the pain shooting up from my foot. 'It's Frank Tipple from A to Z Removals. I've come to give you an estimate for your removal.'

The narrowed eyes regard me with suspicion.

'Who do you say you are, mate?' she responds, her voice barely audible. 'What do you want?'

Gritting my teeth, I position my head as close to hers as possible. 'A to Z Removals,' I bellow. 'Mrs Grant from the council has asked us to provide an estimate for your removal. A to Z Removals, estimate, Mrs Grant.'

She continues to peer suspiciously through the rapidly misting window. 'Who? Who did you say you are?' she asks again, doubt etched all over her worn features.

This is one careful mama. Methinks she's been watching a bit too much of *Crimewatch*. 'Patience, Frank, patience,' I mutter. 'You'll be old yourself soon enough.'

I quickly rummage through my presentation folder and extract a business card. 'Frank Tipple, A to Z Removals,' I shout, holding it up against the glass. In response, Mrs Oglethorpe's presses her nose close to the window and screws up her eyes as she attempts to read the small print. As her elfin head nods from side to side, the corner of the net curtain settles across the top of her hair. She looks like a reincarnation of Mother Teresa.

'Hold on a minute, mate,' she cries, her voice carrying faintly from behind the glass. So saying, she disappears from view, the net curtain falling back into place.

I wait expectantly, my toe throbbing with the regular beat of a drum. A sudden, sharp gust of wind whistles down the passageway between the two houses, toppling next door's rusting metal dustbin onto its side. At the same moment, the shed door flies open and smashes against the side of the shed. Due to the commotion, I barely hear the faint tapping of the glass window behind me. Mrs Oglethorpe's face is back at the window, but with a pair of large horn-rimmed glasses perched precariously on the end of her nose. From where I'm standing, one of the lenses appears to be missing.

'Sorry, mate,' she mouths. 'I had to find my glasses. I never know where I've put the buggers. Now, who did you say you were? And what's that you're showing me?'

Here we go again. Still no key. And, God help me, she's not only deaf – she's as blind as a bat.

For the second time, I hold my business card against the pane, frantically pointing at the company name. She scrutinises the card carefully and I detect a hint of recognition in her eyes as she draws her head back.

'Oh, okay, mate. Can you come round to the front door? I can't find the key to this door.' With that, she withdraws her head, the net curtain falls back into place and she disappears.

Feeling like Mr Grumpy, I limp round to the front entrance, carefully skirting the icy patch. The scene around me is changing for the worse. Large snowdrifts are rapidly building against walls and fences, while gigantic black clouds dominate the sky. The street is bereft of life and the area has the look and feel of a ghost town.

'This is not where you want to be, Frank, my old son,' I hiss, arriving at the front door. Agitated, I flap my arms in an effort to keep my circulation going. Meanwhile, the snow continues to pile up on my head.

My ears perk up as a bolt is drawn back from the bottom of the door, then another bolt from the top. All internal activity suddenly ceases and silence again reigns. The door remains closed.

I wait a couple of minutes but there's no sign of further activity from inside. She's disappeared off the scene. Bending down, I position my head adjacent to the brass letterbox then carefully push the flap open to peer into the hallway.

A small, crescent-shaped hall table with a telephone on top is sited to the edge of the stairwell. But there's no sign of Mrs Oglethorpe.

'H-e-e-l-l-o-o-o, Mrs Oglethorpe, are you there?' I cry through the flap. I lower my head and peer through the narrow slot. But there's still nothing to indicate anyone's at home. Becoming increasingly uncomfortable due to my posture and the strength of the spring attachment, I carefully release the flap, stretch myself, then again crouch in front of the letterbox. My frustration at the lack of action from indoors is now tinged with concern for Mrs Oglethorpe's welfare. Her disappearance is unusual to say the least. I push the flap open then emit another strangled holler from vocal cords that seem to have taken on a life of their own.

'H-e-l-l-l-o-o-o, Mrs Oglethorpe. H-e-l-l-l-o-o-o, are you there?'

I lower my eyes to the level of the letterbox, beginning to feel like a Peeping Tom.

'Sorry, mate. I couldn't find the front door key.'

Startled by the voice behind me, I try to withdraw my fingers, unfortunately not fast enough. The sharp edge of the brass flap clamps onto my frozen fingers, snaring them like a mouse in a trap and causing me to cry out. Simultaneously, my feet slip backwards on the snow-covered path, my head bangs the front door and I end up on my knees like a devout Muslim, my fingers still caught in the letterbox.

It's only with difficulty that I'm able to extract four bruised fingers. Scrambling awkwardly to my feet and waving my injured hand up and down, I turn to address the source of my latest mishap.

Mrs Oglethorpe is facing me, grimly holding on to a Zimmer frame. She is regarding me with alert, twinkling eyes, tinged with concern. Or is it amusement? Having observed my doorstep acrobatics, maybe she's attempting to suppress a bout of laughter.

She must be eighty if she's a day, four feet five short and skinny as a rake. Her only protection from the elements is a light, grey plastic macintosh, similar to the old dears' macs at the bus shelter. As if that's not bad enough, her feet are clad in a flimsy pair of house slippers. House slippers and a plastic mac, in these conditions. Has she got a death wish?

'Sorry to frighten you, mate,' she says, not looking sorry at all. 'I couldn't find the front door key, and the back door key was on the hall table where the front door key should have been. God knows where that's gone, I'm always losing the bleeding things. I hope you haven't hurt yourself, mate. And I didn't keep you waiting, did I?'

My inclination is to take a hold of her bony shoulders and give her a good shaking. Not a good idea. It wouldn't look good to be seen wheeling this poor old soul round my head, singing 'Shake, rattle and roll'.

Taking a couple of deep breaths, I give myself up to a moment of rare honesty. I remind myself of the numerous times I've mislaid my own house keys. So how can I blame her for losing her keys? Or for being deaf? Or for being shortsighted. Or for the state of the weather. She deserves better than this. She is a plucky old dear, showing a positive resolve that would put many a younger person to shame.

'No, no, not at all, Mrs Oglethorpe' I shout at her gallantly, lying through my back teeth. 'No problem. I haven't long got here. I just wasn't sure what was happening inside and whether you'd forgotten me, and you sort of took me by surprise. Can we go inside now please, so that I can discuss your removal with you?'

Not certain she can hear me due to the noise around us, I gesticulate hopefully towards the house interior.

She shakes her little Noddy head in the affirmative, performs a complicated turning manoeuvre with her Zimmer frame then shuffles around the side of the house. She is seemingly oblivious to the danger of the slippery patch, skating over this while I carefully negotiate a detour.

We arrive safely at the back door, thankfully still ajar, and enter the kitchen. Mrs Oglethorpe carefully extricates herself from the Zimmer frame then removes her mac before sitting down at a small gate-leg kitchen table. I pull up a second kitchen chair and seat myself, facing her across the table. She looks across expectantly, waiting for me to make the next move.

Back in my professional persona, I officiously open my presentation folder then extract my pen from my top pocket with an exaggerated flourish. 'I'd first like to get a few details from you, Mrs Oglethorpe,' I declare, somewhat pompously.

Her brow furrows with wrinkles as numerous as a newly ploughed field. 'Deals? What deals?' she replies quizzically, cocking her head sideways like a baby bird waiting for its worm, her mouth open.

She has no teeth. And apparently no dentures. It won't surprise me to find she's mislaid these as well.

'No, no, not deals. Details, details,' I reply testily, raising my voice by ten decibels. 'Details, facts I need to know about your forthcoming removal. Like, for example, have you got far to go?'

'Have I got a car to go?' she responds in puzzlement. 'I haven't even got a bleeding bicycle, mate. And what would I do with a car? A bit of drag-racing through the estate?' So saying, she emits a strangled cackle, like a goose about to lay an egg.

Jesus. She is as deaf as a post. And daft as a brush. I know it's not the old dear's fault, but do I have to suffer this sort of shenanigans? 'No, not car. F-a-r, have you got far to go?' I shout, enunciating and spelling each letter slowly, clearly and loudly. 'Where are the council moving you to?'

Her face lights up. 'Oh, I see. Far. Where am I moving to?' she says, placing her scrawny elbows on the table then resting her chin on top of her clamped hands. She thinks for a moment, her eyes raised to the ceiling. I wait expectantly, my pen poised.

'Just a minute, mate.' She removes her chin from her hands and heaves herself up from the chair. I watch helplessly as she and her Zimmer frame disappear into the hallway.

Chafing at the bit, I utilise the time productively to note the few items of kitchen furniture. I've just completed my notations when she reappears. Tucked under her arm is a sheaf of papers which she deposits on the table. She awkwardly removes a rubber band from around the papers, licks her thumb then slowly commences to leaf through the documents with knobbly, arthritic fingers. 'The new address is in here somewhere, mate. I can't remember where they're sending me.'

I watch helplessly as she sifts laboriously through the pile, eventually reaching the bottom without having found the relevant information. 'It's here somewhere, mate.' She adjusts her glasses – one of the lens is definitely missing – before starting the process once again. Her inspection is conducted in a haphazard manner, some of the documents missing her attention completely. At this rate, we could be here until midnight.

'Can I help?' I shout in desperation, checking the time on my watch. 'Maybe

I can find it.' I point towards the papers and then at myself, my finger vaguely waving to and fro to emphasise my intention.

'Help yourself, mate.' She pushes the pile of papers towards me and sits back with her arms folded.

Within a couple of minutes I find the one I'm looking for, the council letterhead guiding me. Quickly I scan the instructions.

She's only moving to sheltered accommodation round the corner. I shake my head then quickly note the relevant details. 'If it's okay with you, Mrs Oglethorpe, I'll just go upstairs to see what's got to be moved. It'll only take a moment, so you don't need to get up.'

'Sure, mate,' she says. 'But there's not much going from upstairs, so I better come with you.'

I've just lost an opportunity to speed things up. But it is her home. I can't barge ahead and do my own thing. She slowly disengages from the kitchen table then shuffles into the hallway. As we pass the hall table, I spot a key lying on the floor. Bingo, the front-door key.

'There's your front-door key,' I shout, retrieving it, showing it to her and then placing it on the table top.

'Bless you, mate,' she says. 'So that's where the little bugger was hiding. It's got a life of its own.'

She turns to the bottom of the stairway and I note the automated chair-lift which has been installed in the stairwell.

'I need this to get me up and down the stairs, mate,' she advises me needlessly, pointing at the chairlift. 'Had it three or four years now, couldn't do without it.' She slowly extracts herself from the Zimmer and settles into the chair. 'My legs aren't what they used to be,' she rabbits on, totally immune to my restlessness. 'You wouldn't believe it, but I used to have a cracking pair of legs.' She emits another loud cackle, the wrinkles on her face creasing in merriment.

My eyes are inexorably drawn to her legs and I'm again struck speechless. A cracking pair of legs, she says. At one time, maybe. But now, they wouldn't look out of place sticking out of a bird's nest. Feeling it inappropriate to respond, I instead give her an imbecilic, fixed grin, fervently wishing she would activate the chairlift.

Ready for departure, she looks up at me with a silly grin on her face. 'Do you want a lift, mate?' she asks, pointing teasingly at her lap.

I'm being chatted up by an eighty-year-old geriatric with a sense of humour. Is she taking the piss? I'm not amused.

'No, that's all right, thanks all the same. You go on up and I'll follow you, I need the exercise.'

With a smirk as wide and generous as a large slice of Wensleydale cheese, she rests her Zimmer on her lap and activates the starter unit. The chair slowly begins to rise followed by my own manpowered ascent. It eventually stops on the top landing and I hastily squeeze round her outstretched legs before she can lever herself out of the chair.

'No need for you to rush, Mrs Oglethorpe,' I cry into her right ear. 'I'm just going to check what you've got. Okay?' Without waiting for an answer, and neglecting to assist her, I move quickly into the front bedroom and begin to note the few items of free-standing furniture.

My notations have just been completed when Mrs Oglethorpe shuffles into the room.

'You're wasting your time in here, mate. None of this stuff is going,' she says without preamble. No room for it where they're sending me. The Salvation Army are coming and take this lot away.'

'What, nothing at all?'

'That's right, mate. Mind you, I'm sorry to see that go.' She points at the double bed and emits another cackle with a look of pure lechery that would put the frighteners on Casanova. 'I've had a few cracking times in there over the years.'

Looking at the condition of the mattress, it's not difficult to imagine what activities might have taken place on it. But whatever she's got up to in the past, it's all in the mind now, unless she's on Viagra. Perish the thought.

Giving her an imbecilic grin, I quickly erase the information relating to the unwanted bedroom furniture then, failing to learn the lessons of the past, again squeeze past her towards the second bedroom.

This is half the size of the main bedroom and contains one small wardrobe, a chest of drawers, a bedside cabinet, a single bed and a few personal items strewn untidily around the room. This is obviously her bedroom. She should be able to accommodate these pieces in her one-bedroom flat nicely. I have begun to note the relevant items when Mrs

Oglethorpe appears, puffing and blowing.

'Nothing going in there either, mate,' she says without hesitation. 'One of my daughter's sons is having the lot. He's picking it up next week. At least he's supposed to be. He can hardly pick his nose,' she concludes, chuckling like a mother hen.

More of my precious time wasted. I briefly consider whether it might be appropriate to send a donation to the Euthanasia Society. Uncharitable, I know, but it has been a trying day.

'And there's no point in rushing off to the third bedroom. There's only a suitcase with clothing in there,' she tells me. 'I'm having new bedroom furniture delivered. I did tell you downstairs there wasn't much going from up here, but you didn't seem interested.'

I take a deep breath and count to five. All she had to do when we were in the kitchen was say those six magic words, 'Only a suitcase from upstairs, mate.' And now she's implying it's my own fault.

'Pretend it's your dear departed mother, Frank,' I mutter, attempting to readjust the contours of my face into a more friendly and considerate repose. 'Okay, Mrs Oglethorpe, whilst you're making your way down, I'll just go ahead and see what you've got downstairs. I presume you've got some goods in the lounge to be moved?' I add, unnecessarily sarcastically.

'Food in the lounge?' she questions, nodding her head from side to side like a drug-induced hamster. 'There's no food in there, mate. It's all in the kitchen.'

'No, not food. G-o-o-o-o-d-s. Goods, like as in furniture. Three-piece suite, dining table, TV, that sort of thing,' I roar.

She surprises me by laughing, her mouth a small, black, toothless cavern. 'Sorry, mate, when you mentioned food, I thought you wanted to stay for lunch. Yeah, you go ahead. As far as I can remember, everything down there is going. I'll be down in a jiffy.'

Leaving her and her Zimmer frame to negotiate a tight turning circle within the confinement of the small bedroom, I make my way downstairs and into the front room where I take note of the few items of furniture, all in reasonable condition.

Relieved that there's something to be retrieved from the ashes, I replace my pen in my pocket and close my presentation folder. 'Right, Frank, done and dusted. Time to scarper.' I head for the hallway, but she's nowhere to be seen. I'm about to check the kitchen, when I hear her voice drifting from the direction of the stairwell.

'Are you still there, mate? Can you help me?'

Thinking she may have injured herself, I quickly make my way to the bottom of the stairwell and peer up the stairs. To my surprise, she's still on the landing, sitting rigidly in her chair lift.

She looks down at me from over the top of her horn-rimmed glasses, then gives me a royal wave of her hand, happy she's got my attention. 'Good to see you, mate,' she calls. 'I thought you'd buggered off.'

'What's the problem?' I shout, craning my neck backwards.

'My chair's not working,' she replies. 'Something's gone wrong with the electrics. The same thing happened a couple of months ago. I was stuck upstairs for a day and a half before my daughter came round to rescue me. I wasn't able to get to the telephone.'

Muttering dark thoughts, I make my way to the top of the stairs. She settles back in her chair then gives me a whimsical smile but says nothing, cool as a cucumber. You'd think she was at a Sunday tea party.

Her misplaced confidence in my ability to do something is causing me some concern. Changing an electric plug is, for me, mentally challenging. If Mrs Oglethorpe isn't careful, she may find I've hot-wired her chair.

I make a preliminary visual check around the chair, trying to spot any loose cables.

'Are you sure you're pressing the right switch,' I bellow, more in hope than expectation.

She commences to play about with two switches on the arm of the chair. 'Yeah, I think so. Look, this one should take me down, and this one brings me up. But nothing's happening, see?'

I turn to the light-switch on the landing wall and quickly flick it on.

'I don't know what's wrong with it, Mrs Oglethorpe, but it's not the electricity supply,' I shout, my throat in need of lubrication. 'Can I phone your daughter? She could stay with you until the engineer gets here.'

She raises her eyebrows. 'My daughter?' she snorts derisively. 'There's no point in phoning her, mate. She's gone off down to the south coast with her husband. Gone to see his mother. And a right old cow she is.'

'Okay then, what about your daughter's sons?' I ask, desperate to find a quick fix.

'What, Albert and Gerald? No chance, mate. Albert's in Aberdeen on the oil rigs, and as for Gerald – the one that's supposed to be picking up the furniture – he's a good-for-nothing lazy little sod. The pip-squeak's more likely to try and electrocute me. Thinks I've got a few pounds stashed away and is always trying to touch me up for a few quid. Thinks I'm daft.'

I'm beginning to run out of options. 'Oh, right, okay, then,' I shout, with a hint of hysteria. 'What about your neighbours?'

'No way, mate. Don't get along with them. Anyway, don't want them knowing my business.'

She looks up at me from the comfort of her chair, a mischievous expression on her face and a twinkle in her eye. 'Tell you what, mate, if you give me a lift downstairs, I'll be able to phone the council and they'll sort it out.'

Now, why didn't I think of that? Mr Shifter, expert remover of all antiques, animate or inanimate.

But what does she have in mind? A piggy-back, a fireman's lift, or a swing-round-my-shoulder, up-over-my-head, *Strictly Come Dancing* number?

The prospect of physically carting Mrs Oglethorpe down the stairs is not one that fills me with glee. She may be small but with that lift installation occupying a considerable amount of stair space, it won't be easy. And I'm not even in the best physical nick.

I'm struggling to find another solution. 'I've a better idea, Mrs Oglethorpe. How's about if I walk down the stairs in front of you while you lean on my shoulders?' I emphasise my intentions by pointing wildly at my legs, her hands, my shoulders and the stairs. 'We can take it nice and easy.'

'Walk down the stairs? Sorry, mate, no way can I do that. Not even holding on to a big, strong boy like you. My legs wouldn't support me. But there's no need to get your knickers in a twist. You must be used to a lot of lifting and I'm only seven stone, so you shouldn't have any problem. And I promise not to take advantage of you.' She chuckles lecherously, not in the least concerned about our predicament. 'Just give me a piggy-back and after that I'll be alright.' Brooking no further discussion on the matter, she rises slowly from the chair and stands shakily, supporting her skinny frame on the Zimmer.

Lacking any alternative solutions, I'm resigned to the inevitable. I'm also thinking if something goes wrong, we could be lying helpless at the bottom of the stairs for a week until Gerald turns up to collect his furniture. God help the both of us.

Reluctantly preparing for action, I roll my shoulders then give my thighs and upper arms a quick massage. Like it or not, Mrs O has decisively set the agenda for the next few minutes.

Chapter eighteen

THE NEXT FEW MINUTES remain a blur in my mind. But if Jane, Alice or any of the lads had been present, I wouldn't have lived down the embarrassment for the rest of my natural-born life.

While Mrs Oglethorpe hitches up her skirt, I hunker down on my haunches, lock my hands under her bony thighs and hoist her onto my back. With her skinny legs wrapped around my waist and her arms clasped firmly round my neck, I'm bent over at the waist, feeling like an old nag destined for the slaughterhouse. She may have been small and delicate, but it still felt like I was lifting a two-hundred-pound bag of King Edward spuds.

I begin to totter down the stairway, one slow step after another, with her perched on my back like a champion jockey. Her bony, intertwined hands are positioned directly over my Adam's apple, nearly throttling me. My face is showing increasing signs of toil and I'm beginning to sweat profusely, but there's not a single peep from behind me. If she's any sense, her eyes will be shut and she'll be saying her prayers.

We're halfway down the stairway when she suddenly releases one hand from my throat, then leans backwards. 'Giddy up, mate,' she shouts in my ear, giving my backside a sharp smack with her free hand, at the same time clacking her tongue in horsey fashion. 'You're doing fine. Another furlong and we're past the winning post.' This is followed by a bout of laughter, causing her skinny frame to rattle about on my body. She readjusts her position, her hands intertwined back over my gullet.

Here's me struggling to preserve our very lives yet she thinks she's riding the winner at Royal Ascot. For two pins, I could have dumped her on the stairs there and then. Resisting the temptation, I complete my descent and deposit her safely on the ground floor.

Gasping and spluttering, I turn to face her. She's leaning against the hall table, hysterical with laughter, her little frame shaking like a leaf, the tears rolling down her cheeks like a river down a mountain.

I rearrange my clothing, brush my dishevelled hair with the palm of my hand then observe my face in the hall mirror. A grumpy, rounded, sweating beetroot looks back at me with a weary look of resignation, two large, glazed eyes protruding and staring back at me like I've just landed from Mars. I rummage around in my pocket, extract my grotty hanky then mop a film of sweat from my brow. Then, taking a leaf out of Mrs Oglethorpe's book, I lean against the wall for support.

Her laughter has ceased and her forehead is creased with wrinkles of concern. 'Are you okay, mate?' she asks. 'I must say you did a great job there. If any of my friends ever need a lift, I'll definitely recommend you any time.' With that tongue-in-cheek comment, her face again dissolves into laughter. 'Now, can you be a good lad and bring down my walking frame? Then I can do the rest.'

She leans away from the hall table, removes her glasses and wipes her tears with the back of her hand. She then adjusts her skirt and stockings, extracts a comb from the table drawer, and starts to draw it through her hair, all the while regarding me with obvious amusement. She is displaying such a positive reaction to events that all my antagonism towards her is suddenly erased and my heart melts. I'd have to have a heart of steel not to admire her spirit. She really is a plucky old dear. And that crazy laughter of hers is infectious.

A broad grin creases my face. It's time to show her my better side. 'Mrs Oglethorpe, if you can't find a horse to ride at the Grand National, just give me a call. I'm your man.' In return, she gives me a broad, toothless beam followed by a playful dig on my arm. If we carry on like this, we could become real mates.

Leaving her to comb her hair, I take a deep breath, then retrieve the Zimmer.

'Are you okay to sort things out?' I ask her, mouthing the words quietly, hoping that lip-reading is an additional talent to her bareback riding.

'Yeah, I'm fine now, mate. Now, would you like a cup of tea before you go?'

'Thanks, Mrs Oglethorpe,' I tell her with a croaky voice. 'But I've really got to go now. I've got two more appointments. Glad I could help out with the stair problem. I'll put our estimate in the post to the council tomorrow. Give us a ring when you're ready to move. Hope you get the chairlift sorted out soon. And make sure you don't lose those keys of yours again.' I put on my best face, wave my hand limply in the air then make my way back out into the cold and towards the car.

Part of me feels guilty that my impatience got the better of me. That was inexcusable and an unnecessarily harsh response to her disabilities. I'm also uneasy about leaving her to sort things out for herself. If I wasn't so hard-pressed, I'd have ensured all the necessary telephone calls were made before leaving.

But the more I reflect on the situation, the more I'm reassured. Humping her downstairs was above and beyond the call of duty. Who else in their dumb mind would have even attempted it? Not the Pickford's man, that's for sure, and not without charging for it. So, despite my own shortcomings, I can hold my head high. My reputation and innate sense of goodwill towards my fellow man remain intact. And yet a nagging doubt concerning my attitude persists.

If I'm incapable of showing sympathy and understanding to the likes of a sweet, innocent, elderly lady like Mrs Oglethorpe, then why should I automatically expect my customers to be tolerant?

As ye sow, so shall ye reap. Do onto others as they would do onto you.

As these biblical teachings come to mind, drummed into me from an early age by my ma, I can't help but wonder if my failings in this regard are going to bounce back and give me an enormous kick up the bum.

Where Crinkley and McIntosh's damage complaints are concerned, it's not going to be long before I find out.

Chapter nineteen

I RETURN TO THE CAR knackered, like I've just completed a marathon. Neglecting to clear the thick blanket of snow smothering the windscreen, I plump myself down within the interior then check the time. Despite everything, I'm ahead of schedule. If I go straight to Bracknell to see Crinkley, I'm going to arrive early. More than likely I'd get there and find they're out, which means sitting around for forty minutes or so freezing my butt.

I consider another option that would kill two birds with one stone: return to the office, catch up with Alice on what's been happening and grab a coffee at the same time. With a bit of luck, Alice may have replenished the biscuit tin.

Decision made, I switch on the ignition and watch anxiously as the wipers take the strain of moving the mass of snow. Slowly pulling away from the kerb, I carefully negotiate my way back to the main road then, twelve minutes later, into the comparative safety of my compound. I retrieve my presentation folder and make my way towards the entrance. At long last, the snow has stopped and a thin shaft of sunlight is trying to break through the clouds.

At the front door, I step warily over the pool of water, its surface now disguised by a thin layer of snow and ice, awaiting the footsteps of the unwary. The back of Alice's head is visible through the hatch as she beavers away at the typewriter. 'It's me, Alice,' I announce through the window hatch, unnecessarily. She'll have seen and heard me returning. Without getting, or expecting, a response, I make the kitchen my first port of call and fill the kettle, surprised but thankful that the water pipe hasn't frozen.

A few minutes later, I enter the warmth of the office with my hands cupped around a steaming cup of hot black coffee. A glow of hot air immediately envelopes me like a blast from the Sahara. Without further ado, I remove my three-in-one and throw it carelessly over the back of my chair before sitting down. Anticipating a short, but beneficial, period of recuperation and reflection, I take a welcome sip of the coffee.

'You didn't by any chance buy any biscuits over the weekend?' I ask Alice, more in hope than anticipation. 'The office tin's empty and my stomach doesn't know whether it's coming or going.'

'Yes, as it happens, I did,' she replies. 'But I forgot to bring them in. I'll try and remember them in the morning. Sorry, Frank.' With that, she continues to work, totally unaware of the critical nature of her omission.

Resigned to my loss, I toss my folder onto the desk, spread my legs across the top of the desk and savour the aroma of my coffee. Despite the lack of anything more substantial, I'm beginning to feel human.

'Anything of consequence happen since I left?' I ask, aware that Alice doesn't like to be interrupted partway through a task. She turns to face me, reaching for her message pad. 'I was going to bring you up to date as soon as I finished this bit of typing,' she replies testily. She refers to her message pad, squinting through her glasses as she closely scrutinises her scribbles. It crosses my mind she's going to morph into a clone of Mrs Oglethorpe in another fifteen years or so. God help her, and me, if I'm still around. Especially if her hearing fails.

'It's been pretty busy, surprising for this time of the year,' she says. 'I've fixed up a couple of estimates for tomorrow. That's now five you've got in total: three in the morning and two in the afternoon. I haven't been able to get hold of Mrs Arnett about her boxes yet. I'll try her again later. Oh, and Mr Jameson phoned in to thank Herbie and the crew for the job they did last Wednesday. He thought they were polite, courteous and very helpful. He will have no hesitation recommending us.'

She again checks her pad. 'Oh yes, Mr Evans from Cookham Boy Scouts phoned to see if you would support their charity fair by taking advertising space in their programme, just twenty pounds. Apparently you took some space last year. I said you would call him.'

'Now, what else?' Alice again consults her message pad, held about five inches in front of her face. I'm thinking a trip to Specsavers wouldn't be amiss. 'Oh yes, Mrs Spencer and Mr Wilkins have accepted our estimates, but haven't been given any dates yet. They'll call us as soon as they know. I've told them to try and avoid a Friday move if at all possible.'

While I'm digesting the information, Alice has turned the page of her message pad. She now drops a nice big spanner into the works.

'Sorry, Frank, but you're not going to like this. I've also had a call from Mrs Walmsley-Brown about ten minutes ago. As you know, we're doing her removal today. Anyway, she sounds extremely agitated and, I must say, a bit strange. To be honest, I didn't know what to make of her. She's complaining about the lads. Says they're working very slowly, feels they're taking too long on the job. She's asked you to ring her. I've tried to put her at ease but she doesn't sound happy with the situation. I think you need to have a word.'

Having delivered this unwelcome news, she closes her pad, ignores me and turns back to the typewriter. My lips are pursed as tight as a camel's backside in a sand storm.

'Any more cheerful news, Alice?' I ask sarcastically, feeling sorry for myself. 'Or would that be too much to ask for?'

Alice being Alice – having heard it all before – says nothing, my sarcasm running off her like water off a duck's back. She ignores me and continues to pound the keyboard like a concert pianist playing at the Albert Hall.

I'm taken aback by the nature of the complaint. It makes no sense that Herbie, Jim and Kev are going too slow. Never in all the years I've been doing removals has anybody previously made such a complaint. Herbie and Jim are as solid and dependable a crew as one could hope to have, and while Kev may be a novice, he's shown no signs of being a slacker. They've also only been there a couple of hours, and there's still over a day and a half to go. There's got to be some other reason for the complaint.

A nagging pain has returned to the front of my head. I rub my forehead while morosely sipping my coffee.

I try to recall the Walmsley-Browns, following my initial visit a few weeks back. From what I can remember, they were in their late-fifties, and both extremely pleasant. I wondered at the time whether Mr Walmsley-Brown might have been a professor or lecturer at the local college. Or, given his demeanour and obvious wealth, someone high up in the financial world. Unfortunately, I can't check my notes on the worksheet as this has gone out with Herbie. But I'm pretty certain they received a positive rating. Whatever's gone wrong, I need to establish who, or what, is gumming up the works.

With no digestives to eat, my teeth automatically seek remnants of those fingernails still worthy of a bite. It's a lifetime habit that I've tried to beat many, many times, but with only short-term success, each crisis quickly overcoming my resolve. Like the crisis brewing at the Walmsley-Browns. But the sooner the sooner the matter is resolved, the sooner I'll have piece of mind.

I remove my legs from the desk and pick up the telephone, muttering under my breath like a gormless halfwit. Dialling the Walmsley-Brown's number, I'm oblivious to the look Alice is shooting over her shoulder. She returns her attention to the typewriter, trying to convince herself she's not working in a lunatic asylum.

'Walmshley-Brown shpeaking, who'sh calling?' A male voice.

I'm relieved it's not Mrs Walmsley-Brown. If there is a problem, I'm more likely to make an accommodation with the man of the house, and have a more objective and sensible dialogue. Not a view which Jane or Alice would accept. But they're from that other planet, so they wouldn't, would they?

'Ah, good morning, Mr Walmsley-Brown,' I respond, attempting to inject some warmth into my voice. I get straight to the point. 'Frank Tipple, from A to Z Removals. My secretary advises me your wife has expressed concern about the crew's work-rate this morning. Can you tell me exactly what the problem is, please?'

There's no immediate reply. All that can be heard is an indeterminate rustling noise and some heavy breathing. I'm beginning to think the line is faulty when he finally responds. The voice is hesitant and laboured, the words distorted.

'Ah,yesh, Mishter Tizzle. Hervie's bosh. Mishter Tizzle, indeed, I shee, yesh. Thanksh for ringing. Yesh, shure enuf. My wife phoned your offish earlier, yesh, indeed she did. Now what wash it she wished to shay?'

His voice tails off into silence. I'm wondering if he has a speech impediment, or suffered a recent stroke, caused by the stress of moving. It could also account for Mrs Walmsley-Brown's behaviour. She may be stressed up to her eyeballs, having a defective husband to care for, in addition to moving house lock, stock and barrel.

My patience is rewarded as Mr Walmsley-Brown begins to hesitantly confirm the nature of the complaint. 'Well, you shee, Mishter Tizzle,' he says.

'The men sheem to be shitting in the van a lot, shmoking. Yesh, thash ish it, shitting and shmoking. We jushed wondered whash whas going on. Can you pleash shpeed them up a bit, Mishter Tizzle?'

I'm not impressed with the continued mutation of my name. And the manner of his speech and the slurring of his words is making it difficult to understand what he's saying. But he doesn't sound well. That stroke has left him with a pretty serious disability. He'll need to be treated gently. Any additional undue stress at this point and Herbie could have a dead body on his hands. If that happens, he won't have a box big enough to fulfil that extra bit of packing.

'Sorry to hear your removal isn't going as fast as you believe it should, Mr Walmsley-Brown. To be honest, it may be partly my fault. I told Herbie before he left this morning that your furniture is of extraordinarily special value and specifically instructed him not to rush your removal. I'm certain both you and your good wife wouldn't want my crew to rush about like bulls in a china shop, so to speak. That said, could I just have a quick word with Herbie, my foreman, so I can keep the lads on their toes?'

There is a further moment of hesitation. 'Yesh, yesh. Okay, Mr Tizzle, but if you could shpeed them up a bit, I'm shure everything will be shatishfactory. Yesh, yesh indeed. I'll get Hervie, jush a minute, pleash.'

A chink of light suddenly penetrates my grey matter: has he been on the booze?

With this sudden insight, I sit bolt upright and spontaneously unleash a profanity loud enough to cause the click-clack of the typewriter to cease and the light-bulb in the ceiling to flicker. I'm unaware that Alice is staring stonily at the window pane, her lips pursed and her head nodding from side to side in disbelief.

The more I think about it, the more I'm certain Walmsley-Brown's been drinking something stronger than orange juice. His speech pattern mirrors those late-night drunken messages of Cyril. But if true, I'm surprised, when he's in the middle of a house removal.

'Hello, Frank? It's Herbie. The customer says you want to talk to me.'

'Listen, Herbie,' I mutter quietly into the receiver. 'Are you okay to talk openly, or is the old boy standing there beside you?'

'No, Frank,' Herbie replies after a short hesitation. 'I think he's gone back into the kitchen. I'm in his study.'

'Right then, Herbie,' I say promptly, choosing my next words carefully. 'And whatever I'm about to say, don't get the hump. Just hear me out.

'I don't know whether you're aware of it, but your customer phoned the office about thirty minutes ago, complaining the job's going too slowly. They're also complaining you've been sitting around in the van a lot, smoking.'

There is a momentary pause before Herbie replies, 'Jesus Christ, Frank. I don't believe you just said that.' His voice is raised sufficiently to make me withdraw the receiver from my ear. Alice has also heard. Aware that Herbie has not taken the news kindly, she turns her head towards me, her eyebrows raised, wrinkle furrows prominent along the length of her brow.

Trying to look cool in the face of Alice's facial inquisition, I shrug my shoulders, the palm of my left hand turned upwards. *What else was I supposed to say to him?*

Herbie continues his tirade, 'And you expect me not to get the hump. Well, I'll tell you straight out, Frank, I could be a bloody camel after what you've just said. That one with the two humps, a bloody dromedary.

'That sitting around, as you call it, was only our second break of the morning. We were out there for five minutes having a fag when the old bag came out fussing. Jesus Christ, Frank, are we not entitled to a break now and then?'

Herbie is beginning to get wound up tighter than Jane on a bad-hair day. And if he and his crew are being accused of being anything less than diligent in carrying out their duties when he knows better, he'll fight his own corner, and that of his crew. And I respect him for that.

'Listen, Herbie, forget that for the minute. Of course you're entitled to your breaks, you should know me better than that. But I need to make sure there's not going to be any further problem. Now tell me, are Jim or Kev giving you any trouble? When the old dear phoned, she seemed to think you were all on a go-slow.'

Herbie's response is instant. 'No way, Frank. I'm not having any of that bullshit,' he replies, indignant and vociferous. 'As far as I'm concerned, we're doing what we normally do and things are going okay – apart from them and the bleeding weather. We should be packed and loaded up in another five hours or so. I don't know what the miserable sods are complaining about.'

'Sure, Herbie, I understand. But keep your hair on, and your voice down,' I answer quickly. It won't do for Herbie to get his knickers in a twist along with the old lady.

'Listen, Herbie,' I say reassuringly, trying to inject a sense of purpose and optimism into my voice. 'I'm sure the job's going fine. And I know I'm asking a lot, but can you keep the tea breaks to a minimum, and do what you have to do to keep the customer sweet, even if they are a pain in the arse. I don't want to have to pick up the pieces. Or a bouncing cheque.

'Oh, by the bye, when I spoke to the old boy just now he was talking a bit funny and sounded like he'd had a stroke or something. Is that how you read it?'

'A stroke? Is that what you think, Frank? You really think he's had a stroke?' he asks, emitting a short, grim squawk like a strangled chicken. 'You've got to be joking. The man's pissed, that's what. I thought you of all people would have known that. In fact, they're both pissed, pissed out of their cotton-picking little minds. They've been on the booze ever since we arrived this morning. They haven't even offered us a cup of tea all morning. Totally peed off we are.'

No wonder Alice thought Mrs Walmsley-Brown sounded a bit strange when she phoned. And here's me worrying about my alcohol intake. They're making me feel like I'm Mr Temperance personified.

'Sorry you're having hassle, Herbie,' I tell him with genuine sympathy. 'So they've both been on the bottle, then. Listen, I know it can't be easy. And I know how you must feel about the lack of tea. Anyway, I think I've managed to reassure the old boy everything is going fine, so you shouldn't have any more trouble. But whatever they do, try to keep your cool. Don't forget that big tip you'll be getting tomorrow if they're happy.'

With an indecipherable grunt from Herbie, I replace the phone on its cradle and lean back in my chair, weary, frustrated and angry. I've a horrible feeling in the pit of my stomach that this may not be the last I've heard from them. And as the day wears on, if they continue to treat every hour as Happy Hour, their attitude towards the crew could become even more unpredictable.

'What was all the fuss about?' Alice asks, looking at me quizzically.

Despite not wanting to relive the past few moments, I feel some explanation is due. 'Herbie reckons the customers are piddled out of their minds. And here was me thinking he'd suffered a stroke. I tell you, Alice, I sometimes wonder whether it's worth all the bleeding effort. And who's the arsehole who said the customers always right?'

Halfway through my emotional outpouring, Alice decides there's nothing further to interest her. She's heard this particular script at least once a week over the course of many years.

I push my empty coffee mug to the back of the desk, open my folder and extract Fred and Priscilla's worksheet. Folding the estimate into a makeshift aeroplane, I twist round in my chair and launch it towards Alice's desk. After one circuit of her head, it lands directly onto her in tray. James Bond couldn't have done it better. Alice looks at the tray and then turns round and looks at me, her expression a mixture of bemusement and pity. I can tell what she's thinking: *is that stupid little boy ever going to grow up?*

'That's the Watson's estimate,' I advise her smugly. 'There's no need to rush it out. To be honest, I don't give a toss whether we get the job or not.'

With that out of the way, I turn my attention to Mrs Oglethorpe's worksheet. It only takes a moment to decide my removal charge. One hundred pounds plus VAT. If only all my estimates were so simple to assess.

Mindful of the reaction to my previous childish action, I get up from my desk, place the worksheet gently into Alice's action tray and make a big show of smoothing out the sheet, like it's the most important document in the office.

'That's the Oglethorpe estimate,' I advise her. 'A nice old dear she is but deaf as a post and batty as a brush. You won't believe it, Alice, but her stair-lift broke down. I had to give her a piggy-back down the stairs. Nearly bloody throttled me to death, she did. If ever I deserved to get a job, it's this one. Anyway, can you send her estimate directly to Mrs Grant at the council?

'Oh, and did you know that that estimate you arranged for Mr Fettucini was for the removal of a safe? And you never told me. You know how I feel about safes. I nearly wet myself when Fettucini told me.'

'Sorry to hear that, Frank,' she replies nonchalantly, turning away from me, lifting the Watson worksheet from her tray, extracting a blank pro-forma estimate form from her middle drawer and inserting it into the typewriter. 'Now that you mention it, I do remember him saying he wanted a safe removal. I thought he was concerned about his furniture and just wanted reassurance that everything would go smoothly. I merely confirmed that if he used A to Z, that's what would happen – a safe removal, that is.' She commences to fill in the relevant blank spaces on the Watsons' estimate, any further discussion of the matter deemed unnecessary.

The memory of Fettucini, added to the lack of any moral support from Alice, have only succeeded in nettling me, as does the sight of her back. 'Well, I'll tell you this, Alice. He was a right ignorant ratbag,' I opine, falsely injecting an emotional tremor into my voice. 'He wouldn't even let me see the bloody safe. Said he'd set his bloody rottweiler on me then told me to eff off. A total waste of time, that estimate was.'

In a childish pique of anger, I take Fettucini's worksheet and loudly and dramatically tear it into small pieces before throwing it towards the waste bin. Most pieces miss their target and land on the carpet. But bugger me if I'm going to pick them up. Alice can clear this up in her own time, as due penance for her lack of sympathy.

Having exhausted my litany of woes for the time being, I return to my desk, plump back down into my office chair, and stare vacantly at the wild and wintry scene outside, feeling like an Inuit in an igloo. The thunder of a passing train jolts me from my reverie. It's time to get a move on.

'Right, Alice. No rest for the wicked.' I gulp down the dregs of my coffee and heave myself out of my chair. 'I've got to get off to see Crinkley about his damaged settee. You probably won't see me back until about one o'clock. That's assuming I survive this damage assessment and get back at all. If you don't see me, I'll have either suffered convulsions at Crinkley's and been carted off to the hospital, or clocked him one and be in a cell at the local nick.'

I watch Alice's back for any sign of understanding of the heavy responsibility borne by a Commander In Chief. I wait in vain. Undeterred, I continue to deliver my instructions, knowing full well that, despite her lack of interest, Alice will be absorbing everything. 'And don't forget: after I've had some lunch, I've got to go and see McIntosh at around about two o'clock, to find out what that little tosser's fussing about.'

I pause for a reaction but nothing is forthcoming.

'Anyway, that probably won't be of any great concern to you. I'm sure you have enough of your own problems,' I mutter petulantly whilst injecting a heavy note of sarcasm. 'But, whatever else you do, don't make any other appointments for me today. I'm planning to have an early finish. But before going home, I'll just pop in quickly to make sure there've been no more repercussions from the Walmsley-Browns.'

'One further big favour, Alice: maybe you could find me just one customer who isn't a complete and utter arsehole. See you later, then.'

Throughout, I've been addressing Alice's back. She surprises me by ceasing to type. She turns round with a neutral expression on her face.

'Sure, Frank. No problem. I'll do what I can. Have a nice day.' With that, she resumes typing.

I regard her suspiciously. Is she taking the piss or what? Disgruntled, I pick up Crinkley's claim form from my in tray, place it in my folder and once more check the wall clock. Eleven thirty-five. As my high-noon duel draws ever closer, that earlier black-and-white celluloid image of Gary Cooper flashes to the forefront off my mind.

About to hand out retribution, he's standing tall and steadfast in the middle of that dirty, dusty, tumbleweed-strewn, mid-Western, hillbilly town. Directly facing him is his nemesis. It's showtime.

I'm suddenly overcome by a desire to replicate that same scene, unaware that Alice can see my reflection in the window. Drawing myself up to my full height, I square my shoulders, spread my legs and adopt Gary's gunslinger stance. My arms are hanging loosely, my hands poised inches from my imaginary holster belt, in a state of readiness for the shoot-out to come.

'Bite the dust, *hombre*,' I mutter quietly in my best Gary Cooper impersonation.

In one lightning movement, I draw my imaginary guns from their holsters, aim at my reflection in the window and fire. 'Bang,bang!' I mouth silently, a smug grimace creasing my features. Satisfied my target has been downed, I puff the imaginary gun-smoke from the end of my smoking barrels before deftly replacing each gun in its holster. In my mind's eye, the body of Crinkley lies prostrate at the other end of the street, two bullet holes in the centre of his forehead. Job done.

I nonchalantly tip my imaginary Stetson to the back of my head with a raised forefinger, tuck my presentation folder under my arm and without further ado, stride purposefully from the warmth of the office.

I'm blissfully unaware that a perplexed Alice has begun to pound furiously on the typewriter keys, pondering the wisdom of sharing an enclosed space with someone so obviously showing classic symptoms of being deranged.

Chapter twenty

FOLLOWING MY CHILDISH performance, I step outside the Portakabin with a warm inner glow. In tune with my mood, the arrival of sunlight has contributed to a small but significant increase in temperature. The thick layer of fluffy snow lying on the roof is beginning to thaw, the process accelerated by the Sahara-like conditions generated from within. Small droplets of water are dripping off the roof, forming a line of blots in the surface underneath; piss-holes in the snow, as the lads would call them. And if they were at the rear of the Portakabin, that's probably what they'd be.

I briefly consider whether to return to the office and give Alice a timely reminder of the need to reduce our heating bill. It's unlikely she'll pay any attention, though. At her age, the last thing she'll want is to sit in a freezing office and contract a bout of influenza just so I can save a bob or two. Especially when she sees me drawing a substantial director's dividend every time the company bank balance shows a reasonable surplus.

Preparing to leave, I quickly check the location of Crinkley's new home, the map provided by one of the local estate agents. Although Herbie has already given me directions, he didn't seem certain.

Satisfied that the map and Herbie are in agreement, I engage the gear lever and bump my way across the water-filled potholes, through the yard gates and into the snow-covered lane.

As I pass under the railway bridge towards Maidenhead Bridge, my attention is drawn to a proliferation of estate agent signs on my left. There are ten in total, each varying in colour and size and vying with one another for prominence.

The signs prompt me to dwell on the vast home-ownership sector, a major driving force of the national economy and creating employment for a front-line battalion of personnel: town planners, architects, surveyors, construction workers, solicitors, insurers, estate agents, and tradesmen of all descriptions. And, behind the front line, a devouring army of ravenous ants in the retail and service sectors, gorging off the temples of aspiration and materialism, with each outlet offering every conceivable product under the sun in a bid to skim off their own piece of the action.

When I'm feeling a bit holier-than-thou in terms of my perceived importance in the scheme of things, Jane has to remind me I'm merely one of those very same ants, intent on ensnaring my own small piece of the entrails of home ownership.

Approaching the Grenfell Road and King Street junction, I begin to review the circumstances surrounding the Crinkley claim.

Although I'm trying to keep an open mind, I'm not convinced that it's genuine because Herbie and Speedy are emphatic they caused no damage. Although he can't remember much about the sofa – he's moved quite a few since then – Herbie is adamant they had no difficulty whatsoever getting it out of one property and into the other. Crinkley was apparently keeping a close eye on them when they completed both stages of the operation, so would have been well aware if anything untoward occurred. And while it was on the van, it was well protected by heavy-duty removal blankets. As far as Herbie was concerned, it was another removal job well done and deserving of due recognition by the customer.

And Crinkley did just that: he gave the lads a generous tip. There was no indication he was unhappy with any aspect of the removal. Yet eight days after the removal, and out of the blue, he suddenly submits his claim for damage which, technically speaking, places his claim outside the limit of our contract.

When I questioned Herbie further, he reinforced my doubts. When the lads were having a mug of tea before heading back to the yard and Crinkley was praising the lads for a job well done, he told them that his previous removers had difficulty getting the settee into his last property. Apparently it took three or four attempts before they managed to manoeuvre it through the door.

'A bunch of cowboys' is how he described them to Herbie, although I'm never entirely happy to hear any member of my profession take a hammering from anyone without hearing both sides of the story.

The upshot of Crinkley's story was that he submitted a substantial claim for damages. He told Herbie this claim was finally settled, but only after much dispute with his removers and their insurers.

He then went on to say that he was only renting that particular property whilst his new home was being completed. As it was partly furnished, he had to utilise one room as a temporary storeroom for some of his own goods, these being surplus to requirement. The settee was one of the items stored there and before Herbie and Speedy could move it, they had to shift numerous boxes that had been placed around it.

This leads Herbie and me to believe that the damage could have been caused by the previous removers, either when they were manoeuvring the settee into that room or when stacking the boxes around it. Either way, Crinkley wouldn't have been aware of any damage, with the settee surrounded by boxes for the best part of a year. That would also account for his not submitting a claim at that time. It's also feasible that Herbie and Speedy didn't spot it as they were there to shift furniture and effects, not to inspect each item for previous damage.

It's glaringly obvious that either Herbie or Crinkley are singing out of tune. But given Herbie's account, allied to the eight-day delay in submitting the claim, my belief is that Crinkley is the one striking the bum notes.

With my digital clock showing eleven fifty-five, I spot the large billboard erected to identify the development I'm looking for. The large, garish lettering across the top – barely legible due to the combination of snow and grime – invites the general public to BUY YOUR OWN PIECE OF PARADISE. Paradise, according to the billboard, being one of the 145 detached and semi-detached housing plots available for sale.

Much of the site is still in the early stages of construction with building equipment and supplies strewn across the each plot. How could anyone equate this hell-zone with a state of bliss or a life in heaven? The entire area looks like it's been submerged in a landslide.

I bump and grind my way slowly over an uneven surface of snow-covered hardcore and builders' rubble. Attempting to avoid a large pothole, my front wheel hits a raised manhole. With a sickening clunk, I'm rocked in my seat, nearly losing control of the steering. The suspension judders under the strain of the impact.

I swear to God, if I've damaged my suspension, I'll sue the developers. Or Crinkley. That would give him something to think about other than his own bloody claim.

Pissed off with developers, Crinkley and anyone else who should happen to cross my path, I turn into a small cul-de-sac comprising eight detached homes. There is absolutely nothing to distinguish one house from the next. They're certainly not properties I'd consider as my personal idea of paradise. But no doubt the owners would take a different view, having forked out up to four hundred and seventy five thousand pounds of their hard-earned cash (as the billboard at the entrance tells me). With no house numbers visible, I pull into the driveway of the third property on the right in accordance with Herbie's instructions and park behind a brand-new, four-wheel-drive Mercedes-Benz. A closer inspection tells me it's a GL Class roadster. Fifty thousand pounds' worth or thereabouts.

I'm thinking Crinkley could be a man of more than reasonable means. And a bit of a poser. Most four-wheel-drive owners are, in my opinion. How else can these gas-guzzlers be justified for urban use?

Having unwisely revived another long-standing grump – and blind to this further demonstration of my ill-informed prejudices – I leave the comfort of my sensible saloon car with my claim pad tucked safely under my arm. Walking past the Mercedes-Benz, I give it a look of contempt before squelching through the snow-covered path to the front door.

It's twelve o'clock on the dot. Another image of Gary Cooper and that iconic film scene inevitably flashes across my mind.

Gary is standing motionless in the centre of the dirt road, the brim of his Stetson pulled down over his forehead to shield his eyes from the glare of the midday sun.

Doors and windows fronting the ramshackle stores and saloon bars are boarded up and the townsfolk have long since withdrawn indoors. They know what's coming.

Gary begins to move along the street, his arms dangling loosely by his side and his manicured hands poised over revolvers already loosened in their holsters. His prominent jaw is set like a piece of granite, his eyes blue chunks of ice. His whole demeanour projects serious intent.

Small, whirling clouds of hot, blinding dust and wind-swept tumbleweed swirl around him. With concentrated deliberation, Gary wipes a piece of grit from his left eye, all the while keeping his other eye resolutely on the menacing figure of the bad guy, now facing him at a distance of approximately ten metres.

The bad guy is clad from head to toe in black, his face in my image distorted. He's a mean-looking son of a bitch.

Mean enough to be a tax inspector. Or a traffic warden. Or my landlord. Though it could also be Crinkley.

Arriving at the front door, the vision disappears as quickly as it came. Taking a small and pathetic leaf from Gary's book, I wipe an icy tear from my own eye, set my jaw in what I believe to be a replica of granite, draw myself up to my full height of five feet eight, take a deep breath, and count to five. My metaphorical pistols are cocked and ready for firing. My very own high-noon duel is nigh.

Chapter twenty-one

I STARE AT THE white PVC door, feeling like a delinquent schoolchild about to face the wrath of the headteacher. The small Georgian-style panes of glass set within the upper section of the door are frosted, obscuring my view of what lies within. Reminding myself that kicking the door is not an option, I take hold of the small knocker and knock briskly.

Although impatient to be out of the cold, I'm increasingly apprehensive. To make matters worse, my toe is reminding me of my previous mishap. Come the beginning of next week, one toenail will be missing. On the bright side, that leaves nine nails operational. And if a satisfactory, amicable settlement with Crinkley can be reached, I'll bear the loss of that nail willingly.

There's been no immediate response. Given my earlier experiences with Mrs Oglethorpe, I'm wondering if Crinkley could also be hard of hearing. That would really make my day. But I wish he'd get his finger out, because it looks like we might be set for another snowstorm.

Instinctively, I pull the collar of my three-in-one jacket tighter around my neck. Not that that will stop the heebie-jeebies I'm now experiencing.

I'm about to give the knocker another rap when the door opens. Standing in the doorway is a slim, dapper gentleman of medium height, aged somewhere in his early forties. He is instantly recognisable from our previous meeting, mainly due to his pencil-thin moustache. This reminds me of his resemblance to David Niven, another of my favourite black-and-white film stars of days gone by.

A strong waft of aftershave assails my nostrils. He not only looks like a cool dude but he smells like one. There's no doubt that this sweet-smelling *hombre* is Mr Crinkley, my *bete noire* of the moment.

Although he must know who I am, he gives me a quizzical look, eyebrows raised. 'Morning, Mr Crinkley,' I say cheerily, extending my hand in anticipation. 'Frank Tipple, from A to Z Removals. I'm here to view the damage to your settee as arranged.'

He takes a firm hold of my proffered hand and smiles. A thin smile, but a smile nevertheless. I find this reassuring.

'Ah yes, good morning, Mr Tipple. Thanks for coming down on such a rotten day. Come inside, please.'

Carefully wiping my shoes on the doormat, I step past him into the welcoming warmth of the hallway. As he closes the door behind us, I'm observing him closely, attempting to form some additional impressions.

He is attired in smart casual wear, comprising a trim navy-blue sweater worn over a blue-and-cream-striped shirt, grey flannels with a crease you could shave with and a pair of black leather shoes, polished to the nines. Very presentable indeed. But I'm not enamoured with men who smell like they've just climbed out of a vat of perfume or dress like a poncing male model. But perhaps that's because they expose my own shortcomings.

Of similar age to me, though a bit shorter and slimmer, he has, unlike me, an immaculately groomed head of hair. This sweeps luxuriantly round the sides of his head like waves from the bow of a ship. On the downside, he isn't the healthiest-looking specimen. His complexion is sallow, his skin dry, and blue veins run across his forehead like contour lines on an Ordnance Survey map.

He leads me towards a door which presumably leads to the settee in question. 'How was your journey?' he asks considerately, still smiling. His teeth are whiter than white. 'Did you have any problems driving down in the snow? I hope I haven't disrupted your work programme. It's very unfortunate really. I mean, your lads did a really good job and it's such a pity it was spoiled by the one instance of damage.'

Despite my first impressions, I'm beginning to relax and take a real shine to him. He couldn't be more courteous. I'm thinking that my early rainbow categorisation of his claim may have been a mistake.

'Right, here we are then,' he says, waving his left hand vaguely in the direction of the settee.

As I look at the item in question, my jaw drops, my dentures are in danger of spontaneous ejection, and I'm unable to disguise the look of disbelief etched all over my features. My original doubts about Crinkley and the merits of his claim are instantly revived.

The settee looks like it's been resurrected from a council tip.

When I was telling Jane about it the next day, she was trying to watch one of her favourite costume dramas on the television. 'No kidding, Jane,' I said. 'That settee was so old, I'm certain that Noah's bum-print was on the cushions. And if we had invited a second-hand furniture dealer to view this particular antiquity, he'd have laughed his socks off, then told us to stick it up a receptacle in no way designed for an item so large.'

While Jane wasn't enamoured with my quaint way of putting things, she was sympathetic, before quickly turning her attention to the antics of Jane Austen's *Emma*, a matter of much greater importance.

Crinkley and I are now looking intently at a tatty, bottle-green, faux-leather, buttoned-backed settee with low back and arms. His look is one of unadulterated love and affection. Mine is one of utter astonishment.

It's immediately obvious the settee doesn't sit well with the other furniture. It's presence is akin to a prostitute plying her trade in a nunnery. And this particular prostitute has seen a lot of use over the years. The imitation leather is considerably faded and cracked, the blemishes particularly noticeable on the cushioned seats, where numerous crinkles crisscross the surface like dried-up river beds, and on the arms, which are worn and scuffed. In addition, at least three of the buttons to the upright section of the settee are missing.

Irrespective of any tear that has been caused, he's got to be living on another planet if he feels justified making a claim against this dilapidated piece of furniture.

Oblivious to my thoughts, he has strolled nonchalantly to the side of the settee and is observing it with a look of pride and affection, tinged with the concern and reverence you might show a sick dog or a dying granny. Discreetly as possible, I try to identify anything which could come under the general heading of 'Further damage caused by A to Z Removals'. Whatever it is, it's certainly not apparent to the casual eye.

As small trickles of sweat form under my armpits, I circle towards the back of the settee, still seeking to spot the damage. The smell from behind tells me that Crinkley and his aftershave are following in my wake.

Yet I still can't see the tear.

'Do you think you could show me exactly where the damage is, please?' I request, trying to contain a note of impatience.

'Oh, sorry, Mr Tipple, I expected your secretary would have told you,' he replies, looking suitably astonished and pointing vaguely towards the top back corner of the settee. 'There, that hole there.'

My gaze follows the tip of his pointing finger. I'm still unable to see anything untoward. As the absurdity of his claim hits me, goose bumps are forming on my skin. To think he's had the temerity to bring me out in these gruesome weather conditions to assess this tattered lump of shite. On top of which, he's expecting some form of compensation.

Moving closer to the settee, I hunker down and carry out a thorough inspection of the area he has pinpointed. I'm beginning to think I'll need a magnifying glass, when I detect a tiny puncture. It's half-way down the back and about half the size of a five-pence piece; not really a hole, but rather a miniscule tear, less than a quarter of an inch long.

It's easy to understand why Herbie thought the corner of a box could have penetrated the fabric. But it's also possible the settee could have been pushed against the corner of a radiator or a protruding wooden window sill, the fabric punctured without anyone knowing it. But whatever the cause, having now seen the damage, my initial reaction is one of relief. My contact in the upholstery trade could seal this up for about forty quid or so. The repair may not be perfect, but given the settee's overall deterioration, it should be enough to keep Crinkley happy. At the same time, I'm asking myself why I should have to lay out forty quid of my hard-earned money for damage my lads didn't cause in the first place.

The growing possibility of a dispute is causing butterflies to develop in my stomach.

'Right, Mr Crinkley,' I begin, successfully diverting his attention away from the settee. As he turns to face me, a thin smile still playing on his lips, I look him straight in the eye. 'May I just say it's regrettable that your settee has, somehow or other, been damaged. I suppose we can only be thankful that it's of such a minimal nature, taking into account the overall condition of the settee. However, having considered all the facts relating to its removal, and having now seen the damage for myself, I have to say that I'm not convinced my crew can be held responsible.'

For the first time since arriving, Crinkley's mask slips. His mouth closes, his bottom lip curls downwards at the corners and his thin moustache bobs like a frayed shoelace. He gives me the evil eye, clearly displaying the first signs of outright hostility.

'Excuse me-ee, Mister Tipple,' he croaks, as he begins what is indubitably a rebuttal of my opening declaration.

I don't give him the opportunity to elaborate. He can respond to my pot-shots when my own bullets have been expended. Recognising that I've now reached my own *High Noon* moment, I brusquely interrupt. 'No, excuse me-ee, Mr Crinkley. Before you say anything more, it's important you hear me out.

'Firstly, both my lads are adamant that no damage was caused during the course of the removal. I've got no reason to doubt them, given that they've worked for me for a considerable number of years. You are also aware they had no problem moving it during the course of the operation. In fact, I'm led to believe you were so struck by their expertise that you commended them on conclusion of the removal. At no time did you express any concern.'

Crinkley is now watching me closely, his hatchet face wooden, his eyes icy cold. The first hint of a pink flush has appeared on his sickly cheeks. Preparing a response, his top lip quivers as his mouth opens.

Without drawing breath, I resolutely press home my conclusions.

'Secondly, Mr Crinkley, as I understand it, your previous removers had difficulty getting the settee into your old home. Apparently their performance was so poor, and you were so displeased, you submitted an extensive claim for damages.

'Taking these factors into consideration and looking at it from a purely objective viewpoint, it seems pretty clear to me this damage was probably caused by your previous removers. It's not that I want to cause more trouble for them, you understand, but I'm certain that the last thing you'd want would be to lumber me with a claim for which we are not responsible.'

Having presented my case with as much sincerity and conviction as possible, I await Crinkley's reaction with trepidation, unaware of the red glow suffusing my own cheeks. I've also inadvertently cracked the tip of my ballpoint pen due to pressure exerted by my fingertips.

Crinkley's previous air of composure has disintegrated, to be replaced by an increased state of agitation. One eyebrow has developed a spasmodic twitch, both lips are trembling like a baby denied the sustenance of its mother's tit and he has begun to rock on his feet like an agitated wallaby.

'Okay, Mr Tipple, you've had your say. I must say it's extremely generous of you to permit me the opportunity to speak in my own home,' he says, his high-pitched voice filled with sarcasm and emotion, his eyes as cold and shiny as the surface of a mortician's trolley. 'I can tell from your accent that you're not from these parts, originally from Ireland, I'd guess. So I understand how you may have a penchant to talk the hind legs off a donkey and a quaint, romantic and rose-tinted attachment to your staff.

'However, let me make it perfectly clear I can't possibly accept your totally unjustified, biased, illogical analysis of what happened. My wife and I checked everything thoroughly when the furniture was brought into our last home. And yes, my previous removers did have difficulties. And I wasn't very pleased with their services. And we did make a claim against their insurers. But I must also say we were duly compensated to our satisfaction, without unnecessary obstructions, obfuscations or other difficulties being put in our way. And this is what I expect from you.' To emphasise his point, he pounds the arm of the settee with a puny clenched fist.

I'm needled, not only due to what he's said but the patronising manner in which he's said it. And as for that reference to my origins, that's a put-down which maligned the entire Irish nation. My immediate inclination is to tell him to eff off. But that's not going to help matters. Instead, in order to give me breathing space to think, I make a show of opening my presentation folder then pretend to scribble meaningful notes. Meanwhile, my mind is racing around like a drunk trying to get off a moving carousel.

There's no way that he and his wife were able to check all their furniture thoroughly, given the hustle and bustle of a removal. On top of that, he's gone and told an out-and-out porky: maintaining his previous removers and insurers were quick to settle his claims. Yet he told Herbie there was a considerable dispute before it was settled.

It's obvious that we have reached a stand-off. And it would appear I'm left with two choices: to cave in to my principles and accept this little dandy's account of what happened, or stand my ground.

The decision comes easily. The settee's a load of crap, tear or no tear. So there's no way I'm going to toss in the towel for this devious, dandified poser, whatever the loss of goodwill or the aggravation caused. I conclude my meaningless scribbling and bang my presentation folder closed.

'Now hold on a minute,' I reply indignantly, only just managing to keep a rein on my temper. 'Are you really trying to tell me that, in the hustle and bustle of your removal, you and your wife were able to check every inch of each item? In any case, that tear is so small you'd have needed a magnifying glass. And once your removers had stacked those boxes around it, it would have been impossible for you to see it.'

As I pepper Crinkley with these shots from the barrel of my Smith & Wesson 357 Magnum, I raise my eyebrows dramatically to the ceiling and shake my head in a show of disbelief.

There's a moment of silence, then a smirk suddenly crosses his face. 'The removers didn't put the boxes there, Mr Tipple,' he fires back triumphantly. 'I did, after the removers had gone, as I needed more space.'

Instead of being crushed by this piece of news, my spirits instantly lift and a rush of warm blood rises to my head. The bugger has just shot himself in the foot.

'Oh right, I see, you put the boxes there yourself, did you?' I respond, my tone suddenly conciliatory.

I again open my folder and pretend to make some notes. The last pieces of the jigsaw puzzle are finally coming together. A pound to a penny, the silly sod punctured the settee when he stacked the boxes around it. He may conceivably be unaware of having done anything wrong.

My head is still spinning with contradictory thoughts and potential resolutions. Although it's my firm belief that A to Z is not liable and that, in any case, the condition of the settee makes such a claim ludicrous, a tiny but persistent voice is becoming inexorably louder and more dominant in my head.

It's telling me to set aside my dislike of the man, forget my principles and ignore the spurious nature of his claim. It's beseeching me to accept responsibility with good grace, offer him the choice of a repair job or a small cash settlement as a goodwill gesture and get the whole sorry business done and dusted, with the good name and reputation of A to Z intact.

Resigned to the wisdom of this pragmatic approach, I put my cards on the table. 'Okay, Mr Crinkley, as I see it, there are a couple of options: I could get the hole mended by my qualified upholsterer or, alternatively, we could agree a cash sum as compensation, say twenty pounds. Would that be acceptable to you?'

Crinkley's eyes narrow into thin elongated slits. His pinched sallow complexion transforms into the colour of a raw steak and he sways on the balls of his feet, his movement like a harbour buoy in a heavy ocean swell.

'Repaired!' he shrieks in a squeaky voice, at the same time laughing derisorily, his mouth twisted in a bitter grimace. 'That's it? Is that's really the best you've got to offer. I suggest you think again, old son.

'I can assure you, Missstterr Tipple, I have no intention of accepting any repair or cash compensation. The settee will need to be totally re-upholstered. Nothing more, nothing less.'

My stomach heaves and rumbles as the overnight mix of Guinness and vindaloo continues to create havoc within my innards. Involuntarily, a small puff of wind escapes from my backside with a squeak, like a mouse trapped in a cat's paws. In deference to good taste and customer relations, I slowly distance myself from Crinkley, casually wafting my claim folder behind my backside. Caught up in his own emotions, Crinkley continues to give me the evil eye, his body as tense as a five-year-old on a first visit to the dentist.

The significance of his claim has finally struck home. He's had a beneficial claims outcome from his last remover's insurance cover and now he's after a second helping from my insurers. And at a guesstimate, that's going to be somewhere in the region of one thousand pounds and counting. As Herbie suspected, I've now got all the makings of a major claim on my hands, that's going to end up with the insurers and cost me my excess. Well, bugger that for a school of soldiers. Does Crinkley take me for a complete mug?

I've been executing so many U-turns as events have evolved, that I feel my head's been doused in a bucket of Harpic. Yet there's one thing that's now crystal clear: there's no way we're going to see eye to eye on this. So there's nothing to be gained by prolonging further discussion on the matter. That will only result in more, unnecessary aggravation and resolve nothing. And I might also say something I'd regret later. So I'm going to deal with it my way. A strategic withdrawal is therefore now in order. The heavy firepower can be turned on Crinkley later, when the sheriff and his possee arrive and I'm safely removed from the line of fire.

Resolute in my course of action, I strive to mould my features into a form that conveys conciliation. 'Okay, Mr Crinkley, I hear what you say,' I respond in as reasonable a tone as possible, pensively stroking my chin to suggest contrition. 'I very much regret that events have panned out as they have. What I'll do now is refer your claim to my insurance brokers, with all the relevant information. If they have any further questions, I've no doubt they'll be in touch with you shortly.'

Crinkley is observing me closely; suspicious but relieved that he appears to have achieved his objective. My unexpected withdrawal appears to have taken the wind out of his sails. The tension between us has eased perceptibly.

'Oh, I see,' he responds lamely. 'As long as the matter isn't dragged out, Mr Tipple. I would like it sorted as soon as possible.'

'No need to worry on that account, Mr Crinkley,' I reply glibly. 'You can rest assured I'll pass your claim to our brokers today. They will decide the best way to proceed.' Now I know how Pontius Pilate must have felt.

Without further ado, I close my claim file, bid him and his aftershave goodbye, and let myself out the front door. The biting cold wind hits me, but for the first time today, I'm grateful for its cooling presence. As I make my way back to the car, I'm more than ever convinced that my analysis and judgement of this particular claim has been the correct one. I'm also confident that a jury of twelve men, good and true, would reach the same conclusion.

Feeling pleased with myself, I'm brought back to earth when I see my front tyre. It's as flat as a pancake. Jesus! As if it's not bad enough getting a puncture on a hot, sunny day, I've got to deal with one when the temperature is freezing, there's snow underfoot and the wind is whistling up my pipes. Even Victor Meldrew never had to put up with what I've endured this morning.

To add to my woes, the snow suddenly starts to cascade from the heavens, blown into blizzard conditions by the increasingly strong wind.

For the next fifteen minutes, I berate the weather, the developers, the car jack, the manhole covers, the hubcap, the tyre bolts, the tyre itself and Crinkley, totally unconcerned that my voice is echoing around the close.

My spare tyre is finally and successfully fitted, the punctured tyre laid in the boot, ready for the repair shop. My fingers are numb, my hands are covered with oil and grease and a goodly flow of blood is seeping from the knuckles of my right hand. What with the loss of this morning's blood from shaving and now this, I'm going to be a candidate for a blood transfusion. Or end up looking as anaemic as Crinkley.

The meeting with Crinkley and the efforts expended in changing the wheel have left me in a wretched state. From cold to hot, hot to cold, cold to hot and now back to cold, my body has taken a pounding. The will to live has deserted me.

I stagger into my car and turn on the ignition, the heater set on full blast. If I don't thaw out fairly quickly, my demise could occur at this very spot. And, if that happens, how long will it take before someone finds me?

The headlines and copy from Friday's *Maidenhead Advertiser* flash up:

Frozen corpse of local removal proprietor found in Rover car in the centre of large urban development. Industrial heater needed by emergency services to thaw the body prior to extraction.

As hot air begins to circulate round the car, I make a valiant attempt to shake off my depression and focus on the positive things in my life.

I think of Jane and the good times we have together.

I think of my ongoing good health, relatively speaking.

I think of the satisfied customers I've moved over the years.

I think of the director's dividends I'm able to draw when the business account is in surplus.

I think of the Scotch and ginger I'm going to enjoy later.

And lastly, I think of my plan to thwart Crinkley's preposterous claim.

Feeling more positive, I release the hand brake and set the gear shift to drive. But before releasing the brake pedal, I take one last steely-eyed look at Crinkley's residence, noticing movement as one of the front curtains falls back into place.

The sly little toad has been watching my ordeal, and probably enjoying every minute of it. I console myself with the knowledge that, if all goes according to plan, he's going to get his comeuppance.

Gary would be proud of me.

Chapter twenty-two

IT'S TWELVE FORTY-FIVE. Nearly five hours at the coal face, and there's little to show for it but a lot of grief.

I make a rapid reassessment of where I'm at. Having wasted precious time on that flat tyre, I've got one hour to get back to the office, have something to eat then tie up the Crinkley loose-ends before setting out for my McIntosh appointment.

Then, when that hurdle has been surmounted, and I've checked in with Alice, I can go home and treat myself to a hot bath, a couple of drinks and a home-delivery pizza. What could be better than bath, booze and a full stomach to put a man to rights? In tandem with my thoughts, my tummy grumbles and my mouth salivates. I can't wait.

My foot is hard down on the throttle as I exit from the Bracknell development. The radio is tuned to the Jeremy Vine show, not ideal listening, but something to take my mind off the last few minutes.

Tammy Wynette is encouraging the sisterhood to stand by their men, causing me to snort. I'm thinking the little strumpets are more likely to drop their knickers at a vicar's tea party than stick with their men. Not that Jane would accept that chauvinistic assessment. Indeed, she'd promptly remind me that my own sex is just as quick to jump ship when it suits. And in my more objective moments, I'd have to admit she's right on that one.

As Tammy's record fades and Jeremy waffles about the state of the economy, the swirling snow has reduced visibility to fifteen or twenty yards. Oncoming vehicles emerge then pass quickly out of sight, like mechanical ghosts wafting in and out of a white cloud. But the drive back to Maidenhead is uneventful.

Three records and some meaningless chitchat later, I head up the narrow lane towards my premises. Veering through the gates at high speed, I recklessly bounce the car over the pot-holed surface and skid to a stop, the bumper barely two inches away from a collision with the Portakabin.

I shake my head at my own folly. I just hope Alice hasn't witnessed this latest demonstration of my immaturity.

Catching my breath, I sheepishly extract myself then enter the heat of the office, shaking the snowflakes from my three-in-one onto the carpet. Alice is on her lunch break, vacantly observing the scene through the side window. She's seemingly unaware of my reckless driving or how close she was to getting a new air conditioning panel in the wall. And I'm not about to enlighten her.

She's chomping away on a sandwich. The powerful odour polluting the office confirms that it contains her favourite garlic sausage and onion filling, a light repast which hasn't varied since she started to work for me. Though not sickly sweet like Crinkley's aftershave, the smell is bad enough to make the hairs in my nostrils wrinkle. She must be getting a good deal at the local supermarket, or buying the stuff in bulk. Either way, the smell now reminds me I've been functioning throughout the morning on an empty stomach. Major replenishment is required forthwith.

But before heading off, I feel the need to share my latest experiences. While it's not a burden Alice should have to bear, my present emotional instability needs to be salved any way possible. And she's the only option at my disposal.

Up to this point she has totally ignored my return. Sitting with her back towards me, she continues to munch on her sandwich, blissfully unaware of my dishevelled state.

'Hi, Alice,' I say loudly, striving to get her full attention before stating the obvious. 'Back safely. But what a bloody awful morning it's been. And I'm not just talking about the weather. You don't happen to have any anti-depressant pills handy, like a couple of bottles maybe? Or a large bottle of Scotch? I tell you, Alice, the way things are going today, I wonder whether it's worth carrying on, or whether I should just jump off Maidenhead Bridge and end it all.'

I allow a deep swell of emotion to rise up in my throat, followed by a very loud and prolonged sigh. Where my dramatisation and acting skills are concerned, Tony Blair could learn a lot. Not that Alice can be easily fooled.

She sets her sandwich on the desk, stops munching then turns to face me. She regards me quizzically, but says nothing. She's heard and seen my play-acting many times before. Having got her full attention, I update her further on my latest tribulations. 'Crinkley turned out to be a right little shit. A real con-man he is,' I advise her, with as much scorn in my voice as possible. 'I tell you, Alice, he's a real twanker of the first degree. And his claim is a bloody joke. I'm sure he's trying to take us for a ride on the dodgems.'

This reminder of my meeting with the little dandy is once again causing my dormant hackles to rise. 'Listen,' I continue, now upping the gears and getting into my stride. 'Crinkley's wound me up good and proper. After lunch, I'll want to get a letter in the post to our brokers and put a spanner in the little bugger's works. I'll explain later, but first I'm going to nip over to the cafe.'

I temporarily run out of steam. 'Anything else happen since I've been out?' I add lamely as an afterthought.

Having just retrieved her onion and garlic sausage sandwich and taken a further large mouthful, Alice chews frantically with her remaining teeth, purses her lips and gives me her *Can-I-not-have-my-lunch-in-peace* look. She chews for a few seconds before she's able to reply.

'Just one more request for an estimate, the lady can't see you until Friday. I've put the worksheet in your tray. Also, someone from an estate agent phoned about advertising. I told them the usual: much as you'd like to, you're overspent on your advertising budget, so no point in calling again.'

She checks her message pad. 'That's all. It's been pretty quiet since you left.'

I digest this piece of non-news and part of me is relieved. To some extent, no news is good news, particularly where the McLaughlin and Walmsley-Brown removals are concerned. Billy and Herbie must have sorted things out nicely on both fronts. No news from the other two removals either, so hopefully these are progressing according to plan. That means three nice cheques to look forward to in the morning, with Walmsley-Brown's cheque due later.

Cancel the anti-depressants, Alice. I'm feeling better already.

Alice finally notices the condition of my hands. Not surprising, as I've been energetically waving them in front of her. Like the big kid Jane tells me I am, I'll do practically anything to ensure the appropriate attention and sympathy.

'What's happened to your hands?' she asks, with minimal concern, all the while continuing to bite away on her sandwich.

I look down at the clotted blood, grease and dirt. 'Oh, that?' I reply, pretending the matter is of no greater significance than having a heart replacement. 'You probably won't believe it, Alice, but on top of everything else, I had a puncture outside Crinkley's house. The bloody developers haven't tarred the roads yet, and they've left a sodding great manhole jutting about three feet in the air.

'I was trying to avoid a hole as large as the Grand Canyon when the car hit it. Shook me to the core, it did. But that's what probably caused the damage. This mess you see here is the result of a twenty-minute wrestle trying to change the wheel. Bloody freezing it was and all. That's why I'm late back. Do we have a plaster in the house, by any chance?'

Having capably demonstrated my well-versed ability to exaggerate, and having milked my injuries to the limit, I say no more. Instead, Alice gets my best begging-dog look and she dutifully, if reluctantly, responds, leaving her desk and the remaining portion of her sandwich to go to the kitchen. There's no reason why I couldn't have got it myself, but, like a big baby, I'm always expecting someone to look after me.

When she sets the first-aid kit on my desk, a wry smile crosses my face. I'm thinking, *God help anybody who needs an amputation.*

The first-aid kit comprises a small white plastic container, the original Walls ice-cream label still stuck to the lid. In addition to half a dozen plasters, the box contains one small bandage, a packet of aspirin, a roll of adhesive tape, a pair of nail cutters, a small jar of antiseptic cream (past its use-by date) and a tube of KY* Jelly (who put that there, and why, I've no idea).

This kit is the firm's sole concession to health and safety. And if the Health & Safety inspector should happen to come a-calling, well then, it's a safe bet that A to Z and its managing director will most likely end up in a pile of manure, sufficient to fertilise a bed of roses.

But do they really believe I'm going to equip the office with an expensive first-aid kit? Just to satisfy some faceless bureaucrats, with nothing better to do than burden us with more unnecessary legislation, and when none of them have any idea what it's like to run a small business. At the rate those pen-pushers in Brussels and Westminster are drawing up rules and regulations, I'll soon be required to set up an operating theatre and employ a full-time nurse in order to meet their legislative demands.

Alice, miffed that her lunch break has been interrupted, has returned to her sandwich and is declining to show any further interest in my injuries.

Feeling neglected – she could have offered to put the Band-Aid on for me – I leave the warmth of the office and make my way into the kitchen, plaster in hand. I set about the task of scrubbing my hands. Liberal doses of Fairy liquid and lots of cold water eventually remove most of the grease and clotted blood, plus a bit of loose skin. Satisfied I'm unlikely to pick up any infection, I dry my hands and awkwardly apply the Band-Aid.

Revitalised by this trivial exercise and with my stomach crying out for food, I bid Alice and her garlic sandwich good-bye then gingerly make my way through the snow and slush towards the cafe. My mood is one of quiet reflection. This morning's chain of events scrolls across the small screen sited between my ears, launched by that early morning premonition: *it's going to be one of those days.*

One mishap after another. Is it any wonder I've been in a constant state of stress? Yet I'm old enough to know better. Bad experiences invariably sort themselves out, one way or another. All of today's setbacks will be well and truly forgotten by tomorrow. It's not even as if the incidents have been life-threatening, apart from the encounter with the old ladies at the bus shelter and Fettucini and his dog.

Oblivious to the presence of the few people making their way to and from the shops, I talk to myself, caught up in my own little world. 'Why, Frank, why oh why?'

The answer is simple: it's the way I am. I'm a silly, sensitive old sod, sufficient confirmation for any psychiatrist that my feminine side has come to dominate my behaviour.

Gaining some inner satisfaction from my perspicacity and with another blanket of snow perched on my head like a halo, I turn into the cafe and join the queue of eight other hungry souls waiting to give their orders. Although minor concessions have been made to cater for those rare members of the vegetarian species who stray unwittingly into its domain, the menu is dominated by a selection that bears an impressive cholesterol load: eggs, sausages, bacon, beans, mushrooms, fried slice, black pudding, pasties and chips, all served in whatever combination or quantity required.

The proprietor greets me with his normal enthusiasm. Sammy and I go back about ten years, since he took over the running of the cafe. With the amount of custom he's had from me, you'd think a discount would be on the cards. Not bloody likely. Sammy's not as daft as he looks.

'Morning, Frank. Good to see you. And what's it to be today?' he asks, giving me one of his broad tooth-filled smiles.

'Afternoon, Sammy,' I reply, melting snow dripping off my head onto the counter. 'I'll have my usual: vegetarian special with a pot of tea. As fast as you can, if you would, please, I'm in a bit of a rush.'

'Vegetarian special it is, Frank,' he replies straight-faced as he commences to write on his order pad, his soiled apron hanging from his fat, jowly neck. It's obvious to everyone but Sammy that he's indulged in too many of his own meals. He turns to the serving hatch into the kitchen. 'Rose,' he shouts, tearing off my order and pushing it over the small hatch window to the kitchen. 'Vegetarian special for Frank as usual, plus a pot of tea, and as quick as you can.'

'What?' I hear Rose, his wife, query from the bowels of the kitchen.

'Frank's here, wants his usual, vegetarian special,' Sammy shouts back. 'It's on the order slip: bacon, sausage, black pudding, two eggs, baked beans, toast, a large chip and a pot of tea. He's in a hurry.' He turns back to me. 'Right, Frank, take a pew. It'll be with you in a few moments. That's four-fifty, three-fifty to anyone else. Cheap at twice the price, okay?'

In reasonable good humour following this imbecilic piece of dialogue, I settle the bill. Receiving some loose change from Sammy – and feeling more generous towards mankind in anticipation of the forthcoming meal – I slip a ten-pence piece into the staff tips tin. From the sound my coin makes as it hits the bottom, it would appear mine's the first to grace the tin today.

I set about trying to find a table in the non-smoking section. As a minor concession to the laws of the land, Sammy has allocated five tables to the non-smoking section, from a total of thirty. As there's no barrier between smoking and non-smoking sections, anyone sitting anywhere enjoys the dubious benefit of passive smoking. And with the majority of smoking tables continually occupied, that's an awful lot of smoke. The chance of anyone exiting the premises with a clear set of tubes is zero. It's the people's choice, as far as Sammy is concerned. No political correctness in his insular view of life.

Fifteen minutes later, my plate is empty but for one piece of burnt toast. I exit the cafe, sated. The freshness of the air outside does nothing to dispel the competing smells of chip fat and stale cigarette smoke which cling to my outer clothing. But there is a renewed spring to my step as I glide over the snow towards the office. I'm bright-eyed and bushy-tailed, like a squirrel on the pull, blissfully unaware of what the afternoon has in store.

If I had known, I'd have bypassed the office door, climbed the snow-covered embankment, prostrated myself across the frozen railway tracks, then waited impatiently for the 13:30 Paddington express to bring the day to an inglorious but relieving finale. Death, the ultimate stress-buster.

Chapter twenty-three

THE HEAT IN THE OFFICE hits me like a blast from a coal-fired furnace. If Alice isn't careful, she'll morph into a molten pile of flesh and bones. And serve her right for bumping up my electricity bill.

Shaking the snow from my three-in-one, I drape it loosely over the back of my chair then seat myself at my desk. A disconcerting rumbling in my stomach tells me that Sammy's baked beans are not reacting well with the remnants of Guinness and tikka masala. His ingredients might well have the same effect as a match to a keg of gunpowder. But hopefully nothing will ignite until I'm clear of the Portakabin.

With Crinkley at the centre of my universe, I remove his claim form from my folder and listlessly scan the mass of meaningless scribbles. The memory of the meeting immediately resurrects the dormant anger which has been smouldering since leaving Bracknell. Hyped-up and primed for affirmative action, I turn to check Alice's state of readiness.

Hunched over her desk, she is still making the most of her break, her concentration centred on a paperback book. Her cheeks are suffused with a ruddy glow and she is seemingly unconcerned about the pervasiveness of the heat or the odour from her sandwich, which hangs in the air like an indissoluble fog.

Curious to see what she's reading, I peer over her shoulder, to find her reading her latest Mills and Boon acquisition. Love and romance, at her age. You'd think she'd find some better way to spend her time than on soppy material more suited to spotty-faced schoolgirls approaching puberty. But who am I to judge?

As she turns over another well-thumbed page, she finally deigns to acknowledge my presence.

'Hi, Frank, hope you're feeling better now,' she says, surprising me with her concern for my welfare. She peers at me myopically through her glasses, sticks her narrow little nose in the air and makes an extravagant show of sniffing loudly. 'Had your vegetarian special again, I gather.'

Pragmatic to the core, I ignore her last comment and peer over her shoulder, this time to check the message pad. From the absence of additional notes, it would appear no further telephone calls have been received during my brief absence. 'Sorry to be a pain in the arse, Alice. I know you're still on your lunch break, but is there any chance we can do this letter about Crinkley?' I request tentatively. 'I'm really pushed for time and it needs to be drafted today, while the facts are still fresh in my mind. If you take it down and type it up later, I can double-check it in the morning. Is that okay?' With that, she receives another of my best hang-dog looks.

I'm pushing my luck, because if Alice is not in the mood she'll waste no time in putting me to rights. But I don't have the luxury of waiting another ten minutes whilst she immerses herself in romantic codswallop.

She gives me another of those *God give me patience* looks, and emits a long audible sigh. She resignedly places her book-mark between the pages of her novel, lays it to the side of the desk and, sighing again, picks up her pen and pad.

Despite this minor show of petulance, I feel no guilt. She knows that if things are slack in the office, she can read as much as she wants. The four or five Mills and Boon books in her bottom drawer are testament to that.

With Alice now waiting impatiently for action on my part, I pick up a pencil from my pen and pencil holder and absently twiddle it between my fingers while collecting my thoughts.

Fortunately for me, Alice is one of that ever-decreasing band of secretaries who has achieved an excellent standard of shorthand via the School of Pitman. My dictation can be reeled off as freely and spontaneously as my thought processes permit. Then, when Alice has done the donkey work – edited and censored my work as she deems necessary while typing an initial draft – all that is required on my part are last-minute adjustments.

Unfortunately for Alice, I've never had a natural ability to dictate. On the contrary, my attempts to articulate thoughts clearly and authoritatively leave a lot to be desired. This excruciating process is hindered even more by my ingrained habit of interspersing irrelevant comments and interjecting unnecessary instructions on punctuation and grammar, making Alice's task of deciphering my outpourings more difficult.

Right now, she knows what's coming. She is waiting impatiently for me to begin, her pen poised over her pad, the fingers of her left hand lightly drumming the top of the desk. The Mills and Boon lies discarded to the side.

'Right, Alice, here goes,' I say, beginning to pace slowly round the office.

'To Richardson & Co, Insurance Brokers, you know the address. Send it for the attention of Steve. He'll know what to do. And can you put this heading: "Pending Damage Claim, dash, Mr Arsehole." I make a point of spelling each letter of the name slowly and clearly, at the same time closely observing the back of Alice's head.

She has begun to transcribe the name on her pad when her biro suddenly stops in mid-air. She's not daft. Not for nothing is she acquainted with some of my more dubious practices. With an imperceptible shake of her head, she turns and throws a questioning glance in my direction. *And which arsehole are we referring to, Frank?*

I can see what's going through her mind. Impervious to her reaction, I snigger quietly, pleased at my moronic attempt at humour, yet, at the same time, feeling like a naughty child caught peeing in the outside drain.

She gives another exaggerated sigh then turns back to her pad.

'Okay, sorry about that, Alice. Let's start again,' I say, my face as inscrutable as a Japanese samurai. 'Right, heading, damage claim, dash, Mr Crinkley. Oh, and a copy for me, of course? Make sure you don't send Crinkley a copy, I don't want the bugger to know what I'm up to. Right then, here goes.'

I commence dictation. 'Dear Steve…'

That's the easy bit. Circling the floor space with the pencil still twiddling between my fingers, I struggle to formulate a suitable form of words to express what needs to be said. Although it would be easier to discuss the matter over the phone, Steve will want something in writing, if for no other reason than to cover his own back. So if I'm to expect him to support my case, it's important every relevant detail is included. He's got his own reputation and that of his employers to think about.

Endeavouring to collect my thoughts, I abstractly watch the snow. At the rate it's coming down, we're going to need a team of huskies to get out of the yard.

For Alice there follows an excruciating six minutes or so, as I attempt to put my thoughts into words. My dictation is punctuated with numerous stops and starts, the result of which can be seen in Alice's writing pad. The blank pages have evolved into a sea of shorthand waves flowing around and over the rocks of deletions and corrections.

Throughout, I'm required to put up with an extraordinary amount of huffing and puffing as Alice strives to cope. Her noisy, drama-queen sounds of consternation are accompanied by a range of facial expressions, each morphing rapidly and designed to further ensure that I'm fully acquainted with her state of martyrdom.

There's her *What have I done to deserve this?* look.

That's followed by her *Can you stick to the bloody point?* look.

Then, after the briefest moment, her *Jesus, Frank, do you think I'm a bleeding clairvoyant?* look.

Finally her *Of all the places I could have worked, why did it have to be for an incomprehensible Irish bummer like you?* look.

That's a lot of interpretations to put on facial expressions, but, as I have to keep reminding Jane when she scoffs at my interpretations, Alice and I know each other too well. I'm sympathetic to her difficulties, so I suffer her posturing in silence. She's merely taking a leaf out of my own book where the drama-queen performance is concerned.

We're three-quarters through my dissertation when an un-associated problem raises its ugly head, causing further disruption to my dictation and testing Alice's patience even more. The imposition of Sammy's vegetarian special on top of last night's Guinness and tikka masala has resulted in a build-up of gas in my nether regions, a buttock-clenching build-up which is perilously close to explosion point.

'Excuse me, Alice. Back in a minute,' I croak in desperation, compressing the cheeks of my arse before hurriedly rising from my chair and exiting the office, leaving a perplexed Alice staring after me. *What the bleeding hell is he up to now?*

I have barely reached the sanctity of the toilet when there is a prolonged expulsion of wind from my bottom, sounding like a high-powered steam whistle from a coal-fired locomotive.

Hoping the partition walls or a passing train have disguised the nature of my problem, I wait for a few moments then, satisfied the worst is over, sheepishly return to the office. Hanging in the air behind me is a heavy, depressing cloud of noxious curry smells.

Alice is facing the door, her feet impatiently tapping the floor. She regards me with a mixture of pity and amusement.

'Hell's bells, Frank, I thought you were going to blow the roof off the Portakabin,' she says caustically then points her pen towards the wall clock and her writing pad. 'Now, any time you're ready, be my guest.'

There's nothing else to do but look suitably bashful. 'Sorry for the hiccup, Alice,' I reply, ignoring her sarcasm. 'I think Sammy overdid the baked beans. But don't worry, imminent danger has passed. No need to call the Army Explosives team. Right, where was I?'

A few seconds passes whilst Alice considers whether a further cutting comment is appropriate. Instead, she refers to her writing pad and brings me back up to speed.

I digest what she's said then try to pick up the pieces. 'Right, Alice, that sounds good so far. But can you underline the bit about Noah and the Ark. And don't put those other bits in, those bits about exaggeration, underlining the point. That was basically me talking to myself, clarifying and confirming the gist of my argument, if you know what I mean. I'll try to be a little more precise from hereon in.'

With the minor misdemeanour of the explosive gas tank now behind me, so to speak, I recommence circling the office. I need to get this task done and dusted and be on my way to McIntosh.

For the first time since beginning my dictation, there is clarity to my thoughts and words start to tumble from my mouth with the minimum of effort. The transformation hasn't come soon enough for Alice. She is now totally concentrated on keeping pace, her histrionics on hold.

'The bottom line, Steve, is this: I don't want to accept liability for this claim. And also, if at all possible, I don't want Crinkley approaching our insurers direct. I fear they'll take the easy way out and settle this claim without an argument, or without making life difficult for him. Which is why I'd prefer it if this claim goes no further. You know it's not often I ask you to take this sort of action on my behalf, but this is one time I need some unofficial official backing. In any case, he's more likely to accept a rejection coming from an authoritative, independent third party like yourself.

'I'd appreciate it therefore, Steve, if you would pen one of your officious letters to Crinkley – on your letterheading, of course – rejecting his claim outright. Although the various factors I've raised are, I believe, more than sufficient in their own right to justify rejection, I suggest that, rather than getting involved in the minutiae of the claim – and the question of his word against ours – we reject his claim on one simple basis only: his failure to submit his claim on time. This is a clear breach of our terms and conditions that we could defend in court.'

I pause to take a well-earned breath and allow Alice to catch up. Her pen has been flowing fluently across her writing pad as my progress towards my destination has continued at breakneck speed. As her pen comes to a stop – with my engine fairly scooting down the line and the coal scuttle nearly empty – I conclude my dictation. 'If you wish to clarify anything, give me a call. Regards, Frank.'

Alice appears to have kept pace with my improved efforts. She now turns over another page, in readiness for any postscripts. For once, there aren't any.

'Right, that's about it, Alice. If you could type that up, I'll have a look at it tomorrow. But you'd probably like to finish your lunch break first.'

She now gives me her *So considerate of you* look then, without further comment, pushes her pad to the side of the desk, picks up her Mills and Boon, and recommences reading.

Ignoring her, I return to my own desk and stare vacantly out the window, lost in my own thoughts. I'm satisfied with the course of action initiated. An official rejection letter from the insurance brokers should do the trick and bring matters to a close without the need for any further personal involvement with Crinkley.

But if Crinkley does stand his ground and tries to pursue his claim directly with our insurers, I'll make sure they send an assessor. Alternatively, if he chooses to pursue the matter through the Small Claims Court, then I'll insist we pick up the settee and produce it in court as evidence. That should be enough to clinch it in my favour. And I'll charge the costs to Crinkley.

Whatever action he does take, I'm definitely not prepared to let him win this one. It's nigh impossible to please all customers all of the time. Especially when they are dipsticks like Crinkley.

A further black-and-white image of that earlier Wild West scene scuds across my mind. Events have moved on since my last screening. At this point, the high-noon duel has reached its scripted conclusion.

Gary is now standing motionless, his hands hanging loosely by his side, his guns back in their holsters. Lying prone on the dirt is the still form of a black-clad figure, a pool of blood slowly spreading from under the body. The face is distorted in death. But it's clearly identifiable. It's Crinkley.

The deed is done. Justice has been served.

As the image fades, I offer up a silent prayer that McIntosh will also recognise the superiority of the forces lined up against him, and will scuttle to safety with his bagpipes intact and his sporran tucked securely between his legs.

Chapter twenty-four

'YOU'RE GOING to be late for your appointment.'

Alice's hectoring warning, abruptly delivered through pursed lips, breaks into my deliberations. It's obvious she's keen to see the back of me. And who can blame her, when her Mills and Boon is demanding her undivided attention and I've been a misery guts since she arrived for work.

Accepting the wisdom of her warning, I slowly disentangle myself from my chair, the muscles of my legs responding lethargically to the mixed signals emanating from my brain.

The mild euphoria generated by my vegetarian special is now gone, replaced by a mood of gloom and doom. It's the prospect of a second unpleasant confrontation of the day. Mr McIntosh's surly attitude on the phone hasn't exactly warmed me to the man. It also concerns me that the removal crew haven't given me prior warning that there might be repercussions from the removal. They're normally the first to realise something has gone wrong, and the first to let me know about it.

But if I'm being shafted again, there's no way I'm going to turn the proverbial cheek, unless it's to drop my trousers and do a moonie. Twice in one day would be too much to take. Besides, customers are not always right, and sometimes it's necessary to tell them so, unpalatable as it may be. But the inevitable result is ill-will and rancour. And I've had enough of that for one day.

I retrieve McIntosh's paperwork, which Alice has left on my desk. 'Right Alice, I'm off now. Don't forget, no more appointments today, please pretty please. After I've seen Tosh, I'm planning to go home and put my feet up. After the crap I've taken today, some quality time won't go amiss. But first, I'll drop in to make sure everything here is okay.'

The thought of beating the retreat produces a rare moment of benevolence. 'Listen, if this snow continues and you're getting worried about driving conditions, head off early yourself. Just put the answering machine on. But for the time being, can you stick with it?'

Alice, sufficiently surprised at the generosity of my offer, sets aside her Mills and Boon, her craggy face transforming into the closest thing I've yet seen to a genuine smile. 'Ta, Frank,' she replies. 'I'll see how it goes, and how far I get with this letter. Anyway, thanks for the thought. I hope all goes well with Mr McIntosh.'

It's not often Alice gets the opportunity to step outside the Portakabin door before prescribed work times are completed, poor weather conditions or not. But she won't take advantage of the offer unless it's absolutely necessary. One of the old school she is, bless her. She'll be hard to replace, if and when she finally decides to hang up her typewriter ribbons.

Without further ado, I leave the Portakabin and step into the fresh embrace of the winter cold. The snow has ceased, apart from isolated flakes drifting slowly to the ground. On the downside, the sky overhead is still heavy and threatening. If those clouds discharge a deluge of cats and dogs instead of the white stuff, the present Christmas card scene will deteriorate rapidly and the surface of the yard will resemble a mud bath. Now might be a good time to approach the landlord and ask him to experience the problem for himself. A layer of mud over his Jaguar and highly polished Italian shoes could go a long way to solving the issue.

I walk slowly round the car to check my tyres. With no spare available, it's going to be a matter of crossed fingers and a fair wind until the old one is repaired.

Satisfied I'm operational, I install myself within the refrigerated interior, switch on the ignition and heater, engage the gear lever and steer carefully round the potholes and into the lane.

On autopilot, I trace the route to Maidenhead Bridge then along Ray Mead Road towards Cookham, Bourne End and the final lap to Marlow Bottom.

I resolve to show Tosh the happy-go-lucky, sensitive and tolerant side to Frank Tipple. The one beloved by Jane; the one seen by Alice when she adds a substantial dividend to my monthly salary cheque; and the one that beams back from the office mirror after a customer has complimented the managing director on a job well done.

With this positive philosophy and a temporary feeling of goodwill, I pull up in front of Mr McIntosh's residence.

His property is situated within an established residential area, as different from Crinkley's development as would be possible to find. Two- and three-bedroom bungalows are interspersed with four- and five-bedroom two-storey houses on either side of the road. Each home is different in design and size from its neighbour, with variable sizes of gardens, the majority landscaped and nurtured over many years with loving care.

Ascending steeply to McIntosh's single-door garage is a snow-covered driveway, twenty to thirty yards long. Rather than risk driving up the steep, slippery incline, I decide to leave my car where it is. Retrieving my claim file, I crunch my way up the steps adjacent to the drive then branch off onto another short path to the front door.

A loud belch escapes my lips. But better out than in. And better out from top than bottom. And better out here than indoors.

I take a deep breath then ring the doorbell. I'm reminded of my amateur dramatic days, waiting nervously in the wings for my appearance onstage. I can only hope that my performance will be well received.

After a few uncomfortable moments, the door opens. My immediate reaction is one of surprise. The person facing me is not the customer I'd envisaged. And how I didn't remember him, even after all these weeks, is a mystery.

It's his ears. They're enormous, sticking out from the side of his skull like the wings of an albatross. They're so huge they wouldn't look out of place hung from the mast of an ocean-going schooner. And with receptors like these, he certainly won't need a satellite dish. Stick an aerial cable up his backside, plug himself into the mains, and his television will be up and running in no time at all.

Insensitive as it may seem, I'm finding it difficult not to smirk. I'm thinking that if Tosh moves out from the protection of that doorway and is hit by a gust of wind, he's likely to embark on a spontaneous airlift to outer space.

He's a youngish bloke in his late-twenties or thereabouts, about the same height as me, but skinny as a rake.

His small oval head is topped by an unruly mop of ginger hair. This not only fails to disguise the enormity of his receptors, but emphasises the pallid nature of his complexion and the zits dotting his face. A knobbly Adam's apple protrudes from his scrawny neck like a small escarpment. He looks like he's recently been discharged from a Somalian hospital specialising in anorexic and dermatological disorders.

He's also drawn the short straw where his dress sense is concerned. His upper body is enclosed within a baggy, woollen, polo-necked sweater, which has all the hallmarks of a home-knit effort by a blind, arthritic grandmother. The sleeve-ends protrude beyond his hands and the uneven bottom flops over his skinny waistline to within a few inches of his kneecaps. It has also seen better days. One elbow has a hole in it and it's stained in the front with what looks like tomato sauce. The frayed polo-neck fails to disguise his scrawny Adam's apple.

What he's wearing below waist level is no improvement. His grey, over-sized corduroy trousers are worn and crinkled, the frayed turn-ups drooping over a pair of open-topped sandals. Ten misshapen, sickly looking toes stick out through the front of the sandals. All in all, the last time I saw a specimen like McIntosh, it was in the middle of a field and attached to a wooden stake.

While these thoughts are flashing through my mind, Mr McIntosh is observing me intently through hyperactive eyeballs, rolling around his sockets like marbles in a bed of jelly. He appears to be looking in every direction except dead ahead. Despite my best efforts, it's difficult to make eye contact. And someone who can't look me straight in the eye can't be trusted.

Despite my reservations, he now receives the benefit of a full-frontal Frank Tipple welcome. My teeth are displayed to their maximum, my lips curl upwards at the corners, crows feet form at the corners of my eyes and a small dimple appears on my left cheek. My right arm is fully extended in anticipation of a welcoming handshake.

'Good afternoon, Mr McIntosh,' I pronounce in my most friendly and conciliatory tone. 'Frank Tipple, from A to Z Removals, here to assess your damage claim.'

His response is neither friendly nor conciliatory. 'It's nae particularly good afternoon for me, Mr Tipple, nae in the least,' he replies, his lips pursed as tight as the arse of a duck confronted by a randy drake. He extends a bony, long-fingered hand from within his long-sleeved sweater.

His handshake is limp, the skin moist and clammy to the touch, like holding onto a clutch of worms. Finding the touch repellent, I quickly release Tosh's hand then, as he turns to enter his hallway, run my hand down my trouser leg, in a silly and futile attempt to cleanse me from the possibility of contracting Aids, the bubonic plague, zits, or God knows what. Tosh closes the door behind me, his expression a grim picture of grievance. If I'd hoped for an easy ride on this appointment, it looks like it's not going to happen.

'I've spent thae whole weekend trying tae sort things oot,' he shoots over his shoulder, his accented whinging tone already beginning to grate on my ears. 'And my weef is so stressed she's haed to take tae bed. I hae to say, I've gae better things to do than hae this hassle to worry aboot.'

It's obvious that Tosh's attitude has not changed one jot from this morning. This greeting has been extended in a broad Glaswegian accent with all the warmth of a bucket of ice. And it's a bit rich blaming me for his wife's incapacity. But if he doesn't want to bury the hatchet, other than in the top of my head, then that's up to him.

Glancing down the hallway, I can't help but notice some broken ceramic pieces lying on top of a crescent-shaped telephone table. Dark water marks on the carpet indicate that water has recently been spilt. A pound to a penny this is what Tosh knocked off the table when he was on the phone earlier. I hope he's not going to add this item to his claim and expect me to pick up the pieces, literally or metaphorically.

Tosh turns from the closed door, everything but his eyes directly facing me.

'Sorry you've had problems,' I say, friendly-like, prudently refraining from mentioning the broken pieces. 'How can I help you, then?'

'Yae can help me, Mr Tipple, bae quickly sorting oot awe thae damages caused bae yaer crew,' he replies, his eyes dancing the foxtrot and his Adam's apple bouncing up and down like a table tennis ball on a piece of elastic.

As if his demeanour hasn't been sufficient cause for concern, other alarm bells have now gone off in my head, with his confirmation of 'awe thae damages'. 'How many damages are we talking about?' I ask tentatively, mentally trying to second-guess the answer.

'Seven,' he replies truculently, his eyeballs continuing to roll back and forth.

My mind races off at a tangent. What's with this number seven? I've watched *The Magnificent Seven* on television. I've seen Salome perform her sensual Dance of the Seven Veils. As a child, I've enjoyed the frolics of Grumpy, Happy, Bashful, Doc, Dopey, Sleepy and Sneezy. I've succumbed to at least three of the seven deadly sins. I've been fortunate to see two of the Seven Wonders of the World. I've sung along with *Seven Brides for Seven Brothers*. I've read TE Lawrence's *The Seven Pillars of Wisdom*. On a more mundane level, I can quench my thirst with a fizzy bottle of 7-Up. Rome was apparently built on seven hills. And my life is constantly evolving through a seven-day week.

But seven damage claims from the one removal? That's what I'd average in the entire year. It's preposterous. It would take a collision with a bleeding Boeing 707 to cause that number of damages. Not once, in twenty-odd years of lifting and shifting, has there been such a sizeable claim.

Trying to get to grips with the enormity of his claim, I make a show of opening my claim folder, then slowly pen the numbers one to seven down the left margin of the paper.

Whilst Tosh's news is slowly digested along with my lunchtime fry-up, there is an ominous rumbling in my stomach.

I finish my play acting with the claim file and attempt to look him straight in the eyes. 'I see, seven damaged items,' I say lamely, hoping that any colour on my countenance has not totally faded away. 'That doesn't sound too good, does it now? Perhaps you'd be good enough to show me the damages. One at a time if you will, please, so that I can fully assess them.'

Knowing that he's in the driving seat, he puffs out his puny chest, his ears flap like flags ruffled by a breeze and his eyes begin to dance round the maypole. 'Right, Mr Tipple, well, for starters, wae've haed a plant damaged.' As he tentatively volunteers this information, he continues to stand just inside the front door.

My eyebrows rise a half inch. 'A plant?' I query, wondering what sort of plant is worthy of a claim? Perhaps a Japanese bonsai? They cost a bob or two. Or could he mean a mobile generating plant? Is he on home renal dialysis? Given his sickly appearance, that wouldn't surprise me. 'Can I have a look at it, please?' I ask, fearing the worst.

'Look at it? Nae, afraid not,' replies Tosh. 'We threw it oot this morning after we realised it wae damaged. Its leaves were knocked off. Thae binmen hae been here since. I didnae think it wae necessary tae keep it.'

A marked feeling of relief courses through me. It is one of the green-leafed variety. But he's thrown it out, which means I can't assess the damage.

'You threw it out?' I ask, trying to contain my annoyance. 'That's going to make it difficult to assess exactly what damage has been caused, wouldn't you say so, Mr McIntosh?' This is delivered with little attempt to disguise the sarcasm. 'Can you tell me what the cost of the plant was, so I've got some idea of the extent of the claim you're making.'

'One pound fiftae,' he replies confidently, with nary a glimmer of shame or embarrassment.

'One pound fifty?' I question, incredulous.

He nods his head affirmatively, his eyes now doing the samba. 'Aye, thae's whae I said, a pound and fiftae pence. Tae months agae we bought it, at the Church fete it wae. A money plant it wae, one of our favourites.'

From the manner in which he continues to regard me, it's not hard to see that, for him, this is indeed a matter of considerable importance.

Contradictory thoughts spin through my mind. On the one hand, I'm thinking that if each of his seven claims is going to be on a similar scale, then my likely outlay is going to be minimal, ten pounds fifty to be precise. On the other hand, the thought that this stingy little weed may have called me out for the likes of a plant which cost him one pound fifty, causes a deep well of anger and resentment to build up within me. How many leaves is a one pound fifty plant likely to have in the first place? Christ, he'd be lucky to get a stem and a couple of roots for one pound fifty, never mind expect bloody leaves to be hanging from it. My stomach continues to groan and churn. A couple of Immodium tablets may be needed later to control precipitate emissions.

Coinciding with this thought, a small puff of wind escapes from my back passage with a barely discernable squeak. If this build-up of gas continues to the extent it did at the office, we're both in deep shit.

Trying to ignore a change to the quality of the air, I make a rapid scribbled record of claim number one. Tosh's other claims may turn out to be more serious, which would put this pathetic and frivolous claim in perspective.

'Okay, Mr McIntosh, if we can leave the matter of the plant for the moment, perhaps you could show me the other problems?'

Without further comment, McIntosh turns and heads down the hallway, his sandals flip-flopping loosely over the carpet, with me following in the slipstream of his ears. At the end of the hall he enters a door leading into the garage. I follow him through the doorway, wincing as his ears barely clear the sides.

There's hardly room to swing a cat in the single garage. The floor space is strewn with crates, boxes, and various pieces of jumble. Casting my eyes around the garage, I'm vainly trying to spot anything which looks like it might have suffered some damage.

'Here we are.' He points a long bony finger towards a bicycle. His tone is triumphant, like someone who's discovered a valuable hoard of jewels. Peering over his shoulder, my eyes focus on the bicycle, leaning against a rusting, metal shelving unit. 'Thae saddle hae bin damaged and I'm nae very happy aboot it,' he informs me with a pronounced show of petulance. 'It'll need tae be replaced.'

Taking care to avoid contact with his left ear, I step round him then give the bicycle a closer inspection. Not for the first time today, a vacuous expression settles on my countenance, a pretty normal look as Jane would tell me in one of her more petulant moments. But as Victor Meldrew would say: *I just don't believe it.*

The bike isn't just old, it's a museum piece. The only thing that surprises me is that it hasn't got square wheels. With its old-fashioned, squat frame and high upturned handle bars, it must be at least forty years old, similar to one I had as a teenager, and one that had originally belonged to my da and his da before him. As rare a sight as a gritter in winter time.

And it's been badly maintained. Severe rusting has accumulated over a large proportion of the frame, two or three spokes are missing from each wheel, one of the braking cables is broken and wound loosely round the crossbar, and there's only half a mudguard to the front wheel. Irrespective of what's happened to the saddle, the bike is already a readymade candidate for the scrap-metal yard.

First Crinkley's settee and now this. My anger boils to the surface. 'Well now, Mr McIntosh, I must say that in my twenty years of running a very successful removal business, I thought I'd seen and heard everything. But I swear to God Almighty, this is the first time ever I've been subjected to the likes of this sort of nonsense from any of my customers. These claims of yours really do take the biscuit.'

Tosh stares at me with disbelief while I make no attempt to control my choice of words. 'My guys have successfully moved furniture and effects valued by your very own insurance declaration at eighty thousand pounds. Yet you've had the gall to call me down here on such a piss-poor day to tell me you want compensation for a piddling little plant that cost you the princely sum of one pound and fifty. And now you have the brass neck to claim for a saddle on a bicycle which wouldn't look out of place in a scrap-yard. Are you sure you wouldn't like me to replace the whole bloody bicycle?'

My voice has reached such a pitch that I'm beginning to sound like a poofter on helium. As for Tosh, he's apoplectic. He's turned yellow at the gills and his enormous ears have taken on a bright orange hue. In the diminished light of the garage they glow like two Belisha beacons on a darkened street. Adding to his increasing floridity, his zits are like miniature volcanoes, red topped and raw, ready to erupt.

His hands have disappeared up the end of his sleeves and his Adam's apple is bouncing up and down his neck like a bungee-jumper. The tension between us is creating electrical currents, sufficient to power the neighbourhood street lighting.

After the briefest moment of reflection, he vents his feelings, his voice shaking with barely controlled anger.

'Well, if yae're finished, Mister Tipple, I hae to say I'm nae enamoured with thae tone of yaer voice, thae way yae're addressing me, and yaer swearing. May I remind yae that I'm aye customer of yours and I expect tae be treated wae due respect and civility and nae like the way yae're probably accustomed tae talk tae yaer staff. Now perhaps *yae'd* be gaed enough to let me tell *yae* something and I suggest yae listen lang and yae listen gaed.'

His eyes are performing the Gay Gordons and his bagpipes are full to bursting.

'No, I dinnae expect yae tae buy me a new bicycle. And yes, of course I wannae claim for a new saddle.' he expostulates, wildly waving the handless sleeves of his sweater. 'Thae saddle wasnae damaged afore we moved and nae it is. Is thae straightforward enough for yae? I get thae impression that this might all be aye bit difficult for yae, but dae yae think yae cae understand that?'

He's winding me up tighter than a piano string. Taking one step forward, I thrust my head aggressively to within six inches of his weedy nose, my face scrunched in a grotesque grimace.

'Dae I think I cae understand thae?' I mimic in a Glasgow accent, rocking my head from side to side. 'Yes, Mr McIntosh. I think I can just about understand that, although you'll appreciate it's not always easy to comprehend a foreign language, particularly one that emanates from the Gorbals.'

In making this pronouncement, I'm totally immune to the irony that my own Irish accent and dialect might be equally indecipherable.

'What is not clear to me,' I snarl, my teeth still snapping within inches of his face, 'is how you expect anyone – me, my insurers, the angel Gabriel himself – to compensate you for this load of crap. Why could you possibly be daft enough to think that? That's what I can't understand.'

Tosh is looking at me warily, incomprehension etched on his zit-laden face and clearly perplexed by the aggressive nature of my response. His enormous ears have become so red he's in danger of spontaneously combusting. On the plus side, he is actually looking me straight in the eye. If I've cured him of his wandering eyes, by God, I'll submit a bill for services rendered.

His lips move and his mouth opens and shuts like a fish out of water as he endeavours to slot a further two-pennyworth into the melting pot. But I refuse to give him that opportunity.

'Now, let me tell you, and yae listen lang and yae listen gaed. It is my considered opinion that whatever the damage to your saddle, it has in no way caused a depreciation of the bike's value. Your bike was in a crap condition prior to the removal and is still in a crap condition.

'So, to make myself absolutely clear, no way am I prepared to make any offer of compensation for the saddle or the plant; nor am I prepared to indulge any further debate on the matter. Now, if you'd care to show me the remaining items?'

Tosh is incandescent with rage and agitated beyond belief. Surpassing all previous efforts, his eyes are performing a convoluted mixture of a Scottish sword dance and Highland fling, his Adam's apple is gyrating up and down his scrawny neck, his zits and boils are pulsating like illuminated traffic cones and his red flaming ears are continuing to flap like fluorescent mainsails.

Regaining sufficient composure to speak, he subjects me to an explosive tirade. The range of his vocabulary, and his ability to articulate his thoughts, is miraculous: a Scottish edition of the *Encyclopaedia Britannica* on legs.

Not that I was able to absorb or understand everything he said. While he is reading me the Scottish version of the riot act, I'm mentally preparing my own response, simultaneously building up a head of steam to counteract the barrage coming my way. It's clear that we have reached an impasse in our discussion. Nothing can now possibly bridge the considerable gap between our opposing views and behaviour.

When Tosh finally runs out of steam, I communicate some ill-advised words and phrases of my own. I'd be hard-pressed to remember exactly what passed my lips. But it didn't really matter. In the midst of my harangue, I inadvertently deliver the *coup de grace*.

Surpassing all previous efforts, the mother and father of all farts explodes from my bottom, the noise reverberating round the enclosed confines of the garage walls with the full-blooded roar of a wounded bull elephant, creating my very own Nagasaki and increasing global warming at a stroke. As it escapes from my posterior, a small grunt of pleasure passes my lips. The thunder roll lasts for approximately five seconds and in the silence that follows, we are both struck rigid as a nauseous, invisible cloud of noxious gas rises rapidly and steadily upwards and outwards.

Tosh's countenance takes on an even more pallid hue and his nostrils twitch like a mouse given a stale piece of cheese. He fixes me with a gaze of consternation then takes an involuntary step backwards.

As the fumes continue to settle on us like a thick blanket, I'm inwardly assessing the inherent dangers of my digression. *If anyone strikes a match, we're in deep shit. The whole street could blow apart.*

Without further ado – ignoring any desire that Tosh might have to continue his litany of complaints – I stiffly bid him goodbye, emphasise the strength of my feelings with a time-honoured two-finger salute and storm out the front door.

Behind me, I leave a bewildered and incandescent Tosh, his face a flaming mass of skin and tissue, his ears a tribute to fluorescent lighting.

Although I wasn't to know at the time, we never hear from him again. Nor did we ever find out about his other five claims. It later crossed my mind that he may not have survived the gas attack.

Chapter twenty-five

MAKING MY WAY blindly down the path, I'm oblivious to the change in the weather. Rain is cascading from the heavens, causing the blanket of snow to morph into a mushy mound of dirty, grey slush.

I collapse behind the steering wheel, drenched to the skin. Droplets of rain pour off my sodden head and down my face and neck. Thankful for small mercies, my tongue greedily seeks and sucks small drops of moisture from my lips. Not as beneficial as a Scotch, but beggars can't be choosers.

The confrontation with Tosh has left me agitated and weak at the knees. I feel physically and emotionally clapped out, worse than at any other time today. If I don't get a grip of myself, I'll be having a heart seizure and end up in the knacker's yard.

Closing my eyes, my imagination runs riot. *Is this what it feel's like to be at death's door? Could I already be dead?* An image of *News at Ten* appears on the blank screen behind my eyes.

The clock of Big Ben fills the screen, the bell pealing thunderously as it counts down the seconds to the hour. On the stroke of ten, the clock face fades from the screen, replaced by the sombre features of Sir Trevor McDonald. He raises his eyes to the camera and begins to speak in his cultured tones.

'This is the Ten O'Clock News. I bring you the major news item of the day.

'News has just come in that the body of an elderly male has been found slumped in a saloon car, parked in Marlow Bottom. At this time, it is not known how long the deceased may have lain there before being discovered.

'Our cameraman has just sent us these pictures.'

The face of Trevor McDonald fades, to be replaced by a close-up shot of a

Rover car. Police, fire fighters and paramedics are clustered round the vehicle.

As the camera pans in for a close-up, four uniformed personnel are seen to extract a corpse through the sawn-off roof, a morose expression clearly etched on its lifeless face. Incongruously, a clip-board is frozen to one hand, a broken biro between the fingers of the other.

Trevor McDonald's voice-over continues against the background of extensive on-screen activity. 'First reports from the scene indicate death may have been due to a combination of stress and hypothermia, exacerbated by the poor medical condition of the deceased.

'Questions have been raised as to why the owner of the adjoining property – at home over the course of the week and apparently acquainted with the deceased – greeted the news of the body's discovery with a broad smile and an immediate demonstration of the Highland fling.

'Due to the weathered and wrinkled state of the body, no identification has yet been possible.'

My thoughts abruptly return to the real world as a passing car throws a deluge of rain and slush against the side of the car.

But I'm finding it difficult to get my head around the catalogue of events which have conspired to make my day such a misery. It's been an unproductive day, by any standards. If I'm exposed to any further shenanigans, I'll definitely end up on a cold marble slab.

My imagination again runs riot as I visualise the reports appearing in the local morning newspapers.

Maidenhead Advertiser:
Well known removal boss bites the dust, only months before taking a well-earned retirement. Diligent and conscientious as he was, his devotion to the satisfaction of his clients proved to be a burden greater than he, or his body, could bear.

Windsor and Eton Express:
Bucks and Berks legend, Mr Shifter, passes on. Experts from his trade organisation have ensured that he will be hand-packed and professionally secured to ensure minimal damage in transit to his storage allotment in the sky.

Slough Observer:
Due to an unforeseen set of circumstances – culminating in his sudden and unexpected death – Maidenhead removal proprietor, Frederick Francis Foster Fidel Tipple, forfeits all rights to a substantial pension pot. According to those present during his final moments, tears were seen to be running down his face as the injustice of his loss became apparent.

I give myself a good shake. All the bad stuff is over and done with, so it's stupid to feel down. In theatrical terms, today's performance has concluded, the cat-calls endured, the bows taken and the final curtain drawn. After checking in with Alice, I can toddle off home to a hot bath, whisky and food.

Cancel the wreaths and obituaries, Alice. Death is not yet imminent. I still have a future and a pension to look forward to.

On this positive note, I glance through the rain-spattered windscreen at Tosh's front window then – in case he happens to be watching – make a final, exaggerated V-sign in his direction. That childish demonstration out of the way, but feeling the better for it, I switch on the ignition, put the gear stick into drive mode and stamp hard on the accelerator.

The car skids away from the kerbside, the rear end shimmying sideways like a bucking bronco. Hanging grimly onto the steering wheel, it's twenty yards or so down the road before the car brings me under control. Relieved that this manoeuvre has occurred without any further mishap, my thoughts return to home sweet home.

In approximately one half of one hour, that familiar house will embrace me to its comforting bosom like a new-born babe. It can't come soon enough.

Chapter twenty-six

I THREAD MY WAY through pouring rain, barely aware of my surroundings or the traffic around me. The dulcet, melodious voice of Karen Carpenter on Radio 2 is helping to dispel the trauma of my meeting with Tosh. And the title of the song she's singing is apt: 'Where Do I Go From Here?' If only I knew the answer.

The music concludes and the presenter introduces his special guest: a professor of psychology by the name of Polaski, Polkadot, Polyfilla, something like that, on the programme to discuss his recently published book.

As Pol-what's'isname gets into his stride, it doesn't take long to fathom the general topic of his subject: mind over matter and the ability each of us has to influence our quality of life, by adopting a positive attitude and banning pessimistic speculation from our minds.

'Bollocks!' I mutter, quickly switching off. I've suffered enough flatulence of one sort or another for one day without having to take more hot air from some arty-farty East European who thinks he's got all the answers to life's insoluble problems. A morning spent with the likes of Miss McLaughlin, the Watsons, Fettucini, Crinkley, Tosh or the taxman would rapidly dispel much of that positive thinking from his patronising little mind.

As if there aren't enough so-called experts already interfering in our lifestyles, continually advising us what's good and not good for us, and taking us all for a bunch of witless idiots.

Having gained the satisfaction of mentally disembowelling Polkadot's measly efforts to turn a fast buck, I turn into the security of the yard and draw to a stop by the Portakabin. The office light is switched on, its faint beam casting a subdued, rectangular light onto the ground outside. But the weak glow from the hundred-watt bulb does nothing to soften the onset of early dusk, now revealing its ugly face.

The grey outlines of the electricity pylons are casting a sombre spectre over the property, which has now lost its picture-postcard look. The heavy rain has washed away large areas of snow, exposing numerous water-filled potholes. These are expanding before my eyes, the separate puddles gradually and inexorably converging to form miniature lakes. Another half hour or so and the total surface will be well and truly obscured.

The top of Alice's down-turned head is visible through the rain-streaked window. As I thought, she hasn't taken advantage of my earlier offer, but obviously intends to see things through to normal finish time. Bless her.

Ensconced within the shelter of the hallway, I allow the excess rain to drain onto the floor then, as buoyant as at any time today, enter the warmth of the office.

It's immediately apparent that Alice has completed her work duties. Her feet are resting on the partly-opened bottom drawer, and her attention is fixed on her Mills and Boon. With her back towards me, she's so engrossed in her novel she has either chosen to ignore me or has reached a critical point in her tale of sex and intrigue.

I cough, which even to my own ears sounds like the dying squawk of a mother hen. She turns away from her book, swivels around in her chair and gives me the once-over, peering myopically through her glasses as she adjusts her vision.

Her forehead furrows in concern. 'Are you all right, Frank?' she asks. 'You look like you've seen a ghost.'

'Well, to be honest, Alice, I've felt better,' I reply tersely, removing my three-in-one and carelessly throwing it over the back of my chair. 'I've just had a pretty disastrous run-in with our friend McIntosh and it's had a draining effect. The only consolation is it's unlikely that he's feeling any better than I am.' I don't feel it prudent to mention that Tosh's condition might be as much due to toxic gas inhalation as to our disagreement.

'It's that claim he was making,' I now contend, the memory of the event causing my hackles to rise. 'You wouldn't believe it, Alice. One of his complaints is about a plant which had a few leaves knocked off. And guess what? It only cost the bugger one pound fifty. And yet he's making a song and dance about it.'

Alice looks at me with a tight expression on her face. She's probably regretting she said anything. She'll be aware that as I relive my encounter, it'll be having an adverse effect on my blood pressure. And there's nothing in the first-aid tin that's going to help.

Unfortunately for her, my racing stallion is now out of the corral and I've got the bit between my teeth. 'But that's only the half of it,' I bluster, angrily tossing my claim pad across the top of my desk, where it slides up against the wall with a thud. 'The silly sod is also trying to claim for a new saddle on a bicycle. I tell you, Alice, if the saddle was one of the horse variety, it would have seen service under General Custer's bottom at the Battle of Little Big Horn. What with the plant and the saddle, I just blew my top and more or less told him to piss off. We won't be getting very many recommendations from that quarter.'

I'm now in full flow. Nothing, or nobody, is going to stop me offloading my tale of woe. Certainly not Alice, who's paid to soak up my remonstrations, even if she shows the common sense to let them quietly wash over her.

'But do you know what really pisses me off?' I expostulate, my use of gutter terminology in the ascendancy. 'It's not the trivial nature of his claims, silly as they are. It's the fact the little shit didn't have one decent word to say about the lads.

'It makes my blood boil. I tell you, Alice, I've seen it all today. Anything that could go wrong has gone wrong. Talk about the Monday blues. Now you know why I'm not looking my best. I can't wait to get home and put my feet up.'

Alice has been listening to me sympathetically, but appears ill at ease. I sense she's waiting for me to run out of steam so she can get back to her Mills and Boon. I couldn't be more wrong.

She gives me a searching look. She's obviously got something else to say, but doesn't quite know how to phrase it. As I raise my eyebrows and nod my head in encouragement, she finally delivers the crunch news.

'I'm sorry to be the bearer of bad tidings, Frank, but Mr Walmsley-Brown has been on the phone again. Sounds extremely agitated, he does. And you're not going to like this.'

She pauses, as if unsure whether or not to proceed, then delivers the punch line. 'He's now complaining that the lads are going too fast. I tried to reassure him, but it didn't do anything to appease him. He didn't seem to be taking in anything I said. He was also talking a bit funny. I found it difficult to understand him.'

Alice can clearly see the look on my face. 'No, I'm not making this up, Frank,' she says earnestly. 'I know it sounds implausible, but he definitely said "too fast". And that's not all. About five minutes after Walmsley-Brown was on, Herbie also phoned. And he's really, really uptight. I haven't heard him as distressed as that before. I get the impression that the lads are seriously considering walking out on the job as they seem to be getting nothing but hassle. Herbie wants you to go over there to sort things out.'

I'm dumbstruck. What the bloody hell's going on? First the Walmsley-Browns are accusing the lads of going too slow, and now they're going too fast. And Herbie's threatening to walk off the job.

Staring blankly through the window but seeing nothing, I'm finding it difficult to come to terms with this latest setback. When is this bloody day going to end? And where's Tosh or Crinkley when I need somebody to throttle?

But could Alice have got the message wrong? She did say she found it difficult to understand him.

'Sorry, Alice, let me be sure I heard you right. And please feel free to tell me I've gone completely da-loo-la-lally. Are you absolutely sure Walmsley-Brown is now saying the lads are going too fast? Like as in quick, speedy, zoom-zoom?'

I'm looking at Alice with what must be the most moronic expression she has seen since the Three Stooges vacated the big screen.

She has risen from her chair and is on her way to the kitchen. 'Yes, I'm afraid so, Frank. He definitely said the lads were going too fast.'

I rapidly weigh up my options. There aren't any. This problem can't be ignored in the hope it'll go away. There's nothing for it but a face-to-face meeting. My home comforts and the attraction of the amber nectar will have to stay on ice.

'I guess I'd better get over there to see what's going on before matters deteriorate.' I tell Alice, with a large lump in my throat and my body like an empty shell. 'Any other good news before I go?' I add, with a marked touch of sarcasm.

Alice regards me like I'm an elderly cow on its way to the slaughter house.

She returns to her desk and refers briefly to her message pad. 'No, Frank, it's gone pretty quiet, apart from those two calls.'

I swear to God, if Alice had been the bearer of any more bad news, I'd have washed my hands of Herbie and the Walmsley-Browns, buggered off home, extracted the whisky bottle, and shut myself off from the real world until such time all memories of the day lay behind me, erased by the flow of alcohol.

I get set to leave. 'Listen, Alice, after I've sorted out Walmsley-Brown and the lads – and got everybody back in the boat and rowing in the same direction – I'm going straight home. If you need to contact me, just leave a message on my answering machine, but only if it's really, really urgent. Please, pretty please.'

'Sure, Frank, no problem,' replies Alice, picking up her Mills and Boon. 'I hope all goes well in Windsor. I'm sure you'll have a better day tomorrow.'

God bless her. Retrieving my three-in-one, I prepare to leave the office for the last time today. Wild horses are not going to drag me back under any circumstances. And although things seem to be going pear-shaped at the Walmsley-Browns, there's been no bad news from the other removals. That's three fat cheques to look forward to tomorrow morning.

The power of positive thinking: perhaps Professor Polkadot is onto something.

With legs that feel attached to a half-ton of coal, I step out to face the murky winter elements. The wind velocity has increased and is sweeping the rain across the yard, splattering the surface with thousands of minute eruptions. At this rate, Alice will be requiring the services of the RNLA to extract her from the office.

Installing myself in the car, I take a moment to meditate. I close my eyes and rest my head against the steering wheel, striving to conjure up something that might reflect the philosophy of the professor and help me cope with what lies ahead.

The picture that plays in my mind is one I've envisaged on previous occasions, normally after having had a few bevies to spark my imagination.

I'm on a British Airlines Boeing 747. As our flight prepares for its final approach to Heathrow, the no-smoking signs have come on and passengers have been requested to fasten their seat belts.

Looking forward to my reunion with Jane, I finish my plastic cup of Pinot Noir, and begin to think longingly of that welcoming kiss that Jane will be planting on my lips on arrival.

My sweet dreams are abruptly interrupted by a sudden announcement over the aircraft communication system. This is delivered by Shirley, our chief flight attendant, in a shrill, high-pitched voice, the message punctuated by a series of racking sobs.

'Good afternoon, ladies and gentlemen. I have to inform you that an unforeseen situation has arisen which may delay our safe arrival at Heathrow. Our captain and co-pilot have unfortunately succumbed to a severe bout of Spanish tummy. This has most likely been caused by the Chinese chicken chop-suey that many of you may also have eaten during this flight. Unfortunately, this has rendered them incapable of handling the aircraft at this critical time as both require constant evacuation of their bowels. Despite exhortations from those crew members still standing, they have securely locked themselves in the forward toilets and are refusing to open up under any circumstances.'

The first hints of panic are clear in the faces of the passengers around me and silence follows before a clearly disturbed Shirley is able to continue.

'There is no need for immediate panic as George, our automatic pilot, has assumed control of the flight. Unfortunately, God help us, George does not have the capability to land this plane.'

My imagination is now running away with me. I'm unaware that Alice has risen from her seat and is now peering anxiously through the office window, wearing one of her *What the hell is the stupid bugger up to now?* looks. Instead, with my eyes closed and my head still rested on the steering wheel, my mind is filled by the clear image of a tear-stained Shirley as she continues to haltingly convey the rest of her announcement.

'Would any passenger who feels capable of taking over the controls of this aircraft, please bring yourself to my attention. The RAF at Brize Norton is dispatching a fighter plane to guide our volunteer pilot down. Thank you for your cooperation. And may your God go with you. Amen.'

At this juncture, Shirley can be heard convulsing into tears, mixed with a bout of hysterical and spine-chilling laughter.

Cometh the hour, cometh the man.

Without further thought of the consequences, I raise my arm then press the service button on the underside of the locker above me.

Apart from a natural instinct for self-preservation, my logic for volunteering is simple: I didn't have the chop-suey, I' m accustomed to driving large vehicles and this 747 has the same basic control mechanisms as a van – steering wheel, throttle, gear-stick and brakes. Surely it can't be that difficult to fly? Especially with a top-gun from the RAF to guide me down.

Shirley hurries me down the aisle towards the cockpit. As we pass the forward toilets, incoherent muttering noises can be heard from behind both closed doors. If we survive this experience, I'll make a point of contacting BA to question the lack of backbone in their flight personnel. This is not how my childhood heroes Biggles and Douglas Bader would have reacted to a bit of food poisoning. 'Never mind the shit,' they'd have cried. 'Let's get on with it and show the dastardly Hun what else we've got tucked down our trousers.'

Settling into the pilot's seat, I try to ignore the remnants of chicken chop-suey and toilet paper strewn haphazardly around the cabin and attempt to assess the flight controls. As I do, a Tornado suddenly appears on my right, the helmeted pilot wiggling his wings to confirm his presence. In response, I give him a thumbs-up then, as Shirley installs herself in the co-pilot's seat, her over-exposed, shapely pair of legs barely inches from my own, I try to concentrate.

I note the inscription George, *situated below one of the numerous switches on the dashboard. This has an* On/Off *facility. Giving Shirley a reassuring nod of my head and a quick pat on the knee, I grip the joystick firmly in my right hand, take a long, deep breath then activate* George's Off *button.*

There follows a tense, roller-coaster ride until, with the guidance of the Tornado pilot and against all the odds, I crash-land the aircraft on its fuselage, the wheels still retracted, creating a fireworks display big enough to light up the whole of London.

As the plane skids to a stop, it's immediately surrounded by five fire tenders. Simultaneously, the ecstatic sounds of joy and exultation ring out from the cabin area as the passengers break into song.

'For he's a jolly good fellow…'

As I bask in this pleasing expression of appreciation, Shirley drapes her arms round my neck, gives me the most passionate of tongued kisses then slips her personal telephone number into my pocket with an open invitation to fly her kite at any time. Naughty girl.

I descend onto the Tarmac to be greeted by an array of cameras, spotlights, journalists and dignitaries.

Huw Edwards from the BBC is the first to reach me. He thrusts a microphone up to my face and asks the question on everyone's lips: 'How did you do it, Frank? What gave you the balls?'

I preen myself for a moment, puff out my chest then reply with an air of supreme nonchalance: 'Positive thinking, Huw. That's all it took. Just some positive thinking.'

I begin to search the assembled crowds, endeavouring to catch sight of Jane when…

The insistent sound of glass being smacked against glass abruptly shakes me from my reverie. Confused, I raise my head from the steering wheel to see Alice's face filling the office window, her nose pressed against the pane. She is hammering the window pane with a glass retrieved from the kitchen.

'Are you okay, Frank?'

As she mouths her concern, I shake my head in the affirmative and give her the thumbs-up. Knowing she won't hear my response, I mouth my reply. 'Fine, Alice, I was just taking a few moments to save a few hundred souls from an untimely death. See you tomorrow.'

Positive thinking. Professor Polkadot would be proud of me.

Chapter twenty-seven

THE FIFTEEN-MINUTE DRIVE to the Walmsley-Browns gives me plenty of time to reflect on this latest predicament to sour my day. I'm finding it hard to accept that Herbie and the lads have been operating like tortoises or racehorses. Neither is Herbie's style and as foreman, he dictates how fast the removal is undertaken. For as long as I've worked with him, I've never seen him vary his speed. He's like a metronome: not too fast, not too slow, and efficient with it. And whatever the composition of crew, they'll invariably adjust to his method and speed of operation.

But that's not all Herbie has got going for him. He'll apply the same high standard of care to each removal, irrespective of the social or financial standing of the client or the quality of the furniture. The salt of the earth he is, worth every penny of the meagre pittance he and his missus both feel he's being paid. Still, he's stuck with me all these years, so I can't be treating him too badly.

Which is more than the Walmsley-Browns seem to be doing. They may be from a well-heeled background, live in a grand house and mix with the upper set, but give a man or his spouse one drink too many and it can turn anyone into a yobbo.

I turn into the Walmsley-Brown driveway and pull into a small parking area inside the entrance gate. The vague outline of the van is just visible, still parked at the bottom of the drive. And that eliminates one major concern: Herbie and the lads are still sticking in there.

Although the combined elements of rain-swept windscreen and murky gloom are restricting my visibility, I can see that the walk-on tailboard is still lowered and the van appears to be nearly full. Whatever other shenanigans have been going on during the course of the day, the lads appear to have achieved what needs to be done within a pretty normal time-scale. So why are the Walmsley-Browns pressing all the wrong buttons?

I view the scene from the comfort of the car, noting that the large oak front door is slightly ajar. A faint chink of light is emanating from inside, casting its dull reflected light onto the front steps. But there's no sign of the customers. If I can nobble Herbie before meeting the Walmsley-Browns, he'll be able to give me an up-to-date analysis of the situation so I know what to expect.

Steeling myself for what's to come, I extract myself from the car and approach the tailboard of the van. Herbie and the lads are ensconced in the back of the van, sheltered from the worst of the elements. Barely visible, their presence is evident due to the red pinheads of three cigarette ends, glowing in the murky twilight like fireflies. As the lads puff away, wind-swept streams of smoke swirl and drift around the van, before dissipating into the night sky.

Although they must have seen my arrival, there's been no discernible reaction to my presence. I find that strange, and also annoying. I'd have thought they'd be on their feet, to welcome me with open arms or to get their grievances off their chests. Instead, they stare vacantly into space, silent, the only movement being that of cigarettes to mouths. Dejected and bedraggled, they are not the most cheerful-looking bunch of bunny rabbits I've seen gathered in the back of a removal van.

I step into the shelter of the van, my heart not really up to the task ahead. 'Hi, lads,' I cry heartily, trying hard to convey a feeling of cheer and optimism. My greeting is received in silence and with blank looks. Dummies in a shopkeeper's window would have more life.

This passive reaction has the immediate effect of winding me up. I'm only here because Herbie asked me to come. He's supposed to be the bloody captain of the ship, so why the hell is he not taking full control as a good captain should?

A deep well of anger bubbles under the surface of my external calm. That sums up my prevailing mood: from Mr Positive to Mr Angry in the time it takes to fart.

I bite my tongue and commit to say nothing that might exacerbate the problem.

Instead, I direct my attention to Herbie, who looks like he's sitting on the edge of a razor blade, his lips drawn as tight as an arsehole undergoing a colonoscopy. Jim and Kev look like they're the ones administering it. They all continue to puff on their fags, giving me the silent treatment and regarding me like I've escaped from the local asylum. I wrinkle my nose in disgust. Being a converted non-smoker – thirty years or so it's been since my last cancer stick delivered its toxins into my lungs – I do my utmost at every opportunity to persuade the lads to give up smoking, to no avail. But I don't think today is a day for sermonising. Not unless I want three lit cigarettes stuck up my backside.

I scan the surrounding area to ensure the Walmsley-Browns are nowhere within hearing distance. The lads' choice of language can be colourful and I don't want an already fraught situation made worse because of a few ill-chosen words.

Satisfied the area is clear, I clasp my hands in front of me, clear my throat and address Herbie, my tone conciliatory. 'Alice tells me you're having further problems, Herbie. I don't know whether you're aware of it or not, but the old boy has been on the phone again, half an hour ago, expressing more dissatisfaction with you and the lads.'

There's an immediate change in Herbie's demeanour. If his face represented a weather pattern, thunder and lightning would be flashing across his countenance. He's about to respond, but I stop him in his tracks. 'Hold on to your reins a moment, Herbie, let me finish. I know this is going to sound a bit daft, but according to Alice, he's now complaining you and the lads have been going too fast for them, causing them hassle. They're in a bit of a tizz and, to be blunt, the way things are turning out, I'm worried they may well renege on payment of their bill.

'So, in your opinion, Herbie, what do you think the problem is?'

Herbie, Jim and Kev simultaneously become extremely animated, each sounding off to such an extent I find it difficult to understand what one or the other is saying.

My worst fears are also realised. Amid the harangue directed at me, profanity and swearing punctuates the air, delivered at a level to be heard a hundred yards away.

I glance furtively over my shoulder to check that no-one has appeared at the front door then hold my arms up at shoulder level, the palms of my hands facing the lads. 'Whoah, lads,' I plead, my own voice raised higher than necessary. 'I surrender. Now can you hold on a minute? And for Christ's sake, can you watch your language and keep the noise down a bit?'

I'm immune to the fact I've just added to the level of profanity, instead gaining some small satisfaction when the harangue stops as quickly as it started. As Commandeer-in-Chief I don't always find my troops so responsive. 'Herbie, you're foreman. What the hell's going on? And can we do without the bloody expletives please?'

Herbie needs little encouragement. His face is twisted in a grotesque mask of pure anger. 'Walmsley is pissed as a newt, Frank. That's the problem, pure and simple. And his missus isn't in much better shape. I tell you, Frank, since we spoke on the phone, they've been hitting the booze hard. They've got to be alcoholics the way they're knocking it back.'

He pauses as he takes a deep breath, followed by a long drag of his rapidly diminishing cigarette. As supporting players in the drama, Jim and Kev are both nodding their heads vigorously, puffs of smoke exiting from mouths and nostrils.

'We thought everything was going hunky-dory, apart from the weather, that is,' Herbie snarls, his lips curling. 'But after lunch, well, I tell you, Frank, that's when the shit really hit the fan. They've both been a right pain in the arse, though she seems to be the one that's pulling his strings. She's done nothing but moan all afternoon. First, she wasn't happy with the way we were getting a bed down the stairs. Just stood there watching us with a drink in her hand and trying to tell us how to do it. How long have I been doing this job? I mean to say, would she tell a bloody plumber how to fit a new washer on a tap? No, she bloody wouldn't, or else she'd be liable to get it stuffed up her pipes.

'Then she was moaning because she needed a cardigan from one of the boxes we'd already taken out to the van. This was after she'd already given Jim the go-ahead to pack it, said she didn't need it. Not only did I have to shift some of the furniture that was already loaded in order to find the right box, but we're now going to have to repack the bloody box. She couldn't bother her fat arse to do it herself.

'I tell you, Frank, what with the amount they're drinking, and all that pissing about, they're not only getting more and more pissed, but are totally pissing us off. And not even so much as a cup of tea all bloody day. Isn't that right, lads?'

With these further expletive-laden observations from Herbie echoing around the back of the van, I wince and furtively check over my shoulder to ensure the Walmsley-Browns are still out of the action zone. If they have heard Herbie's appraisal of the situation, it's not going to make my task any easier. There's quite a few hundred quid at stake here, not to mention the long-term reputation of A to Z Removals.

Jim and Kev are shaking their heads vigorously like marionettes on a string. They remind me of those little nodding dogs you see in the back-window shelf of a car. Happy for Herbie to be their mouthpiece, they are now keeping any opinions they may have on the matter to themselves.

Having drawn sufficient breath to take two long drags on his cigarette, he continues to bare his soul. Nothing, or no-one, is going to stop him getting this off his chest. 'I'm telling you, Frank, if you hadn't come over now, the lads and I were going to close up the back of the van and get straight back to the yard. We've had it up to here.' He holds his hand up to the level of his neck to demonstrate the point. 'I don't want to come back tomorrow, then have to go through the same sort of shit.'

With this final pronouncement, he stands up, takes one last drag then tosses the butt-end on to the van floor. He proceeds to give it a good mashing under his left foot before resuming his seat on the edge of a concrete flowerpot.

If I'm interpreting this action correctly, it's the Walmsley-Browns who have just been pulverised under his size tens.

Glancing back towards the doorway, I'm thinking it's strange there's been no sight or sound of the customers. Given the attention they've focused on the crew during the day, you'd think one of them would have been out here to establish why work has come to a standstill.

I turn my attention to Herbie. 'Where are they now, the customers?'

He cups his hands round the end of a match as he attempts to light another cigarette, then thinks for a moment before replying. 'Frank, I haven't got a bloody clue, and I don't give a toss either.' His face is momentarily obscured by a cloud of smoke. 'The last time I saw the old dear she was heading up the stairs, three steps up, two steps down, she was. If there hadn't been a handrail for her to hold onto, she would have ended up arse-over-heels at the bottom of the stairs. I haven't seen her since, for the first time

this afternoon, thank Christ.'

'And what about the old boy? Any ideas where I might find him?'

'The last I saw him he was in the kitchen pouring himself another beer. With a bit of luck, the miserable sod will have drowned in it.' As he runs out of steam and draws on his fag, his his cheeks momentarily collapse like the bag of a switched-off vacuum cleaner.

'Right, lads,' I say purposefully, reluctantly stepping off the wet tailboard. 'Sit tight and have another fag while I see what's going on. I'll give you the nod when I've got things sorted out.'

With a grunt from Herbie to send me on my way, I pull my three-in-one collar around my neck, take a deep breath then crunch my way over the water-logged gravel towards the faint glow of the front entrance. With each step, the fierce cold wind, combined with the sheeting rain threatens to sweep me off my feet.

Apprehensive, I climb the five steps to the front door, feeling like a lamb being led to the slaughter.

Chapter twenty-eight

IT'S WITH A DEEP SENSE of foreboding that I find myself standing on the Walmsley-Browns' doorstep. Unfortunately, there's no porch to provide protection from the freezing rain, which continues to pelt down.

Cold, wet and miserable, I ring the doorbell then flex my facial muscles in readiness for an appearance. The thin strip of light filtering through the gap between door and door jamb casts a faint but welcoming glow onto the doorstep, inviting me to enter. But I'm reluctant to do that without an express invitation. Daft really, considering my lads have been traipsing in and out all day. But I was brought up to have respect for other people's property.

There's been no immediate response. Fidgeting from foot to foot, I press the bell firmly with one freezing finger. The resonance of the bell can be heard deep within the bowels of the house. And if I can hear it, why can't the Walmsley-Browns?

I wait another half a minute then, frustrated and impatient to be under cover, slowly push the oak door fully open. The light from inside spills outside, transforming the tumultuous, heavy raindrops bouncing off the steps into sparkling clusters of tiny fragmented diamonds.

But there's no sign or sound of life inside. Despite feeling like I've been trampled by a herd of wild elephants, I'm trying to follow the Polkadot formula and remain positive.

Having waited longer than necessary to observe the niceties of protocol, I hesitantly enter the hallway. The rain runs off my head and down my three-in-one before dripping onto the carpeted floor, creating a series of small, grey, damp splotches. But I'm beyond caring.

Within the hallway, the indistinct glow emanating downwards from the single ceiling light bulb is creating a spooky atmosphere straight out of a Stephen King horror movie, the gloomy ambience exacerbated by the absence of furniture, pictures or artefacts.

I sneak a quick peek over my shoulder. The three lads are still visible in the deteriorating light, perched in the same positions. They are gazing in my direction with a healthy degree of scepticism, three small circles of orange glowing intermittently in the dark as they continue to clog up their respiratory systems.

Becoming increasingly agitated, I stride purposefully to the bottom of the stairway, slant my head backwards then commence to exercise my vocal cords. 'Helll-loooo,' I call out loudly. 'Is anyone at home?'

My voice echoes down the hall, up the stairs and around the house before silence settles.

'Heeellllloooo,' I shout once more. 'Mr and Mrs Walmsley-Brownnnn, is anyone there?'

Recalling Herbie's observation about the old dear struggling to get up the stairs, and that she could be the chief string-puller, I commence to climb the stairs, bellowing her name as I go. 'Mrs Walmsley-Brown, helllooo. It's Frank Tipple from your removal company.'

My voice rebounds around the stairwell, my head cocked to the side like a sparrow that's detected a worm. But still there's nothing. I reach the first floor landing and pause to get my bearings.

As my eyes adjust to the dim light, the vague outlines of five white doors take shape along a corridor to my left. All are firmly closed, with no chinks of light to indicate a human presence. Yet she's got to be in one of these rooms. Taking a deep breath, I begin to tread cautiously along the dark corridor. The distorted shadow of my body, cast by the downstairs light, follows me slowly along the wall. It reminds me of my childhood fear of the dark, which, irrational as it seems, hasn't diminished much over the years.

I instinctively pull my three-in-one closer around me for protection. Not that that will do any good if one of Walmsley-Brown's ancestors pops out and hits me over the head with a mallet.

I reach the first door then knock gently, calling out loudly, 'Heeelll-ooo, Mrs Walmsley-Brown, are you in there?' My ear is pressed tight to the door, listening intently for a response.

'Bollocks to etiquette.' Muttering under my breath, I grip the doorknob and energetically push the door open, causing the inside handle to smack against the wall with a resounding crash, sufficient to waken the dead.

The room is in darkness, suffused only by the dim twilight from outside. Swearing quietly, my fingers trace up and down the wall on the inside of the doorway, searching for a light switch. At last, the room is bathed in the soft light from a solitary bulb, hanging in the centre of the ceiling. I find myself in an empty bedroom, devoid of life and furniture.

Bedroom number two is also empty, except for one box, sitting in a corner. The box is open and various items of clothing lie scattered to the side. Probably the one Herbie had to bring back into the house earlier so she could find her cardigan. Two down, three to go.

Door number three takes me into a bathroom. Fortunately, Mrs Walmsley-Brown isn't occupying either the bath or the loo. It would be embarrassing to catch the old dear with her knickers around her ankles or stark naked and up to her neck in soapsuds.

Room number four is also empty and with only one room left to explore, I'm beginning to think that she has found her way back downstairs when – bingo – I strike gold. On opening door number five and switching on the light, I see the main bedroom is empty of all furniture with the exception of a king-size bed.

But spread-eagled on her back across the middle of the bed like a beached whale, snoring loudly, and in a state of undress, is Mrs Walmsley-Brown. I know it's not her husband because he wouldn't be wearing old-fashioned knickers like these. They're large enough to grace the backside of a hippopotamus and balloon out from under her dress like two parachutes manufactured from an old potato sack. Definitely not an item purchased at an Ann Summers party.

She's not a pretty sight, sufficiently grotesque to make a lesser man take the pledge forthwith. Vivid streaks of blue-tinged eye mascara are smeared down both cheeks and her red lipstick is smudged around her mouth like tomato ketchup round the edge of a dinner plate. Her mouth is a wide, open cavern, with trickles of saliva drooling down the side of her chin onto the pillow.

Her clothing is in a state of disarray. A fawn woollen cardigan and white cotton blouse have been partially removed, exposing a bra with cups big enough to contain two large water-melons.

As if the drooling clown's face, the gigantic bra and the huge bloomers aren't enough for sore eyes, her black net stockings – rather inappropriate for a woman of her mature years and physique – are rolled down to her ankles, revealing chubby thighs, and legs speckled with lumpy clots of varicose veins. The toes of one shoe-less foot are pointing upwards to the ceiling like five fat frankfurters.

The odour of stale booze is permeating the room. Half-empty bottles of Bacardi and Coca-Cola, tops removed, are sitting on the bedside table, perilously close to the edge.

Despite the evidence of my own eyes, I'm finding it hard to take in the spectacle facing me. My God, if she'd been having a cigarette in bed, the house would have gone up in flames. She'd have been barbecued to a cinder. And there'd have been enough ash from that frame of hers to fertilise the whole garden.

Neither the bedroom light shining directly into her face nor my presence has disturbed her. It's unlikely that a detonation of Semtex would awaken her. It's no wonder she didn't hear me shouting.

Despite everything, I can't help but feel a small stab of pity that the lady of the house could demean herself in such a manner. If she could only see herself, that would surely be sufficient to put her on the straight and narrow for now and forever.

If only I'd brought my camera. A few candid shots of this could prove useful in the event of a dispute regarding my removal charges, especially if it becomes necessary to pursue payment through the small claims court. Shaking my head, I switch off the light and exit the bedroom, pulling the door shut quietly behind me. There's only one option left: to find the master of the house, then pray he'll be in better condition than his missus.

Moral outrage burning inside me, I quickly retrace my steps downstairs and enter the kitchen. My eyes mist over in amazement as I take in the display of alcohol scattered around the worktops. And here's me worried about my intake.

There's a half-empty bottle of Gordon's gin next to two glasses, both empty. Further down the worktop is a partly-finished bottle of Bell's whisky, an empty bottle of Jacob's Creek red wine, a half-empty bottle of Chardonnay, and two wine glasses. A can of lager is lying on the floor.

I lick my lips. The temptation to help myself to a medicinal shot of Bell's at the Walmsley-Brown's expense is strong. A little booster would do me all the good in the world and steel me for the meeting to come.

I manage to contain myself. Now's not the time. Not until the business of the day is completed. And not until I get home and can settle down to enjoy it.

In a fit of pique, and without any consideration for the condition of my big toe, I give the can on the floor a hard kick, sending it spinning along the floor and pinging against a floor cupboard. Leaving the can where it is on the lager-mottled floor, I rapidly and methodically check the rest of the ground floor, with no success.

Unless he has left the property altogether, without Herbie being aware of it, he's got to be somewhere close to hand. 'Where the bleeding hell are you, you wanker?' I bellow along the length of the hall, my frustration getting the better of me. The only response is my echo, and perhaps that's for the best.

In foul mood, I retrace my steps to the front door, my heart pumping faster than can be good for my long-term survival. But Herbie's going to have to put his thinking cap on, because I'm fast running out of ideas.

Kev and Jim are now propping up the sides of the van, barely sheltered from the elements. Herbie is still sitting on the edge of the flower pot, his head and shoulders bowed, his hands stuffed in his trouser pockets, his feet scuffing the floor of the van. Their cigarettes extinguished, the lads look fed-up to the back teeth.

As they spot me coming through the door, I detect a quickening of their interest.

'She's upstairs, lying on the bed,' I advise them curtly, stepping smartly onto the back of the van to avoid the worst of the rain. 'Fast asleep, she is. And just like you said, Herbie, pissed as a newt. Best to let her sleep till morning. But I'm still trying to find him. Herbie, are you sure he hasn't gone off to the shops or something?'

'I doubt it,' replies Herbie testily. 'He was around about ten minutes before you arrived. We'd have noticed if he'd come out the front door. Anyway, his car is still in the garage and he's so pissed I doubt if he could walk out the front gate, never mind drive out. Have you been around the back? Maybe he's in the shed?'

Why would he be in the shed in this weather? But he's certainly not indoors. Maybe he's got a secret stash of alcohol hidden there. Having one for the road, so to speak. 'Okay, lads, I'm really sorry about all this, but hold tight while I see if I can find him. Have another ciggie and I'll be back in a few minutes.'

I limp towards the decorative black wrought-iron gate leading towards the rear of the property. Swearing under my breath, I push open the gate then, mindful of potential obstacles, head along the narrow concrete path and round the side of the property towards the shed. My last-chance saloon.

Chapter twenty-nine

A SECURITY LIGHT is activated to the side of the house, helping me to see where I'm going. I've covered fifteen feet leading to the rear when my attention is drawn to a sudden movement up ahead. And that's when I finally spot him.

He's standing outside the kitchen door, about twenty feet down the path, his silhouette highlighted by the faint yellow glow from the rear kitchen windows. A small overhead lean-to with corrugated roofing is affording him minimal protection from the elements.

Relieved to have finally pinned him down, I quickly step sideways into a dark corner. As his wife originally showed me round the property, it makes sense to try and get some insight into the type of man I'm going to be dealing with.

But I could kick myself. Only two minutes ago, when I was in the kitchen, we were within three feet of each other, with only the door's wood panelling separating us.

Keyed up, I observe him closely, my eyes slowly becoming accustomed to the darkness. Facing away from me, his gaze is directed across his back patio towards a small privet hedge, the boundary with his neighbour. The hedge is solid enough to keep the neighbour's dogs out, but not high or dense enough to ensure total privacy. Whatever he's looking at, it's obvious he hasn't heard my approach.

He's about my age, but tall and heavily built, with a large protruding stomach. His bare head is exposed to the elements and his grey strands of hair are being buffeted by the wind. He is sparingly but neatly dressed in a blue-striped shirt, tie, black flannels and black leather shoes. No hat, no jacket, no overcoat. Apart from the lack of sensible clothing, everything about him appears normal. If Herbie hadn't already primed me about the booze consumed, and if I hadn't seen his missus and the evidence for myself, I'd have been hard put to say anything was amiss.

But it's apparent that he's not steady on his feet. He is swaying slightly from side to side, his movement like that of a stalk of wheat ruffled by a mild wind. He now executes four shuffling steps that take him left, right, then back to his starting point. If I didn't know better, I'd say he was practising his dance steps for the rumba.

He raises an unsteady hand to his face and the tip of a cigarette glows in the darkness. A cloud of pale-grey smoke suddenly shoots from his mouth like steam from a boiling kettle, to be instantly whipped away by the wind.

I steel myself for action, contorting my face with a loony rictus grin. 'Afternoon, Mr Walmsley-Brown,' I say loudly, announcing my arrival in a cheerful voice.

My unexpected entrance and the sudden sound of my voice cause him to move away from the security of the door. He involuntarily takes two steps sideways before lurching backwards against the wall of the house. He stabilises himself by splaying both legs, like he's preparing to evacuate his bladder.

Squeezing myself under the limited protection of the lean-to, I look him straight in the eyes, which are bloodshot and glazed. Although he's trying hard to focus, it's difficult to know if I've got his attention.

I extend the Tipple hand of welcome and adopt the most conciliatory tone I can muster. 'Sorry to startle you, Mr Walmsley-Brown. It's Frank Tipple, from A to Z Removals. I've been all through the house trying to find you. Thought I'd check that everything is going all right with the move.'

He ignores my outstretched hand and looks at me like I've just landed from outer space, an expression of incomprehension on his face. Instead, he takes a long pull on his cigarette, all the while looking at me blankly.

Jane would recognise that look. She's seen it on my face often enough, after I've had one too many and don't know whether I'm coming or going.

Drink or no drink, genuine complaint or not, the miserable bugger should at least have the basic decency to be sociable. Biting hard on my bottom lip, I strive to resurrect the Polkadot philosophy. Positive thinking could still win the day. At that moment, whether by accident or design, he directs a full blast of smoke straight into my face.

I've a mind to forcibly remove his cigarette and shove it up his nostril. But with nearly fifteen hundred quid at stake, it's essential to retain my composure.

'Mr Walmsley-Brown, it's Frank Tipple, from A to Z Removals,' I repeat, raising my voice to counter the noise of wind and rain. I'm now close enough to give him a large kiss or a Glasgow handshake, should the desire take me. The way things are going, I'm inclined to the latter.

Apart from an odd grunting sound, he remains infuriatingly silent, his expressionless eyes locked on God knows what. Instead, he takes another long drag of his cigarette then exhales with a loud whoosh, enveloping me once again in a cloud of smoke.

Annoyed, I turn my head to the side, holding my breath, then make another attempt to open up dialogue. 'Mr Walmsley-Brown,' I cry, shouting over the noise of the wind. 'It's Frank Tipple. We spoke on the telephone this morning. I've just come over to check everything is going all right with your removal. I understand you phoned again this afternoon.'

For the first time since coming face to face, I detect an encouraging sign of recognition. The pupils of his eyes focus on me and the cigarette is momentarily forgotten, dangling loosely by his side. He strives to draw in raindrops from his lips, which then move in and out in a rapid kissing action, accompanied by a sucking sound as he attempts to formulate a reply. Unfortunately, his mouth is not synchronised with his brain.

Instead, his mouth closes and he shoots me a look of undiluted disdain, like I've just offered him a time-share in Siberia. He then slowly and deliberately raises the cigarette to his face, checks the butt closely to see what remains, then, satisfied he's had value for money, carelessly flicks it past my shoulder onto the patio, at which point he loses his balance. Launching into his rumba routine, he takes a couple of tentative steps in my direction, his hands clasping at thin air as they seek solid support.

I instinctively grasp him firmly by the upper arms, and he grabs my arms in a vice-like grip, sufficiently hard to make me wince. With his height, weight and momentum threatening to bring us both clattering to the ground, we wrestle, like two drunken sailors doing a fan dance.

We eventually stabilise each other, a couple of yards away from the protection of the lean-to, before I roughly guide him backwards to the sanctuary of the door. He lolls drunkenly against the door, a bemused expression on his face, then surprises me by finally responding.

'Ah, yesh, Mishter Tizzle,' he slurs, his lips pursing and sucking like a newborn baby on its mummy's tit. 'Yesh, indeed, Hervie's bosh from the removal company.'

There is a pregnant pause whilst he pulls a crushed cigarette packet and matches from his trouser pocket. There follows a performance worthy of a third-rate comic as he attempts to light up. Three aborted efforts later, he triumphantly waves the cigarette in front of my face before taking a long, slow drag. In expectation of an exhalation of smoke, I avert my head.

'Ah yesh, Mishter Tizzle, Hervie's bosh,' he repeats, unsteady on his feet. 'Ish the removal going shwell, you ask?' He drags, holds his breath then exhales. Again I avert my head. 'Shwell now, Mishter Tizzle, in ansher to your queschton, I'd have to shay no, ish not going shwell. In fact, I'd haf to shay thash I'm not shathisfied one little bit.' Before I can take evasive action, he blows a cloud of smoke in my face.

The ignorant bastard. I give him my most poisonous look, then take a step forward and project my face a foot away from his.

'So what's the big problem then?' I bark, my lips curled in a snarl. 'From what I can see, the men seem to have done an extremely efficient job so far, and, I must say, under the most difficult of circumstances.'

He curls his lips and looks at me like I've just told him his fly is open and his manhood exposed to the public at large. His head commences to bob from side to side in an exaggerated and argumentative manner and he takes an unsteady step towards me. We are now eyeball to eyeball. 'Shwell, Mishter Tizzle,' he slurs, waving his cigarette end in front of my face. 'If you think thash your men were effishent, *hic*, then you are talking crap. And thash ish wash they are, crap. Yesh, thash is it. Crap, *hic*, like ash in shit, *hic*, S-H-I-T. Do you undershtand, Tizzle?'

With that less than enlightening pronouncement, he exhales another lungful of smoke directly into my face.

Incandescent with rage, I finally snap. This arsehole, so drunk he can hardly stand on his own two feet, not only has the nerve to denigrate my crew without good reason, but talks to me like I've just been dragged up from the frigging sewers. On top of that, he's determined to suffocate me with his bloody cigarette smoke. 'Fuck that for a bunch of roses,' I cry out to Walmsley-Brown and the world at large, my earlier exhortations to the lads a thing of the past.

Not even the presence of Polkadot with his positive thinking could have kept the lid on this steaming cauldron.

Chapter thirty

AS HE PROVOKES my verbal declaration of intent, I instinctively move toward him, my left foot stepping directly onto his right foot, effectively pinning him to the spot. At the same time, I grab him aggressively by his shirt front, both hands firmly gripping the thin, wet cotton material. As a pained, perplexed expression spreads across his sozzled countenance, I realise that I've not only got hold of his shirt, but also his nipples. And I'm squeezing hard.

From there on in, it's downhill all the way. My forward momentum, allied to his inability to take evasive action, propels me up against him.

Still holding onto his shirt and nipples, I make a crushing contact with his protruding stomach. The impact bounces him away from the safety of the door, causing him to lose his balance. He swivels on his feet, then back-pedals unsteadily in the direction of the privet fence, his arms flapping either side of his head like he's just walked into a wasp's nest.

Had I any sense, I'd have released my hold on his overweight frame there and then. But despite my anger, the last thing on my mind was to have him bash his brains on the patio tiles. Instead, I propel myself forward in tandem with his backward movement, my nipple-crunching hands still holding onto his breasts like limpet mines to the hull of a ship.

I've little doubt that neighbours would have been astonished by the whole spectacle. There we are, two grown men, performing a *pas de deux* and simulating the mating ritual of two demented ducks dancing on water. This routine takes us at an erratic speed and direction across the patio until Walmsley-Brown backs into the privet hedge, with yours truly still holding onto him like a miser to his last penny.

If the hedge had been higher and denser, then both of us would have come to a full stop, still in an upright position and able to regain some degree of decorum from the proceedings.

Unfortunately, the delicate branches are insufficient to support his overweight frame and he topples backwards through it. He crashes down onto the lawn of the neighbouring garden, letting out a short, loud grunt as his breath whooshes from his body like air from a burst balloon. Unfortunately, that's not the only calamity to befall him.

Still firmly holding onto his shirt front, I follow him through the hedge. As I collapse on top of him, my right knee bangs him fair and square on his privates. Another drawn-out groan escapes his lips, giving me a moment of satisfaction, which is short-lived.

As my knee makes contact with his testicles, his left knee jerks upwards in a reflex action, making contact with my own unprotected jewels. My left testicle takes the full force of his solid kneecap. 'Aaarrggh, my bollocks!' I cry out in pain as tears spring to my eyes and I curse the God that has permitted this latest degradation. I also curse Walmsley-Brown. He's had the benefit of an alcoholic anaesthetic to lessen the pain. I haven't had that luxury.

The soaking wet fabric of my trouser bottoms is clinging to my legs like an ice-cold poultice, and I'm only thankful that my three-in-one is affording some protection to my upper body. But the only protection Walmsley-Brown has is me, and that's to the front of his body. What the freezing, rain-soaked, muddy lawn is doing to his back, I hate to think. Fighting to regain my composure, I lie spread-eagled on top of him, eyeball-to-eyeball, like a bedraggled, gay, geriatric lover. But it's not a comfortable position to be in. His breath stinks like putrid meat marinated in nicotine and stale beer. It's as much as I can do not to throw up all over him. Not that that would do him any favours, but it might well relieve me of the ongoing turmoil caused by Sammy's vegetarian special.

Concerned for his welfare, I gaze into his eyes, which are registering signs of shock, bewilderment, confusion and pain. He looks like a rabbit caught in the headlights of a car.

From where I'm lying, things don't look good in the customer relations department. He's expressed dissatisfaction with the quality of service he's received, I've inadvertently assaulted him, and to cap it all, he's suffering the indignity and misery of being straddled by his removals contractor.

Now the chance of him coughing up payment tomorrow is remote. But more than ever, I'm determined not to be railroaded, or permit him or his wife to short-change me as a consequence of *their* inadequacies. And I still have one ace in the pack to play.

I inspect his eyes closely to ensure he's still in the land of the living. He returns my gaze, but says nothing, his eyes like two large, red-tinted marbles. Satisfied that he's reasonably cognisant, I position my face directly over his, with only six inches separating the tips of our noses.

'Right then, Mr Walmsley-Brown, sir,' I begin, courteous to the last and enunciating each word as clearly as possible. Raindrops stream off the top and sides of my head and onto Walmsley-Brown, adding to his discomfort. 'Can you hear me?'

His marble eyes roll slightly in the sockets as he attempts to focus. A couple of moments elapse before he responds. His tone is subdued, hesitant and dispirited, with no indication of the aggression and bombast of earlier. 'Yesh, Mishter Tizzle, but can you get off me, pleash?'

'All in good time, sir,' I reply politely. This is one bargaining position I have no intention of losing any time soon. 'Now, Mr Walmsley-Brown, can I suggest you listen very carefully to what I'm about to say? But first, I need to be certain you are receiving me loud and clear. Do you understand?'

After a momentary hesitation, he whispers his reply, 'Yesh, Mishter Tizzle, I understhand.' He peers myopically into my face, the combination of alcohol and rain blurring his vision. The initial shock of my assault has subsided and there are now only signs of uncertainty and confusion. If it weren't for what had gone before, I'd feel sorry for the poor bugger and roll off.

'That's excellent, sir,' I reply, self-satisfied, like I'd just successfully potty-trained a recalcitrant child. 'Firstly, regarding your earlier comments about my removal men, I want to make it perfectly clear that there is only one piece of crap in the immediate vicinity, and I happen to be lying on it at this moment.'

I shift my body slightly to ease the needles and pins developing in my arms. 'Secondly, sir,' I continue, relentlessly spelling out my message. 'Given the condition you and your wife are in, I don't believe either of you are in any position to comment on the deficiencies of anyone.

'And lastly, may I take this opportunity to remind you that my name is Tipple. Not Tizzle, or Tiddle, or Tissle. But Tipple. T.I.P.P.L.E. I would very much appreciate it if you would, in future, be good enough to address me by my long-held family name.'

In recognition that he might be having some difficulty drawing breath, I slightly raise my body, using my elbows as levers, then again scrutinise him closely. The possibility that he could have a heart seizure or develop some other fatal malaise never enters my mind. Revenge is sweet and blind.

'Yesh, Mr Tipple,' he replies after a slight hesitation. 'I understand.'

I'm now reassured he's understanding me loud and clear – because the important part is about to come. If he doesn't get this, all my efforts to secure my removal charge will have been in vain.

'Good, I'm pleased to hear that,' I answer encouragingly, the weight of my body holding him immobile on the soaked earth. 'I won't detain you much longer,' I say, sugar-sweetly, my innate goodwill still palpable despite the bruising it's taken.

'I now wish to discuss payment of your removal charges. As you are probably aware, our original contract terms require you to give my foreman, Herbie, a cheque on completion of your removal tomorrow, when you are satisfied with the level of service you have obtained.

'I now have to inform you that a small but important change is required to our earlier arrangement, due to the unfortunate circumstances that have taken place over the course of today, for which both you and your wife must take full responsibility.

'So here's the new deal.' I pause for effect. 'Tomorrow morning, while my crew are loading the remainder of your goods, I will expect you to go to your bank and draw out your removal charge of fourteen hundred and seventy six pounds in cash. Not a cheque, but cash, in pound notes. Do you understand?'

To emphasise my point, I adjust my elbows and apply a little downward pressure on his chest. Five or six seconds elapse. 'Yes'h, Mr Tipple, you want me to draw my removal charge in cash,' he repeats, parrot-fashion, as he gazes at me intently. He is very, very subdued.

'Good,' I reply, encouraged by the clarity of his response. 'When you get back from the bank I will be waiting for you here, and will expect you to place that total amount of money in my sticky little hands. I will then give you a receipt, following which my crew will be instructed to proceed to Woodstock to offload your goods.

'However, if by tomorrow morning you do not pay me in full, in cash, it will be necessary for me to instruct the crew to take your goods to a storage depot. There we will hold them until such time as I do receive a full cash payment. In addition, you will be charged at the relevant weekly rate for storage, plus a further sum for the cost of having to bring your goods into and out of store.

'Now, Mr Walmsley-Brown, would you like me to repeat what I've just said?'

It crosses my mind that Walmsley-Brown could decide to challenge the legality of my revised contract of payment. He and his missus would undoubtedly turn up at court sober, it would be their word against mine, and there'd be no tangible evidence to justify my changing payment terms. Although the testimony of the lads could swing it my way, their presence would mean time off on full pay, plus the potential loss of business due to the unavailability of one crew for a day. But now's not the time for faint hearts, liberal thoughts or legal niceties. Practical, no-nonsense solutions are required for this particular dispute. And to my mind, it's a fair bet that the Walmsley-Browns won't want to be deprived of their furniture and effects for the many weeks or months it would take to resolve the matter.

With the cold and damp really beginning to kick in, a shudder runs through Walmsley-Brown's body before he is able to speak. His voice is a whimper and barely audible against the howling wind and rain. 'Can you pleash get off me? I'm getting very cold and wet and ish difficult to breathe.'

His face has taken on a grey hue and his breathing comes in short, shallow pants. His eyelids droop, close then slowly open. Then close. And stay closed.

Alarmed, I give his cheeks a gentle tap with the palms of my hands. To my relief, his eyelids rise and he looks directly into my face.

'Mr Walmsley-Brown, did you hear and understand what I just said? And if so, can you repeat it for me, please?' I ask, thankful he's still in the land of the living.

There is a pregnant silence whilst he collects his addled thoughts. 'Okay, Mr Tipple, you are coming back in the morning,' he replies hesitantly then pauses to organise his thoughts. 'You want me to go to the bank, draw the money I owe you in cash. C.A.S.H.' Here he spells out the word painfully slowly. 'And then give it to you tomorrow morning. Only then will you give your men the all-clear to deliver my furniture. Now can you pleash get off me?'

All my recent pent-up anger immediately dissipates, replaced by a feeling of responsibility and benevolence towards this sad old man lying in the mud. As far as I'm concerned, the slate is now clean.

I struggle to my feet then proffer my hand to help him up. I manage to get him upright and we stand face to face, holding onto each other like long-lost brothers. My body is racked by a series of shivers and my teeth are chattering uncontrollably. But with no overcoat or jacket to protect him, it strikes me that Walmsley-Brown must be in a worse condition.

From the corner of my eye, I detect movement in the subdued light coming from the side of the house. Concerned that the police might have been alerted to the dust-up, I screw up my eyes and peer through the blanket of rain to determine who has joined us.

But it's Herbie, Jim and Kev, three sets of eyes staring round the corner of the garage. How long they've been watching the proceedings, I don't know. I'm only glad it's them and not some third party that's been observing the brouhaha that's just taken place.

Ignoring the lads, I return my attention to Walmsley-Brown. He has taken root on the spot, swaying on his feet and looking blankly around him like he's searching for someone to guide him out of the mire. It's obvious he's incapable of making any immediate decisions. If he's to survive this afternoon's shenanigans, he's going to need a prod up the backside. 'Right, sir,' I say, more brightly than I feel. 'Now that we have successfully sorted out our little differences, I'll bid you goodbye until tomorrow morning. May I suggest you go back inside, have a hot bath and a change of clothes, then join your wife, who is having a much needed kip in the bedroom? The lads can stop work now and do the rest in the morning.'

I take him by the arm and gently guide him across the patio, past the staring crew, down the path, through the wrought-iron gate then into the safety of the hallway. The three lads follow me like they're escorting royalty. Satisfied he's capable of standing on his own two feet, I direct him towards the bottom of the stairs, give him a gentle push then watch as he slowly and laboriously begins to climb, pulling himself up by the handrail.

'Bye for now,' I call after him, like nothing untoward has just occurred. 'I'll see you at ten-thirty in the morning, then.'

There's no reply and he disappears from sight along the first-floor corridor.

Satisfied there's nothing more to be done, I turn on my heels, close the front door behind me and make my way to the back of the van, where the lads have congregated.

Their attitude has changed. Privy to what went on around the back, they are now regarding me with a certain degree of respect. It'll be the only occasion they'll have seen me uphold the integrity of the firm and its employees in that particular manner.

'Right, Herbie, we're all sorted out,' I say, as if everything that just happened has been a normal, routine occurrence. 'You shouldn't have any further problems. Shut up shop now. I'll be back with you in the morning to make sure all's well that ends well. All right, lads? See you in the morning, then. And keep smiling.' With that, I step smartly off the back of the tailboard and head back towards my car with a spring in my step.

'Nice one, Frank,' Herbie calls after me, his face creased with approval. 'We heard and saw most of that. See you tomorrow, and thanks for sticking up for us.'

Praise for the boss, and from Herbie at that. Pretending that I haven't heard him, I walk towards the car with a John Wayne swagger, my chest puffed out. If Polkadot was here now, he'd give me a gold medal.

★ ★ ★

ON ARRIVING at the Walmsley-Browns' doorstep at ten-thirty the next morning, unsure of the reception I'd receive, not only are they sober, but they greet me like a prodigal son, with no adverse comment or reference to the previous day's events. They then pay their total removal charges in cash, up-front, and without my even having to ask.

As if that isn't a sufficient enough conversion to be going on with, they then go out of their way to treat the lads splendidly, supplying teas and coffees throughout the day and with nary a word of complaint. To put the icing on the cake, they send the crew on their way with the palms of their hands well and truly greased. All in all, a happy ending to a woeful litany of events.

A couple of days after the event, when I had an overwhelming compulsion to recount the whole unfortunate experience to Jane, I was complaining at length about the Walmsley-Browns' lack of restraint in the drinks department, reliving each moment with an exaggerated display of arm waving and histrionics. When my long-winded, theatrical performance was concluded, she remained deep in thought for a few moments then, looking me straight in the eye, took both my hands in hers, squeezed them and delivered what she believed to be a gentle admonishment.

'Frank, dear,' she said in a calm voice, her face brimming with the innate authority of someone who knows she holds the levers of common sense. When I saw that expression on her face and heard the word 'dear', I realised she was about to dish out a reproach of epic proportions.

'Frank, dear,' she repeated to ensure she had my full attention. 'I have to ask you this: does an elephant that drinks copiously from the water-hole have just cause to castigate the rhinoceros that chooses to sup from that very same pool?'

Well, I have to say that that shut me up good and proper. But where that piece of Confucian whimsy came from, I've no idea. And it certainly didn't discourage me from sloshing around the water-hole on frequent occasions subsequently.

Chapter thirty-one

I REACH THE SANCTUARY of my car, feeling like I've been shagged by a hundred and one vestal virgins. Behind me I leave an unnatural wall of silence which, in the all-consuming bleakness of winter nightfall, has an eerie, ghostly content. This is suddenly broken as Herbie turns the ignition key of the van, the roar from the diesel engine momentarily drowning out the noise of wind and rain. The lads will be as keen to get home as I am.

I stare blankly through the rain-splattered windscreen into the blackness of beyond. Illogical as it may seem, the physical confrontation with Walmsley-Brown has been the best possible antidote to the awful day now behind me. The gloom which has been steadily gnawing away at my soul has been released in one fell swoop by this single incident. I'm now drained of all but one emotion: an overwhelming sense of relief.

As Herbie manoeuvres the van down the driveway towards the exit, the glare of headlights shakes me from my stupor.

'Come on, Frank, get your arse in gear,' I muse, switching on the car ignition and heater. 'You're done for the day, mate. Not one of your better days. And although you've probably lost some customer goodwill along the way, sod it, at least you've retained your self-respect.'

With those enlightening words, I slip the car into gear and ease out into the slush-covered road, the wiper blades working relentlessly to clear the rainfall. In my rear-view mirror, the twin beams from the van follow me through the entrance.

In a compulsive, infantile movement, I whip my loyal steed into a gallop. 'Giddy-up, Trigger!' I cry through the windscreen, slapping the steering wheel with the palm of my right hand, simultaneously stamping hard on the accelerator. The rear wheels spin as the tyre treads cope with the wet surface, then my trusty nag takes off like a bat out of hell towards home.

Twenty minutes later, the front door of my property beckons with love and affection. As I enter the hall, a welcoming warmth envelops me and I silently applaud the benefits of modern central heating. I toss my three-in-one over the back of the Windsor chair, then open the door to the lounge. In the darkness ahead of me, the small but distinctive red light of my answering machine is flashing. And it's not a light that's offering the promise of a hot, steamy sexual encounter.

My heart misses a beat. It's not that the answering machine always brings bad tidings. But seeing it flash as brazenly as an old tart in a whore-house invariably has the same effect that a lighthouse beam must have on the captain of a rudderless ship on a stormy sea. I switch on the lounge light and hesitantly make my way towards the bureau. 'Please, pretty please, no more problems,' I beseech both the answering machine and Him up on high.

Waiting for the first message to activate, my wet pinstripe trousers cling to me like a cold compress. To compound my discomfort, my feet are squelching in my soggy socks and shoes. The skin will surely be as white and wrinkled as an old crone's backside.

These issues are temporarily forgotten as the machine spews its first message. 'Hi Frank, Alice here. Just thought you'd like to know all crews got back safe and sound. All the moves seem to have gone okay, except for Herbie's which you already know about. And to cheer you up, there are three cheques now sitting in your middle drawer, ready to go to the bank tomorrow...'

At this point in the recording there is a pregnant pause. In the background, there's the ominous sound of rustling paper.

'Oh, and Miss McLaughlin phoned to say thanks for a job well done. She's asked us to pass that message on to Billy and Stephen.

'I think that's all, Frank. It's been pretty quiet since you left. Yes, that's it, see you in the morning. Oh, I nearly forgot, one other thing...'

Hypnotised by the slowly spooling tape, I'm rooted to the spot, uptight and strung as tight as a fat lady's girdle. It's still hard for me to accept that Alice is the bearer of only good tidings.

'You better bring your wellies in with you tomorrow, as it's getting a bit waterlogged around the Portakabin. I swear I saw a salmon swimming past, chased by a polar bear. Bye, see you in the morning.'

Jesus, she had me going there. But God bless her sense of humour. Just hope she doesn't give up the day job.

I permit myself to wallow in the good news: three cheques in the bag and everybody happy, except the Walmsley-Browns. And they've been taken care of. Thank you, Alice. Thank you, lads. Thank you, Miss McLaughlin. Thank you, God. Thanks, thanks and thanks.

With a second message to come, a partially-chewed fingernail finds its way into my mouth.

'Hi Frank, it's me?'

I recognise the voice immediately. It's Pete, this morning's absentee.

'Sorry I couldn't make it in this morning, but that was one dose of the craps I had. I tell you, Frank, I was shitting bricks for most of the day. Anyway, Beryl tells me I'm feeling much better now, so I'll be in for work in the morning. And don't worry, I'll wear two pairs of underpants and bring a toilet roll in case I get caught short. Only joking, Frank. See you tomorrow, then.'

The tape clicks to a stop. In recognition of the good tidings, I give it an affectionate look. Polkadot would have a field day if he knew how I allow myself to get tied up in knots for no good reason.

I remove my pinstripe coat and throw it over the arm of the nearby chair, quickly followed by my wet shirt and tie. Bare-chested, I loosen my belt before removing shoes, damp socks and soggy, mud-caked trousers. The socks and trousers follow the coat, shirt and tie onto the arm, causing the lot to slide onto the floor in an untidy pile.

I'm now standing in my underpants, with the comforting warmth of the lounge softly caressing my stricken body like a masseuse in a sex parlour. As I suspected, my feet are white and wrinkled. One blackened toenail provides the only contrast. Hopefully, a warm bath and the passage of time will sort out both ailments in quick order.

But before anything else, this morning's debris has to be cleaned up. The last thing I'll want to see at breakfast is a reminder of today's debacles. And those wet clothes have also got to be sorted, ready for the wash and cleaners.

I make my way into the kitchen, to be greeted by an unexpected surprise. The tooth fairy has visited whilst I've been out.

Sitting on the worktop are a loaf of bread, a tin of baked beans, half a dozen eggs, and a box of corn flakes, along with a scribbled note from Jane.

Hi Frank, Noticed last night you were running a bit short on supplies, so took the liberty of calling into the corner shop on the way home for lunch. Hope these will sustain you until your next shop. Milk is in the fridge. Speak to you later. Love you. Jane.

PS. Didn't have time to clear up the kitchen. What in the name of heavens have you been up to? The place looks like a war zone.

Bless her. What would I do without her? A pity she had to see the mess in the kitchen though. Wouldn't want her to think I'm turning into a slob.

Buoyed by this latest display of Jane's love and affection, I methodically clear up the debris in the kitchen, lounge and finally the bedroom. Oddly enough, this proves to be therapeutic, exorcising any remaining demons. All that's now needed to complete my rehabilitation is a hot bath, a stiff drink, and something to eat.

Twenty minutes later, the rapidly cooling bath water brings the first phase of my therapy to an end. Towelled, refreshed, invigorated and clad only in a fresh pair of underpants, I make my way back downstairs and order my regular full-on pizza. With delivery promised within the hour, I approach my cocktail cabinet, licking my lips in anticipation. I remove bottles of Famous Grouse whisky and Canada Dry ginger ale and reverentially place them on the small occasional table situated beside my favourite armchair. I then retrieve my special Waterford-crystal whisky glass and the television remote control, setting them carefully beside the bottles. Satisfied everything is to hand, I flop into the chair, then pour a stiff measure of whisky followed by a small portion of ginger ale. A couple of glasses of this, plus a half-bottle of Jacob's Creek with my pizza should put a cap on my convalescence, but not so much that I'll be in danger of suffering another hangover tomorrow.

With the medicinal benefit of the alcohol quickly spreading through my body, Polkadot-thoughts reign supreme. As long as neither Jane nor the local vicar calls unexpectedly to knock me off my stride, a state of second heaven should soon be beckoning.

With nothing more to do until the arrival of my pizza, I switch on the TV.

The prime minister is addressing the annual conference of the Labour Party. With waving arms and smarmy smile, he's outlining the benefits of his latest 'New Deal' for the unemployed, basking in the applause from his gullible, captive audience.

'New Deal!' I scoff sceptically, drawing sustenance from my fast depleting glass. 'Try telling that to Kev, Tone. I know where he'll stick your "New Deal", and it's where the sun doesn't shine.'

As Tony winds up his speech and prepares to take his leave, the sound of the New Labour election theme bursts from the screen. Against my better judgement, I'm drawn into the spirit of the conference mood. 'Things can only get better,' I sing along quietly, my Famous Grouse working wonders.

Getting into the swing of things and allowing my tendency for drama to get the better of me, I rise from the comfort of my armchair, raise my glass and propound my own deeply felt beliefs to the now-departed prime minister. 'Cheers, Tony,' I cry. 'May God forgive you and your spin-doctors for your preference for style over substance and for treating us like mugs, but, most of all, for your diabolical acting skills. And as for your promotion of New Labour and Cool Britannia, I have only one thing to add: bollocks.'

With this succinct declaration, another swig finds its way down my throat. 'And another thing, Tone,' I exclaim enthusiastically to the moving, indeterminate images on screen, like I'm addressing a motley audience in Hyde Park Corner. 'Wherever you're off to now, spare a thought for those of us who are working our arses to the bone to enable you and your Right Honourable Members to prance about at our expense, pontificating on every subject under the sun, yet achieving zilch for the welfare of the little man.'

Gaining some satisfaction from my less-than-subtle critique of our leader and the political classes, I smugly plump myself back onto my chair, reach for the remote control and switch to BBC1.

The agreeable features of Fiona Bruce appear on screen, fronting the *News at Six*, swiftly followed by the beaming face of the prime minister.

It's him and those teeth again. Grinning at me like he's had a hot poker shoved up his arse. Resigned to the inevitable, I refill my glass then settle back into my armchair. He'll be gone from the telly soon enough.

Right now, it's hard to believe that it was only this morning I had that early morning premonition: *it's going to be one of those days*. And that it certainly was. But from where I'm sitting, the future looks bright.

Caught up in the optimistic mood of the moment, I rise from the comfort of my armchair, puff out my bare chest then raise my glass to the television. 'Ladies and gentlemen,' I cry out in a stentorian tone. 'Please be upstanding.'

In true theatrical style, I pause whilst my make-believe audience on the screen rises in unison. Only when I'm satisfied that I have their full attention, do I proceed with my oration, my voice cracking with emotion.

'Thank you. May I ask you to join me in toasting that one section of our business community which has, since time immemorial, made a significant contribution to the wealth and well-being of our proud nation.'

Tottering slightly on my stilts, I pause for effect.

'Yes, my friends, I refer specifically to that under-rated, under-paid, and sometimes much-maligned member of the home removals industry: the removal man. A rare breed of man that needs to have the skin of a rhinoceros and the wisdom of Solomon, and who has yet to receive due recognition at the highest level for the outstanding expertise of services rendered.

'Ladies and gentlemen, please raise your glasses to each and every Mr Shifter across the land. May you all live long and die oblong.'

Pleased as Punch with this rather ridiculous performance, I flop back into my armchair to resume viewing. A lingering intake of Scotch and ginger languidly works its way past my lips, fondly caresses my teeth and tongue, brushes a flurry of kisses along the length of my windpipe, then slowly meanders down my oesophagus to engage with the remnants of Sammy's vegetarian special.

Epilogue

I'M STANDING IN THE GARDENS of Buckingham Palace, wallowing in the grandeur and historical significance of my surroundings. High on the parapet above my head, the Royal Standard wafts lazily in the slight breeze blowing up The Mall, proudly announcing the presence of the Royal Family. The sky is blue, not a cloud to be seen anywhere, and an intense sunlight bathes the earth in its radiance.

With Jane dressed in her Sunday best and linked demurely to my arm, I'm barely aware of the considerable activity taking place around me, both outside and inside the closely guarded perimeter of the grounds. I am on cloud nine and my inner-self is bursting with pride. The fact that we're both actually here, standing on this hallowed turf, still hasn't fully registered.

But yes, here we are, courtesy of that unexpected communication from the office of the Central Chancery of the Orders of Knighthood, inviting Francis Frederick Foster Fidel Tipple to join the great and good from across the nation at this Investiture ceremony. That invitation is now safely tucked inside my morning-suit jacket, hired specifically for today's ceremony. It – the invitation, not the suit – will be returned to its place of honour on my mantelpiece on my return home later today, to be framed then hung in a prominent position on my lounge wall until such time that its imposition upon friends and family has been stretched to the point of boredom.

As Jane stops to adjust the crimson bow draped around her neck, I pinch myself, trying to take everything in.

Milling around us are hundreds of people, among them numerous celebrities from the world of stage, music, politics, television, sports and big business. The male members of the assembly, famous and plebs alike, are indistinguishable one from the other, attired as they are in their penguin suits and top hats. The females, as is their wont, are vying with each other for prominence and dressed up to the nines in a flamboyant variety of outfits, bought, borrowed or rented. The styling of some outfits is outrageous, the amount of human flesh on display defying all sense of decorum or propriety. But one common factor binds all guests: pride at the honour to be bestowed on husband, wife, brother, sister, son, daughter or friend.

Jane and I are exchanging pleasantries with Prince Philip and Prince Harry, when my name is called over the loudspeaker system, rigged up within the Palace enclosure. The cultured voice of the announcer booms through the speakers, temporarily bringing the hubbub to a halt.

'Would Mr Francis Frederick Foster Fidel Tipple please make his way to the Investiture Chamber immediately?'

The moment I've been waiting for over the past three weeks has finally come, causing my heartbeat to increase to an alarming rate. I gently disengage Jane's arm then kiss her affectionately on the cheek, chuffed that she has been able to take the day off work to be with me on this very special occasion. Prince Harry grins broadly and shakes my hand warmly. Prince Philip gives me an encouraging pat on the arm whilst looking down his elongated nose like he's just discovered a piece of snot hanging from his nostril.

Numb and overcome by the occasion, my mind is taken up with another matter of more immediate concern: my bladder is full to bursting. I should have spent a penny before the call came through. But it's too late now. Her Majesty can't be kept waiting at my convenience, or while I'm ensconced in her convenience.

Waiting to greet me at the entrance to the Investiture Chamber is a tiny, officious gentleman usher. No taller than four foot six in his cotton socks and leather sandals, he's resplendent in brightly coloured tunic and breeches and wearing a hat with feathers. He holds a scroll of guest names to which he refers before looking at me imperiously over a pug-like nose. He reminds me of a gnome at our local garden centre.

To my chagrin, he's unable to disguise the smirk which crosses his countenance as he recites my name. 'Francis Frederick Foster Fidel Tipple?' he queries. Standing on his tip-toes, he vainly tries to look me straight in the eye, his feathers bobbing in the slight breeze.

I nod my head in the affirmative. He bows obsequiously but says nothing more, silently beckoning me to follow him into the ceremonial chamber.

As we enter the packed chamber, there before me, perched majestically on an ornate golden throne, sits Her Royal Highness, Elizabeth Queen of England, the United Kingdom and the Commonwealth. She is resplendent in tiara and jewels, and wearing a shimmering gown of silk, embedded with emeralds, rubies and diamonds. Standing behind her is the Lord Chamberlain, accompanied by five members of the Queen's Yeomen of the Guard. Lounging at her feet are half a dozen corgis in various states of repose.

A nudge from the gnome encourages me to nervously approach the Queen who gives me a broad, welcoming smile. Bless her.

My moment has come. My heart is pounding and beads of sweat are rapidly accumulating under my armpits. I'm thankful that Jane insisted on a double dose of deodorant before heading for London. The last thing one wants is for a waft of BO to spoil this particular occasion, for me or the Queen.

Her Majesty beckons imperceptibly towards the low footstool placed before the throne. I look down towards the Italian marbled floor, humbly clasp my hands in front of me then kneel. I'm praying fervently that the seams of my over-tight rental trousers do not give or that my poorly shod shoes are not visible to the assembled dignitaries and guests.

As I bow my head, one of the corgis raises itself from the floor and nonchalantly cocks its leg against the rear of the throne. A fine and seemingly interminable stream of dog urine erupts and runs down the throne leg to the marble floor then begins to slowly wind its way towards me. Mesmerised, I watch as the stream passes under the stool between my upraised knees. Sympathetic to the corgi's need and his method of dealing with it, I'm hard pressed to control the contents of my own bladder.

Nobody else seems to be aware of what's just happened. If they have, they're unconcerned. The corgi cockily waddles back to its position by the Queen's feet, giving me a look as if to say: 'This is my home, mate. If I want to pee, that's between me and her, nobody else.'

It's only when I hear the rustling of silk and the jangling of jewellery that I'm aware that the Queen has arisen from her throne.

I hear the clink of steel. A long narrow shadow dances across the floor as the sunlight, cascading through the windows of the chamber, strikes the ceremonial sword being passed to Her Royal Highness.

A hush descends upon the chamber.

Only then does the Queen speak, those cultivated and measured tones instantly reminding one of the presence of nobility. Her voice rings out across the chamber, the need for amplification unnecessary:

'Mr Francis Frederick Foster Fidel Tipple, my loyal subject, I welcome you here today for an honour which has been long overdue in coming, for which I offer my most royal, humble apology.

'On behalf of the Nation – nay the Commonwealth, nay the world – it gives me the utmost pleasure to recognise the dedication and outstanding manner in which you have represented the removals industry for nearly two decades.

'For the satisfaction which you have brought to thousands of homeowners over those same years.

'For the way you have protected your employees and nurtured their development through times both rough and smooth.

'For the even-handed manner in which you have attempted to address the conniving, deceitful, scurrilous ratbags you've met during the course of your career, many of whom my husband would have removed to the dungeons for immediate castration.

'For all of these things and many, many more, which unfortunately time does not permit me to dwell on at this time…'

Momentarily the Queen pauses and I feel the blade of the sword make light contact with my left shoulder. Then I hear those magic words:

'Arise, Sir Francis Tipple.'

To the acclaim of the assembled audience, I sheepishly rise to my feet. Tears of joy are streaming down my face in rivulets. Quite frankly, I don't give a toss.

The Queen, acutely sensitive to the intensity of my emotions, ignores protocol and spontaneously reaches towards me. Surprising me with the strength of her grip, she draws me into her bosom and smothers me in a very motherly fashion. 'Good on you, Frank, me old mate,' she whispers in a broad Aussie accent as she gives me a bear hug, nearly squeezing the bleeding life out of me. 'Don't let the buggers grind you down. Go give 'em one!' After which she plants a great slobbering kiss on my right cheek.

★ ★ ★

THE SOUND OF a car back-firing in the street directly outside my bedroom awakens me. Sleepy, tired, and just a little bit inebriated, the images of the past few minutes quickly fade from my mind.

Smiling in contentment, I pull my duvet closer around me and turn over on my side, snug as a bug in a rug. Sleep quickly regains its delicate hold over my fragile equilibrium.

The author

EDWARD DAVIE was born in Belfast in 1939 and educated at the Royal Belfast Academical Institution. During his early career he worked in a variety of sales roles in Northern Ireland, Canada and England before embarking on a new venture, as owner of a medium-sized removal business. He managed this company for over twenty years before retiring in Spain with his wife Ann. His interests include mountain walking, reading and watching rugby.

www.ingramcontent.com/pod-product-compliance
Lightning Source LLC
Chambersburg PA
CBHW031833090426
42741CB00005B/225